Christmas is ⸱

Sharing a kiss under mistl⸱⸱⸱⸱⸱⸱⸱⸱⸱⸱⸱⸱⸱⸱⸱⸱⸱⸱⸱d in a light snowfall. . .gazing at the one of your dreams by candlelight. . .yes, Christmas is the perfect time of year to fall in love. And this season of joy and dreams is the perfect setting for four all-new inspirational romances by four cherished authors.

Christmas is the time for dreams.

Close your eyes and you're there, in a Christmas world where love knows no bounds. Imagine yourself in the beautiful Alaskan wilderness; the rugged plains of the Dakotas; and the fun-filled country excitement of the Ozarks. Close your eyes and you're in love again, for the first time. Close your eyes and see the man or woman God has chosen just for you.

Christmas is the time for treasures.

From the hearts and pens of four of America's best-loved inspirational romance authors—Veda Boyd Jones, Tracie Peterson, Colleen L. Reece, and Lauraine Snelling—to you, *Christmas Treasures* is a gift of love, for a season of love.

Christmas TREASURES

Veda Boyd Jones
Tracie Peterson
Colleen L. Reece
Lauraine Snelling

A Barbour Book

© MCMXCVI by Barbour & Company, Inc.

ISBN 1-55748-883-5 Paperback Edition
ISBN 1-57748-005-8 Hardbound Edition

Published by Barbour & Company, Inc.
            P.O. Box 719
            Uhrichsville, Ohio 44683
            e-mail: books<barbour@tusco.net>

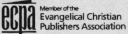 Member of the
Evangelical Christian
Publishers Association

Printed in the United States of America

Christmas
TREASURES

An Ozark Christmas Angel

Veda Boyd Jones

One

"Lyndsay, I have a great favor to ask." Anita Jane Wells' normally powerful voice came across the telephone line as a whisper.

"Just name it," Lyndsay replied without hesitation. "Are you all right? What's wrong?" There was nothing she wouldn't do for Anita Jane, her mentor, who'd paved Lyndsay's way into the country music scene.

"The doctor says pneumonia can be very dangerous."

"Pneumonia? Are you in the hospital?"

"Yes," Anita Jane croaked. "I'm in Branson, and I need you to fulfill my contract. I can't leave the theater in the lurch. I know it's a lot to ask, since this is your composing time, but I'll be on my feet in a week or two. Certainly before Christmas."

"Do you have a show tonight? I don't know if I can get a flight that fast."

"There's a one-fifteen out of Dallas this afternoon.

I've taken it before."

Lyndsay glanced at her watch. Almost ten. "I'll be on it. What about backup singers? Are yours there?"

"Oh, yes. It's my usual Christmas show, and the manager has agreed that you can step in. All you have to do is bring your guitar. My secretary will have a ticket waiting for you at the airport, and someone will pick you up in Springfield. The doctor is here, so I'd better go."

"Could I speak with him? Please?" She knew Anita Jane would gloss over the severity of her illness. Lyndsay had seen her walk on stage when she'd had a burning fever, spouting the line, "The show must go on." She must be gravely ill to have Lyndsay replace her for two weeks.

"Dr. Hamilton," a baritone voice announced.

"This is Lyndsay Rose. How is she, really?"

"She's doing fine and should be out of here soon. Don't be overly alarmed."

"She said pneumonia— "

"Yes," he interrupted. "Pneumonia can be a killer, but I'm certain Anita Jane will be fine. Some rest will work wonders for her."

Lyndsay let out a deep breath, unaware that she had been holding it.

"Okay. Take care of her, Dr. Hamilton. I'll go to the hospital as soon as I get to Branson."

There was a pause on the other end. Then, "She'll be fine, Miss Rose. I'll see you later today."

Lyndsay hung up the phone and pulled suitcases from a large storage closet. She mentally made a list of costumes to take and street clothes as well. What was the weather like in Missouri? Hadn't Anita Jane mentioned wading through deep snow last Christmas?

❧

"She sounds like a nice person and is very concerned about you. Why are you doing this to her?" Dr. Hamilton asked in a gruff voice as he helped his older friend with her coat. He stood in front of the door to the hospital corridor and waited for a reply.

"I told you she needs to be with people at Christmas," Anita Jane said in her normal voice. "For the last three years, since her husband died, she's isolated herself with the pretense of writing songs. I'm doing this for her." Anita Jane chuckled. "Hey, I could be a Christmas angel, going about doing good."

Will Hamilton laughed and studied the country singer. She was sixty-four, but her energy level, her skin tone and her heavy dark hair belied her years. Oh, there were character wrinkles and some gray hairs among the brown, but this woman stayed young without the help of cosmetic surgery and hair dye. Still, she wasn't his idea of a Christmas angel. An exceptional individual, yes. A headstrong woman, yes. An unconventional woman, yes. But never a Christmas angel.

"What about this afternoon when she gets to Branson?"

"Will, I was hoping you'd help me out there."

"I've already lied for you," he said.

"No, not lied. Lyndsay's a stickler for lying. You never said I was a patient here. Or that I actually had pneumonia, and neither did I."

"I was careful about what I said, but that isn't what she heard, and you know it. She thinks you're on your deathbed."

"I'll straighten her out in a few days. After you pick her up at the airport and take her to the theater to sign the contract. And after she's done a couple of shows and realizes how much she needs this."

"I'm going to pick her up?" Will stared at his friend. How had he let her talk him into helping her? Probably because she reminded him of his aunt, who also got her way when something was important to her. This morning, Anita Jane had called and asked if she could meet him at the doctor's lounge. When he'd told her it was his day off, but he would be checking on a few patients, she'd conned him into seeing her. Now she wanted him to pick up Lyndsay Rose?

"Please, Will. It would mean so much to Lyndsay if you reassured her that I would be mending quick." When he didn't immediately answer, she continued. "Remember that benefit I did for the children's ward? You said anytime I needed anything, anything at all . . ."

"Okay. Okay. Then we're even." He didn't appreciate spending his day off driving an hour to the Springfield airport even if it was to pick up the beautiful Lyndsay Rose. He'd planned on fishing.

Anita Jane smiled at him, one of those cat-who-ate-the-canary smiles, and he opened the door to the hallway. Together they walked to the parking lot.

"You're in your bachelor car. Where's your four-wheel drive?" she asked when he stopped at his little sports car.

"At home."

"Better take it. Lyndsay's never learned to travel light."

☙

Lyndsay peered out the window as the plane descended and headed for the runway. What a small place compared to the massive Dallas/Ft. Worth airport she had left a little over an hour ago.

No snow. Maybe she'd been wrong about the weather in Missouri. She'd never played in Branson, although she'd performed in Kansas City on her last tour. But that had been in the summer, and she'd been in that city for less than twenty-four hours before she'd taken off for Denver. Tours wore her out. She much preferred studio work, but it was hard to sell records if she didn't hit the road.

The plane set down with a couple of thumps, not the smoothest landing Lyndsay had ever experienced. She wondered who would be picking her up. Probably Anita Jane's secretary, Rowena. That woman could organize anything on a moment's notice.

The last time she'd seen Rowena was at Trevor's funeral. The cancer had been quick. Four months after it was discovered, her husband had died. Although Anita Jane had been the strong one for Lyndsay, Rowena had been there in the background, quietly organizing everything, making phone calls, and making sure the family were where they needed to be when they needed to be there.

Anita Jane and Lyndsay's mother had been high school friends who had roomed together in Nashville while Anita Jane had been trying to hit the big time and Melinda worked as a secretary for a recording company. Melinda was actually instrumental in getting Anita Jane's big break. But as she'd told Anita Jane countless times, if she hadn't had the talent, getting Melinda's boss to listen to her wouldn't have done any good. Anita Jane had repeated the story to Lyndsay and echoed the same sentiment when she'd gotten a record producer to listen to Lyndsay's demo.

That had been eight years ago, when she was twenty. A lot had happened since then. Her career had skyrocketed, and then her mother had died, later Trevor, and now Anita Jane was ill. Wasn't pneumonia what people got right before they died? Even cancer victims like Trevor ended up with pneumonia. Once the lungs filled, death was inevitable.

With a heavy heart, Lyndsay automatically donned sunglasses, joined the group of passengers exiting the plane, and walked through the tunnel into Springfield's terminal. She should have no trouble finding Rowena in this place.

She looked for the tall redhead in the crowd of some forty people in the waiting area, but she wasn't there. Her first thought was that Anita Jane might be so ill that Rowena wouldn't leave her. Lyndsay whipped off her sunglasses, thinking whoever was to pick her up might not recognize her with them on.

She stepped over to the side to wait when a huge bear of a man approached. He was a basketball coach's dream and a football coach's dream at the same time. He wasn't heavy, there appeared to be nothing but muscle on his tall frame, but he was huge, and she'd guess he was somewhere in his early thirties. She looked up at deep brown eyes.

"Lyndsay Rose, I'm Will Hamilton."

She didn't recognize the name and shook her head.

"Dr. Hamilton. We spoke this morning about Anita Jane."

"Oh, no," she gasped. Had the doctor come to tell her the bad news? *Dear God, please don't let her be gone,* Lyndsay prayed. She groped for the nearest seat and sat down hard.

Will watched Lyndsay's face turn a ghastly white.

"Are you going to faint?" he said and hunched down beside her chair. "Put your head down." He gently pulled her toward him.

"Anita Jane?" she mumbled.

Realization hit him. "She's fine. Anita Jane is fine!" But she wouldn't be for long. He might put her six feet under for what she'd put this woman through.

"She's still alive?"

"Very much alive. I had the afternoon off, so I came to get you as a favor to Anita Jane. We'll talk as soon as you're feeling better."

"I'm okay now."

"You're getting some color back, but sit here a few more minutes while I get your suitcase."

She handed him five baggage claims.

"I'll get these loaded and be back in a few minutes."

Will strode toward the baggage area. Anita Jane had gone too far this time. She'd always been a bit eccentric, but her antics had never harmed anyone before. Maybe he should leave Lyndsay's suitcases and get her on the next plane back to Dallas. No, she should have the opportunity to look a healthy Anita Jane in the eye and ask her what she could possibly mean by getting her to Missouri under false pretenses.

He carried two cumbersome bags to his Suburban and moved his car to the ten-minute loading zone. Two more suitcases and a wardrobe trunk later, he returned to the waiting room to find Lyndsay signing autographs.

For a moment he'd forgotten she was a big star. He'd seen her as the victim of unforgivable meddling.

She looked up and smiled at him.

"Just a moment, Dr. Hamilton, and we can go."

Where had all these people come from? Of course they would recognize her. Dark glasses no longer covered her face, but even with them, her trademark waist-length blonde hair was a dead giveaway. She signed another twenty autographs, giving her complete attention to each fan, before they made their getaway to his car.

He snatched the parking ticket from under the windshield wiper and vowed to bill Anita Jane.

As soon as they were on the road Lyndsay turned to him.

"So Anita Jane is all right? She's responding to treatment?"

Will took a deep breath. "Anita Jane doesn't have pneumonia. She wanted you to think that so you would come down here and not be alone for Christmas."

"What!"

He glanced at his passenger, whose expressive eyes that had earlier held panic and grief now were saucersized in disbelief.

"She says that since your husband died you pretend to write songs in December and become a hermit. She thinks you need to be around people."

"You're not making this up?"

He shook his head.

"It's true that I don't go on the road in December. Trevor died December fifth, we were married on the fifteenth, and his birthday was the twenty-first. That's an awful lot of memories for one month, and sometimes

17

they get me a little down. But I have always spent Christmas Day with family. If I'm not at my brother's, I go to my in-laws." She shook her head. "I'm not lonely, even though I miss my husband. I can't imagine what Anita Jane was thinking."

"I don't know that she's thought it through, but she sees herself as some sort of Christmas angel, spreading joy and good cheer. I just can't picture her sprouting a couple of wings. And a halo is out of the question."

Lyndsay laughed, a bit out of relief and a bit at the improbable word-portrait that Will Hamilton had painted of her friend.

"What's your part in this little farce? You told me she had pneumonia."

"Not exactly." He gave a blow-by-blow of his morning conversation with Anita Jane.

"So she was in the doctor's lounge when she called. She's good," Lyndsay said and nodded her head in thought. "But she has met her match. I'm not sure what I'm going to do, but are you willing to help me?"

"Whatever it is, count me in."

Two

Will drove Lyndsay directly to the theater where she would be performing that evening.

"Her plan is for you to sign the contract right off. Once you've signed, she thinks she'll have you down here for at least a couple of weeks. Do you want to do that?"

"It's okay. Since I'm here, I'll play along until we figure out what else to do. I've already cleared this with my agent. I taped a Christmas TV special last month, so I have a show all worked up."

Will ushered her through a side door into the theater and introduced her to the manager, who had the contract sitting on his desk.

"It's wonderful of you to fill in for Anita Jane like

19

this," the manager gushed. "I'm sure she'll be well soon and can take over before the winter season starts."

Lyndsay exchanged a glance with Will. Was the manager in on this game, too? Will raised his eyebrows as if to say he didn't know. Oddly, she'd known the doctor for only an hour, and yet they could communicate without words.

Lyndsay studied the contract. It ran through the middle of December with no days off. On Sunday she'd lead a gospel music service.

"When does the winter season start?" she asked.

"After the New Year. We take a couple of weeks off before we begin again. Not too many tourists are here for the actual holidays, but they do like the Christmas shows, so this week and next will be busy."

Lyndsay glanced at her watch. Already four o'clock.

"I'd like to check with Anita Jane and then rehearse before the show."

"Anita Jane set a rehearsal for four-thirty. Some of the musicians are already backstage. Here's the program she's been doing and the music," he said, and handed her a stack of papers, "but I'm sure you'll want to add a few songs of your own."

The manager showed them to Anita Jane's dressing room, then a stagehand left with Will to unload her wardrobe trunk and suitcases.

Lyndsay collapsed on the small sofa. What had she gotten herself into? Taking over someone else's show was a monumental task. Well, she wouldn't get it done by moaning about it. With a prayer for help and new resolve, she sat up straight and flipped through the sheets of musical numbers, mentally matching the music with the costumes she'd brought. They would work. The songs were mostly traditional Christmas carols, so she knew the words. A few arrangements had an Anita Jane twist, but she could mimic that. She'd grown up with Anita Jane's music, and she knew her musical mannerisms and show style.

"Do you want all of these?" Will asked from the doorway.

"These two have street clothes." Lyndsay pointed to the smaller suitcases.

"I'll take them to your suite," Will said. "Anita Jane has a cabin out at Big Cedar, but she's arranged for you to stay in the main lodge."

"Why don't I stay with Anita Jane? Doesn't she have an extra bedroom?"

"I'm sure she does, since those cabins have several rooms, but she asked that. . . Oh, good idea, Lyndsay. She's supposed to be in the hospital anyway. Let's see her wiggle out of this one."

"Exactly. She'll have to fake her illness and stay in bed while I'm there or confess. As a matter of fact," she said as she picked up the phone from a small end table, "I think I'll ring her right now and let her tell me she's been dismissed from the hospital."

But it wasn't Anita Jane who answered. Rowena told Lyndsay that Anita was in the hospital.

"I have a rehearsal in a few minutes, but I'd like to check on her. Do you have the hospital number?" Lyndsay wrote it down. "Rowena, Will says I'm booked at the lodge, but I'd much rather stay at Anita Jane's. While she's in the hospital that shouldn't be a problem, and while she's recuperating, I can help take care of her. Will can drop my suitcases by there. . . No, I insist. I want to be near her." Lyndsay grinned at Will. "I've got to run. See you soon."

Lyndsay read the phone number to Will. "Is this familiar?"

"That's the hospital. I wonder what she's up to now."

The information desk answered the call. "The receptionist says she's in room 255," Lyndsay told Will as she waited for the connection.

"There isn't a room 255. She's probably. . ."

Lyndsay waved her hand to shush him. "Anita Jane? How are you? . . . I'm at the theater now. Will's going to take my things to your cabin, but I'll come to the hospital immediately after the show."

Lyndsay handed the phone to Will. "She wants to talk to you."

She couldn't tell much from Will's half of the conversation. It was partly in code, since most of his answers were of the "yes" and "no" variety. He motioned for her to go out of the room, so Lyndsay stood in the hall outside the open door.

"I can talk freely now. She's stepped out for a minute." Will winked at Lyndsay. "No, she's determined to stay with you and take care of you. Are you sure you know what you're doing, Anita Jane? She's stressed out about this. . . . All right, but I don't approve. Where are you now?"

He motioned Lyndsay back into the room. "Lyndsay's back. Did you want to tell her anything else? Fine. I'll be over to see about your release." He hung up the phone.

"Well? Where is she?"

"She's been standing at the information desk waiting for your call. Now she's decided I can dismiss her with a private duty nurse, because she hates hospitals. That means the extra bedroom is out for you. She sure covers all the angles."

"All right. I'll stay in the lodge, but I'll be dropping in on her at all hours."

"She'll expect you tonight after the show, and she'll try to arrange any other visits. What we have to do is decide where she wants to be, and be there first. That way she'll have to stay home. Last year, she made all the Christmas parties. I'll make a list and see what we can do. This is going to be fun."

"Excuse me." A woman stood in the doorway. "Miss Rose, I'm from wardrobe."

Lyndsay held up one finger. "Just one minute and we'll get to work." She turned her attention back to Will. "Why did you have me step into the hall?"

He shrugged. "Anita Jane said you were a stickler about lying. So, I'm playing the game by your rules."

He glanced at his watch. "I'm headed to the hospital to check on patients and see Anita Jane. I'll be back here when your show is over and take you to the lodge. Around nine?"

"Okay."

He carried her two suitcases with him as he left.

A whirl of activity engulfed Lyndsay. A makeup artist, the wardrobe mistress, and the band leader swarmed in. She carried on three conversations at once and tried to take direction herself.

By five forty-five the rehearsal ended so the entertainers could get dressed for the seven o'clock performance. They'd run through most numbers once, but hadn't practiced any of the songs Lyndsay would be adding to the show. She felt comfortable enough to sing them without backup, but tomorrow she'd make sure they rehearsed. Harmony added to the depth of her music, and she wanted the audience to get their money's worth. As it was, she worried they would feel cheated that they didn't get to see the legendary Anita Jane Wells.

❧

So, this was how a double agent felt, Will mused as he prepared to take on Anita Jane. Because he knew she would expect him to protest, he did just that and with a vehemence, since his heart was in it.

"You should have seen her at the airport. She thought you were dead, and I was there to break it to her," he explained as they sat at a table in the doctor's lounge. "You should be ashamed of yourself."

"Will, you don't understand. In the long run Lyndsay is going to thank me for this. She's a beautiful woman, isn't she?"

That was an understatement. Her beauty wasn't just physical; it was in the depth of human understanding in her eyes. Not that she had merely survived some hard emotional times, but that she had accepted them and gone on with her life. He didn't know exactly how he knew that, but he did. She had inner peace. That's what he'd seen in her deep blue eyes.

"Yes, she's beautiful, but I think you underestimate her. She's grieved for her husband, but she's come to grips with it."

Anita Jane gave him a long look. "I know her very well, and I believe I know what's best for her. I was there when she was born, I was with her when her mother died, and I was there right after her husband died. In a couple of weeks, she'll be a different person, and she'll have me to thank for it. Now, are you available to take her to the lodge tonight? Or do I need to get someone else? Dave Robbins would probably do it."

Was she crazy? He wouldn't trust Dave Robbins within twenty miles of Lyndsay. The man might be a professor at the College of the Ozarks and be one of his good friends, but he wouldn't welcome any competition from Dave. Competition? Now why would that enter the picture? He pushed the thought out of his mind. "I've already arranged to pick Lyndsay up after the show."

"Fine. Here," she said and dug a ticket out of her purse, "in case you get there early. Well, I've got to run. Rowena's interviewing nurses for me since Lyndsay's thrown a kink in some of my plans. I thought of just getting someone from a temp agency, but Lyndsay's sure to question her about her credentials. This is getting to be an expensive ordeal. I just hope Lyndsay appreciates what I'm doing. After all, I am her Christmas angel." She straightened an imaginary halo and laughed, then turned and left.

"Christmas angel—bah, humbug!" Will exclaimed to the empty room. No self-respecting Christmas angel, even a pretend one, would introduce Dave Robbins to Lyndsay Rose. His friend might be a charmer, but Will wouldn't trust him with his sister, and he certainly wouldn't trust him with Lyndsay. Oh, he was going to enjoy teaching Anita Jane Wells a lesson about meddling in other people's lives.

He ordered opening night roses for Lyndsay, made his rounds, then drove to his home on Lake Taneycomo and studied his calendar. There were the usual number of Christmas parties and special events held around Branson, and they were all important to Anita Jane.

She prided herself in being not only a country singer, but being part of the community. That was how he'd met her in the first place. She'd volunteered for a committee to study the traffic situation in Branson. With all the music theaters on the strip, there was a continual traffic jam from April to November. While the highway department put in new roads, the committee came up with alternate routes for the locals and smart tourists. They'd also requested that the music shows stagger their hours so all the shows wouldn't let out at the same time. He'd met Anita Jane at the first meeting, and they had hit it off. She wasn't at all what he thought of as a celebrity but was a down-to-earth person. This was her third year to return to Branson for part of the tourist season and to stay through Christmas. Twice she'd come to him as a patient—once for asthma and once for a sprained wrist. But their relationship wasn't really professional; it had been sparked by mutual respect and genuine friendship.

But that was in the past. Now he was ready to do battle with Miss Christmas Angel. She had hurt an innocent young woman, no matter what misguided good intentions she'd had. She should learn to think matters through before acting on them.

He made a list of events Anita Jane wouldn't want to miss and canceled other plans he'd had so that he could attend them, escorting Lyndsay Rose. Anita Jane would have to stay away from the festivities or give away her deception in getting Lyndsay to Branson.

He fixed a quick sandwich, showered, dressed, and drove to the family theater where he saw the marquee announcing Lyndsay Rose in a Christmas Spectacular.

Before the opening curtain, the manager made a quick appearance and announced that Lyndsay Rose was replacing Anita Jane Wells; however, he didn't give any reason. The audience didn't seem to care. They sat spellbound as Lyndsay's clear, sweet voice gave new meaning to old carols. The sets sparkled with artificial snow and Christmas greenery, giant red bows and ornaments. Backup singers wore elaborate costumes that glittered and shone.

But the star was Lyndsay Rose. Whether flanked by others or sitting on a stool alone on the stage, she commanded attention. At one point she asked a couple of children from the front section to join her on stage. They sat in a sleigh while she sang "Jingle Bells" and two mechanical horses pulled them across the stage. After the song, she handed each child a present she selected from those under the giant Christmas tree at stage left.

She ended the show with "Silent Night," and a more eloquent version he'd never heard. The audience burst into applause. Lyndsay bowed again and again. The stage manager presented her with a bouquet of roses and the audience clapped even louder. Lyndsay read the card attached to the ribbon, looked directly at Will in the second row, mouthed "Thank you," and smiled, then walked gracefully off stage.

Three

"**W**onderful show," the theater manager said. "They loved it."

Echoes of the same sentiment came from all sides as the cast congratulated each other.

"And that was with one rehearsal," a backup singer told Lyndsay. "Imagine what we'll be doing by next week."

"It's Anita Jane's program," Lyndsay said. "She's great at developing a show." She looked down at the roses she held. Will was a real sweetheart. She'd seen him the moment the curtain had opened. It was hard to miss a man that big.

"How about dinner?" another backup singer asked.

"Thanks, but my ride is here, and I've not even checked into my room yet. It's been a long day."

The singer squeezed her arm. "Yeah. And I'll bet the delicious Dr. Hamilton is your ride."

"You know Will?" Lyndsay asked.

"I saw him bring you this afternoon. He's a friend of Anita Jane's, so he's been backstage before. He's a hunk and eligible." She raised her eyebrows in speculation.

"He's very nice," Lyndsay said. "And I need to get out of this outfit, so I can go. I'll see you all tomorrow—around six?" With the success of the show, she decided they didn't need to rehearse again before the evening performance. The cast members' cheers of agreement followed her to her dressing room.

Will was leaning against the wall beside her door.

"Wonderful show," he said. "You were marvelous."

"Thanks. And thank you for the roses. You're very sweet."

Sweet? Will couldn't remember that he'd ever been called sweet. It didn't sound like a masculine characteristic, but coming from Lyndsay, it sounded like a great compliment.

"I'll only take a minute to change," she announced and disappeared inside the dressing room.

Will exchanged hellos with cast members as they drifted to other dressing rooms. Within five minutes Lyndsay reappeared, this time devoid of stage makeup and dressed in the jeans and sweater she'd worn when he'd picked up her at the airport.

"Well," she said when they were settled in his car. "Did you release Anita Jane from the hospital?"

"She's home all right. And I think she'll be there for some time. I have a plan."

He explained his schedule of events and how he'd arranged for them to attend festivities that Anita Jane would normally attend.

"I realize you won't be able to go places during your performances, but when you're finished for the evening, we can make an appearance, just like Anita Jane would have done."

"Are there events during the day that I could attend on my own?"

"Well, there are some, and I'm on a light schedule, so I can take you around." He didn't mention that he'd rearranged his on-call time and traded time off with his partner in his family practice so he would be available to squire her around.

"This sounds crazy, but medicine is a cyclical business. People would rather spend money on Christmas presents than on doctor bills, so in December they don't always go to a doctor when they should. Of course, many end up in the emergency room."

"And do some get well without medicine?" Lyndsay asked.

He glanced over at her and saw her teasing grin.

"Yes. Some do. But you've got to admit there's a lot to peace of mind, and that's what some people get from visiting a doctor."

"Can't argue with that," Lyndsay said. "How much further? Haven't we gone several miles?"

"We're almost there. The lodge is on Table Rock Lake, and the drive is worth the great view you're going to have. Another night, when you're not so tired, I'll show you the million Christmas lights."

"Sounds great. Don't you think I should spend some time checking on Anita Jane? Otherwise she might get suspicious."

"True. We want to flush her out of her scheme, but not before she has to suffer for it." He didn't mention that he wanted their time together to go on for awhile. He didn't understand why that thought even occurred to him. He hardly knew Lyndsay, but he knew he wanted to know her better.

"You are bad, Will Hamilton."

He grinned. He accepted that as a compliment.

"Is this a town?" Lyndsay asked as Will pulled up in front of a magnificent lodge. They'd passed several cabins and another huge rustic building.

"No, but it appears that way. There are three lodges and a hundred private cabins. Anita's cabin is down that road. Do you want to see her first or check in?"

"Let's go straight to her. That would be my normal reaction."

Will turned the car down the narrow road and soon parked at Anita Jane's. A light blazed from the front window.

Their knock was answered by a woman in a white uniform. Will exchanged a glance with Lyndsay and whispered, "She doesn't skimp on anything."

Lyndsay nodded and followed the nurse into the cabin. A fire burned cheerily in the fireplace, and a robed Anita Jane sat in a recliner, covered with a quilt.

Lyndsay rushed to her side and hugged her.

"How are you feeling?"

"Better, now that I'm home," Anita Jane said in a husky voice. "Thank you so much for coming. I knew I could count on you." She coughed.

Will reached for her wrist and felt her pulse as he looked at his watch. "Could I see her latest readings, nurse?"

The nurse handed a clipboard to Will.

Lyndsay glanced at the fireplace. "Do you think it's wise to have a fire? I know not much smoke escapes, but there's bound to be some. Will?"

"Lyndsay's right. Don't build a fire tomorrow," he instructed the nurse, then turned back to his patient. "Delicate lungs don't need any further complications." Lyndsay was brilliant. Anita Jane enjoyed a fire, more for the esthetic value than the heat. Having no fire would keep her aware of Lyndsay, even when she wasn't there physically. "And the real Christmas tree ought to go," he added. "With your allergic tendencies, you're running the risk of a flare-up with the spores from a live tree. An artificial tree would be okay."

Lyndsay turned to take off her coat, and Anita Jane glared at Will and shook her head.

"You'd better go on to the lodge, honey. I'm going to bed. I stayed up just to see you for a minute."

"Anita Jane, I'll be happy to stay here with you."

"Any other time I'd love that, honey. But the nurse will take care of me, and I'm up and down in the night, taking medicine and all. I want you to rest undisturbed." She coughed again, then continued, "I heard the show went off without a hitch."

"It went fine. You have a good program lined up."

"I'll take Lyndsay to the lodge," Will said, "and I'll check on you tomorrow, Anita Jane." He bent over and kissed his friend on the cheek, then hustled Lyndsay outside.

"She's quite an actress," Lyndsay said once they were inside the car. She coughed in Anita Jane's style.

"No fire. A stroke of genius," Will said.

"Thanks. I thought it was a nice touch. And that bit about the live tree was excellent. She loves the smell of an evergreen at Christmas."

Will parked the car in the lot and escorted Lindsay to the lobby. While she checked in, he returned to the car for her luggage.

He stepped into the lobby in time to hear Lindsay cry out and run into the arms of another man.

"It's so good to see you, Morgan," she said, then hugged the woman beside him—a woman Will hadn't seen at first. "Callie, what are you doing here?"

"Grandma's always wanted to see Branson, so we brought her down for the Christmas shows," Callie said. "We'll be here until Saturday."

"Oh, Will. You won't believe who's here," Lyndsay

said and waved him over to the group. She made the introductions and Will breathed an inward sigh when he learned the couple were married.

"Morgan is known as Trey to his fans," Lyndsay explained, and Will understood why the man looked familiar. "We only see each other at country music award shows," Lyndsay explained, "but we get in all the visiting we can then. Did you bring Daisy?" she asked, then turned to Will again. "She's their darling little baby."

"She'll be one on Thursday, so she's hardly a baby," Callie said. "She took her first step three weeks ago, and now she thinks she's conquered the world. Sorry, I sound like a new mother, don't I? Daisy's upstairs with Grandma. We took in one of the shows tonight, then Morgan and I went for a walk by the lake. Isn't this the most romantic place?"

"I just got here. I'm filling in for Anita Jane."

"What happened?" Morgan asked.

Will shot Lyndsay a warning glance.

"They can be trusted," Lyndsay said, "and they could be good accomplices."

"Okay, but we can't let it be general knowledge or Anita Jane will never forgive us."

"Promise you'll never repeat what we tell you?" Lyndsay asked. "It wouldn't do Anita Jane's career any good."

Callie nervously glanced around. "Is there something illegal going on?"

"You know me better than that," Lyndsay said, then explained the situation. "Don't you agree she needs to be taught a lesson?"

"Wouldn't hurt," Morgan said. "What can we do?"

The foursome walked to a sitting area in front of a massive fireplace. Callie and Morgan sat on one couch, and Will and Lyndsay sat on another facing them.

"We saw Anita Jane's show on Saturday night," Callie said. "She's one of Grandma's favorites. We went backstage after her show, and I know Grandma would love to be in on this scheme. We could visit Anita Jane tomorrow morning and take one of Grandma's home remedies for a cold."

"You have one with you?" Will asked.

"No, but there are all sorts of wild herbs for sale at a store we shopped at yesterday. We can get the ingredients and have Grandma cook it over at Anita Jane's. She'll have to pretend to be sick while we're there."

"Great," Lyndsay said. "I hope it tastes horrible. But can you make sure she takes it?"

Callie laughed. "Few people can cross Grandma. She'll make Anita Jane swallow it."

"I'll watch Daisy while you all take your turn with Anita Jane," Lyndsay offered. She'd fallen in love with the little girl when she'd seen her in Nashville in October at the awards show and welcomed the chance to spend time with her. Trevor had wanted lots of children, and just days before he'd gotten sick, they'd talked about starting a family.

"Wonderful," Callie said. "It might be easier if you came to our suite instead of us carting all of Daisy's belongings to you. Amazing what one little person requires in an hour's time."

They exchanged room numbers, and Will stood up, effectively ending the conversation. Now that tomorrow morning was planned, he wanted to get Lyndsay up to her room. She had to be tired, both emotionally and physically.

"Lyndsay hasn't seen her suite yet," he said as he picked up the two suitcases once again.

They said good night to Morgan and Callie and climbed the wide staircase to the second floor. Will opened the door to Lyndsay's suite and carried the suitcases through the living room and deposited them on the bedroom floor. When he returned to the living room, he found Lyndsay reclining in an overstuffed chair, her feet on the ottoman, her eyes closed.

"Tired?" he asked.

"Exhausted." She was also hungry. She'd not eaten since that sandwich on the plane. "Is there a restaurant here?"

"Of course. Would you like to go there or have something sent up?"

Lyndsay glanced around the pine walls of the rustic room. The stuffed head of a deer stared at her from above the fireplace. "Does the lodge have room service?"

"Don't let the decor deceive you. Although it looks

like a turn-of-the-century hunting lodge, it has all the modern conveniences. Even indoor plumbing," he said with a chuckle.

"Then I'd love to have something delivered."

Will located a menu in a desk drawer, read it aloud, then called in their order. "Fifteen minutes, guaranteed," he said.

Lyndsay leaned back in her chair and closed her eyes again, thankful that Will had ordered some food and would stay to eat with her. Odd how relaxed she felt with him.

"When I got up today I planned on Christmas shopping for my brother's family and working on a new song. Instead I'm here in Missouri, and I've performed on Branson's famous strip. Who'd have guessed it?" She opened her eyes and looked at Will. "What about you?"

"Since it's my day off, I'd planned on making early rounds and then fishing."

"Instead you ended up hauling me around."

He nodded. "And it's been much more exciting than throwing a line in the water."

This time she nodded in agreement. "And more exciting than deciding which scarf to get for my sister-in-law."

Four

"Come get this, Daisy," Lyndsay said. She shook a stuffed raccoon to get the little girl's attention.

Daisy toddled over and grabbed the animal. "Da, da, do," she chanted.

Those were her favorite sounds, Lyndsay had decided, since she said them no matter what they were playing with.

Morgan, Callie and her grandmother were at Anita Jane's, doing their part to make her life miserable. Lyndsay chuckled at the thought of Grandma. She was a wiry little woman whose iron will was apparent at first meeting. Anita Jane had met her match in that woman.

"Da, da, do," Daisy said and pulled Lyndsay's arm.

"Whatever," Lyndsay said. "Want to go for a walk?" She picked Daisy up and hugged her. When Daisy hugged back, Lyndsay sighed. "Oh, precious." What she would give to have a little darling of her own.

She put Daisy's coat on her and carried her down the stairs. A walk by the lake would be a fine morning outing. How could she have associated Missouri with snow? Today was a gorgeous day, bright sun and not a cloud in the blue sky. The temperature must have been fifty and it was the third of December. This was almost Dallas weather.

Lyndsay carried Daisy along the water's edge and pointed out birds and an occasional fish that surfaced for food then left widening circles behind. She let the little girl walk for a few minutes and tightly held her hand. Then she carried her back to the lodge.

Will Hamilton stood on the wide porch.

"Will, what are you doing out here?" Lyndsay called. A wide smile expressed her delight at seeing him again.

"Making a house call." He held out his hands to Daisy and she reached for him.

"I guess she doesn't know a stranger," Lyndsay said, a bit miffed that Daisy would so readily leave her.

"Kids like me," he said. "Actually they like high perches," he admitted. "And deep voices."

He certainly could provide both, Lyndsay thought, looking up at him. Each time she saw him, he seemed bigger, more impressive.

"Da, da, do," Daisy said and pointed.

Lyndsay turned and saw Morgan, Callie and Grandma crossing the parking lot.

"She's fit to be tied," Grandma said after she'd been introduced to Will. "I told her you thought my remedy would do her good. She about choked on it, but she got a tablespoon down. I'm going back this afternoon to give her another dose."

"What's in this potion you've concocted?" Will asked.

"Can't give away my secret recipe or you'll be using it on all your patients, but she'll have garlic on her breath for awhile."

Will laughed and handed Daisy over to Morgan. "I believe I'll pay her a visit. Come with me, Lyndsay?"

"Sure. Callie, you have a little angel here."

"Was she good?"

"Couldn't have been better. I'll stay with her again if you all want to go out during the day."

"Thanks. I'll keep that in mind," Callie said and followed her family inside.

Will retrieved his bag from his car, and he and Lyndsay walked to Anita Jane's cabin. Will pointed to the chimney. "No smoke." Her Christmas tree, now unadorned by lights and ornaments, stood in its stand on the front porch.

They found Anita Jane as they had left her the night before, sitting in the recliner.

She smiled at them. "Good to see you again, honey.

Did you sleep all right?" she asked in her hoarse voice.

"I'm supposed to be asking you that," Lyndsay said and hugged her friend. "My suite is wonderful. Now, how are you?"

"I had a good night. I'll be on my feet in no time. Can't keep me down." This time her voice sounded more normal.

No, but they were going to try to keep her down, Lyndsay thought.

"You don't want to rush anything," Will said. He listened to her heart and her lungs. "Your lungs are doing better. Are you taking your medicine?"

A stubborn look crossed Anita Jane's face. "Of course, Will. And I took some horrible poison from Callie Rutherford's grandmother. That woman's trying to kill me."

"She means well, and there's nothing in her natural cure that will harm you."

"Where's your nurse?" Lyndsay asked.

"She'll be back tonight. I just sent Rowena on a couple of errands, but she'll be right back, and she'll stay with me during the day. About tonight, Lyndsay. My driver will take you to the theater at five-thirty. I can arrange for a friend to bring you back."

"I'll pick her up after the show," Will spoke up. "I promised her I'd show her the Christmas lights."

"Okay. That's arranged for tonight. Tomorrow—"

"Tomorrow we're going on the lake, and Thursday night we're invited to the party at the college. Next week we'll take in the Chamber's bash and the Grand Palace party for the entertainers."

Anita Jane's eyes grew wider with every plan Will announced.

"Sorry you won't be able to go, but right now you need to get some rest. You're talking too much. You don't want to overexert yourself. Can I help you into bed?"

"No. I breathe better sitting up. I'll be fine," she snapped.

"I'll check back with you before I go to the theater," Lyndsay said before she and Will stepped outside.

They didn't talk until they were out of earshot of the cabin.

"She's getting testy," Lyndsay said.

"Sure is," Will said with a grin.

"Will, you said you weren't lying about things, just walking around them. What about Anita Jane's lungs? You said they were better."

Will looked thoughtfully at the calm lake, then looked back at Lyndsay. "What do you know about asthma?"

"Is that an evasive response, so I don't get into the patient-doctor confidential area?"

Will nodded.

"Okay. I know she has asthmatic tendencies that flared up from time to time. I won't ask any more questions."

"There's no need for other questions. She's not having an episode." Will reached for her hand and held it quite naturally as they walked toward the lodge. Lyndsay hoped his medical training didn't allow him to feel her pulse through her fingertips, for she was sure her heart was beating a hundred times a minute.

He was only holding her hand, but a man had not held her hand in this companionable way since Trevor had died. It was both alarming and quite satisfying at the same time.

When they reached the lodge, Will said good-bye and promised to pick her up immediately after the show.

Lyndsay climbed the stairs in a daze. How could a hand offered in friendship affect her this way? Was she actually interested in a man? Wasn't that being disloyal to Trevor?

She paced her living room, restless to go out, yet not knowing where to go. A hike along the lake might be the answer. She pulled back her trademark long hair in a ponytail and stuffed it under a hat. Sunglasses completed a disguise that had worked very well for her for years. The lodge wasn't packed with tourists who had recognized her, but she had noticed a few stares when she and Daisy had taken their walk. She wasn't in the mood for signing autographs.

For an hour Lyndsay strolled along the water's edge, skirting soft areas. She rested on a fallen log and looked up at the tall hardwood trees with their winter silhouettes devoid of leaves. In spring this area would take on a whole new look—green renewal, the promise of new growth.

Maybe it was time for her to have a new growth, too. Her life with Trevor was finished, but her life wasn't over.

As always, when faced with difficult thoughts, Lyndsay turned to God.

Is it time to move forward? Lord, I don't know what to do. And I may be premature in even speaking of this. I've known Will only a short time, but I know I'm attracted to him. What I don't know is how he feels. Even if he isn't interested, I need to know how to handle this new feeling. How do I act? What do I do? I need direction.

Lyndsay bowed her head and cried healing tears. Her tears were for Trevor, for uncertainty, and for loneliness. After a few moments she rose from her perch on the log and retraced her steps toward the lodge. Her heart felt lighter, refreshed.

And she needed to talk to a friend. She followed the narrow road to Anita Jane's. In bringing her here, her older friend had started her on a different road of recovery. Maybe Anita Jane had had her best interests at heart.

Lyndsay rapped on the door and hugged Rowena after she opened the door. Out of the corner of her eye, Lyndsay saw Anita Jane dive for the recliner.

As much as Lyndsay wanted to let her friend off the hook, she couldn't since she'd agreed with Will to teach her a lesson. Maybe their farce wouldn't be carried on much longer. On the other hand, once the pretense was over, she'd be on a plane returning to Dallas and her life there. She frowned at that thought.

"Something wrong?" Anita Jane asked. Her hoarse voice was back.

Lyndsay shook her head. "No. Just checking to see how you are and to ask a question."

A concerned look crossed Anita Jane's face. "Ask."

Lyndsay sat down on the couch. "This is a little awkward, but I'd like to know more about Will Hamilton."

Anita Jane's face lit up like a light bulb.

"He's a true friend. You like him?"

"I don't really know him yet, but he's an interesting man. Tell me about him."

"He's a gentleman. Played football in college, but you may have guessed that from his size. Football and medical school seem a remarkable combination, but he's a remarkable kind of man. Is that the kind of thing you want to know?"

Lyndsay nodded. "Go on."

"He likes fishing, a real nut about it, but I don't know why. What's important is he's a Christian, and he puts others' needs ahead of his own. As far as medicine is concerned, he's an outstanding family doctor. His talent is in diagnosing. One of my backup singers went to him after being treated for diabetes. Will examined him and just by touching him, located a lump. That night they operated on him and found a tumor which had caused the diabetes."

"Pretty impressive. Is the singer all right?"

"He's had chemo and is in remission. And all thanks to Will Hamilton."

"Anything you don't like about him?" Lyndsay asked with a smile.

Anita Jane studied the ceiling. "He works too hard. Even on his days off, he's checking on patients. And there's one thing worse than that. His fishing. He'd rather fish than about anything."

Lyndsay laughed. "That's the worst thing?"

"That's it."

"Well, thanks," Lyndsay said and stood up to leave. "Sorry to have you talk so much. I know Will wants you to get some rest. I'll check back with you later."

Lyndsay enjoyed the walk back to the lodge. She ate a leisurely lunch at the restaurant, took a nap, read part of a mystery, and dropped in on Anita Jane again before time to get ready for the show.

Again the performance went well. As soon as the final curtain dropped, Lyndsay hustled to her dressing room. Will was already there, leaning against the wall and conversing with one of the staff.

As quickly as she could, Lyndsay took off her stage makeup and changed into street clothes. Again she stuffed her hair under a hat, then joined Will, who whisked her into his car.

"We just have time to make it to Silver Dollar City. It closes at ten, and I want you to see the big tree."

"The lights all along the strip are magnificent," Lyndsay said. Every theater and hotel sported string after string of lights. Some trees glistened with white lights only, others were multicolored.

"Just wait," Will said.

When they arrived at the 1890s theme park, they left the car in a huge lot and rode the shuttle to the main gate. Lights sparkled from every possible location, but the wire tree in the village green area surpassed them all.

Animated lighted ornaments, perfectly choreographed to music, brought the tree to life. It positively radiated warmth and good cheer. Lyndsay glanced at others around her. Not a solemn face looked up at the tree, but eyes were filled with wonder, and not just in the faces of youngsters. Senior citizens also gazed in awe at the spectacular tree.

Will held Lyndsay's hand and led her to a tiny wooden church where a pianist played carols. From inside she could see across a valley where lighted figures on the hillside appeared to be suspended in air.

They exited the church and walked the perimeter of the park, with Lyndsay's "oohs" and "aahs" joining the voices of other light-seers.

"I want to come back here again," she told Will when they arrived back at the car.

"We will," he promised. He drove downtown, and they strolled hand-in-hand along the lake where more animated lights held her spellbound.

"The whole place is a wonderland," she said as they stood and gazed on a lighted nativity scene.

"Life takes on a special glow at Christmas," Will said and pulled her into his arms. He looked down at her with tenderness in his eyes, and then he kissed her. Lyndsay thought she'd never breathe again.

Five

"I've wanted to do that since we met," Will said and this time kissed her on the forehead. He kept his arm around her shoulder as they walked back to the car.

"I've wanted you to do that since we met," Lyndsay said, then wondered why she'd been so forthright with him.

Will grinned, an ear-to-ear type of grin. "Then maybe we should try this once more." He turned her in his arms and kissed her again. And again Lyndsay's heart stood still.

When they pulled apart, Will asked, "Would you like to go fishing tomorrow afternoon?"

"Fishing?" she whispered. It was all the voice she could manage.

"I have the afternoon off and thought you'd like to see some of the natural wonders of the area." He didn't add that he'd had his schedule juggled so he could take her out on the lake. "And Thursday night is a party at the college that Anita Jane wouldn't miss for the world. It's one of her charities. I thought we'd make an appearance."

"Sounds like fun."

Will helped Lyndsay into the car and drove her home, detouring by sections of town that had more elaborate light displays.

He walked her to her suite and finally thought to ask, "Did you have dinner? Are you hungry?" He'd been in such a hurry to get her to Silver Dollar City that he'd forgotten that she might not have had time to eat before the show.

"I ate a sandwich around five, so I'm fine."

"Well, then, I guess this is good night." He wasn't about to let her go without a good-night kiss. She felt so right in his arms, even though she only came to his shoulder. He felt protective toward her, and more than that, he felt…love.

That thought jolted through him, and he ended the kiss and turned to leave. "I'll pick you up around one-thirty," he said and bolted down the stairs.

Love? What was he thinking? He'd only known her a couple of days. He'd felt sorry for her because of what Anita Jane had planned for her, and he felt anger at Anita Jane for manipulating Lyndsay, but love?

"Will Hamilton, get a grip!" he mumbled under his breath.

Instead of heading home, he went by Anita Jane's. The light was still on.

She opened the door and croaked a welcome.

Looking behind him, she asked "You alone?" in a normal voice.

"Yes. I just dropped Lyndsay off. When are you going to tell her? Hasn't this gone on long enough?" He didn't want it to end, but he wanted it over. He wished he could straighten out his feelings, but his mind was mush.

"Oh, I think she needs a little bit longer. Not much. She seems to be healing faster than I thought."

"Maybe that's because she didn't need healing. Maybe she's gone through all the mourning steps and is just living her own life in her own way without you controlling it."

Anita sat down in a chair and looked hard at Will, who paced back and forth. She didn't say a word, but raised her eyebrows at him.

"Maybe she should go on back to Dallas. Now. Tomorrow."

"I thought you were taking her out on the lake tomorrow."

"I am, but I can cancel that and take her to the airport instead."

"Why does her being here bother you?"

Will stopped his pacing. "She doesn't bother me. I just feel you shouldn't be so deceitful."

"Oh. So, you're worried about my mental well-being."

"Something like that."

Anita smiled and nodded. "That's very kind of you, Will. But I'll suffer through in my present state of mind for a few more days. Then I'll tell Lyndsay. If she bothers you, stay away from her. I'll arrange for others to occupy her time."

"I told you she doesn't bother me," he said in a forceful voice and walked toward the door. "She doesn't bother me," he said again. "Good night."

He was starting to lie as much as Anita. "She doesn't bother me," he said with a harsh laugh as he climbed behind the wheel. "Right."

❧

Lyndsay was ready by the time Will picked her up the next afternoon. She'd never been fishing in her entire life, so she was looking forward to a new experience. Anita Jane had told her to wear jeans and a heavy coat since it was colder on the water than on the shore. The temperature that morning when she'd walked to Anita Jane's had been just below freezing, but the sun had melted the frost and now the thermometer read in the upper forties.

"Which lake are we going to?" Lyndsay asked.

"I live on Taneycomo. It's actually the White River dammed up on both ends. Great rainbow trout. You'll see."

Will seemed unusually quiet, although Lyndsay reminded herself that she didn't know him well enough to make that determination. It just seemed that her every waking minute in Branson was spent with him.

"This is your home?" she asked, when he parked the car next to a rustic log house. It would have fit in perfectly with the building code at the lodge complex.

He nodded. "What do you think?"

Was it her imagination or did he sound defensive?

"It's so peaceful, and it fits right in with the woods."

He opened the door for her and showed her around the living room and kitchen, then asked if she'd make coffee while he changed clothes. He'd picked her up wearing a sport coat and tie, and she guessed he'd come straight from his office.

When he reappeared in a sweater, jeans and hiking boots, he poured the coffee into a thermos.

"It gets a little chilly on the water," he said and picked up the cashmere coat she'd laid on a chair. "This black coat's a little fancy for the lake. You'd better wear one of mine." He hunted through the hall closet, then handed Lyndsay an old brown quilted jacket. "That's the smallest I have."

Of course it swallowed her, but she rolled up the sleeves as best she could and once they were in his fishing boat and on the lake, she was glad the length came down to her knees. A wind blew steadily and dropped the temperature by ten degrees.

Will gazed open-mouthed at her when she asked him what to do with the pole.

"You don't know how to fish?"

"Well, I've seen fishing in movies, but is there something more than holding this pole in the water? I want to do it right."

"You've never fished?" He still had that disbelieving look on his face.

What was wrong with him? Why couldn't he grasp what she said?

"I'm a city girl. Born in Nashville, but raised in Dallas. I'm sure people there fish, but I don't think my dad did. He died when I was three. And I can guarantee my mom didn't fish."

He let out a long breath. "Okay. Rainbow trout should be biting this afternoon, and they don't care if you have a live worm wiggling at the end or an artificial lure."

Now it was Lyndsay's turn to let out a long breath. Her lucky day. She wouldn't have to fish with live worms.

Once he helped her put her line in the water, she watched Will change the piece of plastic on his hook and throw in his line.

"When the fish takes the bait, you reel him in. You can feel the tug."

"Like this?" she asked. Her pole was bowed from the weight of a fish on the other end.

"You've got one. Reel him in."

"It doesn't work." She tried to wind the string, but she couldn't turn it.

"Unfasten the clamp," he said and reached for her pole. While he wrestled with it, he stuck his pole under his arm and fidgeted with hers. "Wow, it's a big one. Pull up on your pole and wind."

As he handed her pole back to her, a fish bit his bait and jerked the pole out of his precarious hold. All he could do was watch his favorite pole sink into the water.

"I've caught one," Lyndsay shouted. "Look at the size of this fish. Isn't it big?"

Will turned back to her and saw one of the biggest fish he'd ever seen come out of Taneycomo. He helped her land it and stared at it, then at her, then at the spot where his pole lay on the bottom of the lake.

"Should we throw it back in and catch it again?" Lyndsay asked. She didn't want to think about killing the poor fish. And from the way Will was acting, she didn't think he was too excited about it, either. She'd heard that fishing wasn't about catching fish but about appreciating time and nature. The latter fit more into Will's character as she knew him than a hunter who would purposefully kill helpless fish.

"Throw it back?" Will asked. This woman was exasperating. The fish was mounting size, and she wanted to throw it back. She should be wanting to get it weighed. "It'll probably tip the scales at fifteen pounds."

"Well, I sure don't want to kill it, but I don't want to touch it either. Will you throw it back in?"

Will took her pole and unhooked the fish which had been flopping on the floor of the boat. It arched and skimmed the water when he dropped it overboard.

Another boat approached them, and he waved to Kevin, a lake patrol officer, who had another man with him.

"Having any luck?" Kevin asked as he drew his boat beside Will's.

"We caught a big one, fifteen pounds, but we threw it back," Lyndsay said.

Kevin shot a questioning glance at Will. "Usually you throw back the little ones," he said. "This is our new officer, Tom Whiting. I'm teaching him the ropes. Could you show him your fishing license, Dr. Hamilton? Ma'am?"

Will dug his wallet out of his back pocket and showed his license. Lyndsay sat still in the front of the boat.

When the officer turned to her, she held her hands out, palms up.

"I don't live here. I'm just visiting, and I don't have a license."

"Dr. Hamilton?" Kevin said.

"It didn't cross my mind that she'd need a license."

"Well, she does. But it looks to me like only one of you is fishing anyway. One pole, no fish, except the fifteen-pound one that you threw back in," he said and chuckled. "I guess she doesn't need a license this time. But before you drop a line in the water, you need to get a license." He stared at Lyndsay as if trying to place where he'd seen her.

"Okay," Lyndsay said. "I'll get one. Thanks."

The officers shoved off and soon disappeared around a bend in the long lake.

"Where's your pole?" Lyndsay asked.

"I dropped it in the lake," Will muttered.

"Oh," she said, wondering when he'd dropped his pole. "So, what do we do now?"

"Well, since you can't fish and don't want to hurt them anyway, I suggest we go back home."

Lyndsay glanced at her watch. "Could we go for a little ride first? I don't have to be back at the lodge for a couple of hours."

Will took a deep breath and studied the beautiful woman in his old brown coat. He wasn't being a very good sport about this. It wasn't her fault that she'd caught a bigger fish than he'd ever pulled out of the lake. And it wasn't her fault that he'd dropped his pole.

"Why don't you pour us some coffee, and I'll get this motor going. This isn't a speed boat; we'll just take it nice and easy."

He'd forgotten to bring an extra cup, so they shared the cup that served as a lid to the thermos. As they puttered down the lake, Lyndsay watched some ducks drop out of formation and land on the water.

Bare-limbed trees in a thick forest on one shore gave

way to high bluffs. Every curve and bend brought a new sight.

"It's beautiful here," she told Will. "I can see why you love it so much."

"You should see it in spring. There must be fifty shades of green everywhere you look. The summer's good, too. Hot sun, cool water. Fall's gorgeous with all the burnt oranges and red of the leaves."

"You ever think of running an ad agency?"

Will laughed. "I do sound like an advertisement, but there's no place like the Ozarks to live. It's a place of change." He handed her the cup of coffee so she could take a sip and took her free hand in his own.

A place of change, Lyndsay thought. She held his hand and looked at the man who had made her feel like a woman again. Yes, it was a place of change.

Six

"Did you ask Anita Jane to come?" Lyndsay asked Callie.

Daisy's first birthday was being celebrated in style. A private dining room at the lodge had been transformed into a wonderland of colorful balloons.

"Yes, but she declined. I told her we'd take her a piece of cake later."

Daisy sat in a high chair with a pie-sized cake of her own. Most of the icing was on her face, and part of the cake was on the floor.

Her guests were a who's who of performers in Branson. Of course, Morgan knew them, and although they didn't know Daisy, the party was a chance for the entertainers to get together on a personal basis, and that was an opportunity rarely afforded them. The award shows they attended had pre-gala events, but then the singers were too nervous to enjoy each others' company.

Lyndsay had found a log cabin doll house for Daisy. She'd have to be a little older to appreciate the fine craftsmanship that went into it and to have the memory that she'd celebrated her first birthday in Missouri, but Lyndsay knew Callie would put it on a shelf for a few years.

Will showed up at the party for about half an hour, and Lyndsay introduced him to the celebrities he didn't know. Odd to be in his town, yet be the one to know the party guests. Will fit right in, not standing in awe of celebrities like some people did who weren't part of the entertainment industry. Of course, he knew the singers who made Branson their year-round home, but many were booked at theaters for a month or two run, then went back on tour.

Since touring wasn't high on Lyndsay's list of favorite things to do, Branson was growing on her. She performed at night, but she wasn't packing up and flying to a different city during the days. Those hours were free, and she liked having the best of both worlds. The audience gave her affirmation of her talent, and they came to her; she didn't travel to them. She could see why Anita Jane spent several months here.

Will left the party with the promise to take Lyndsay to the local college's Christmas party that evening. With that in mind, Lyndsay wore her red silk dress when she delivered Anita Jane's promised piece of birthday cake and left from the cabin for the theater. As soon as the evening performance was over, she changed into the red silk again and met Will.

"Tonight's party will be a hundred eighty-degree change from that birthday party. A few celebrities might drop in after their shows, the ones who live here year round, but mostly it will be community people and those who teach at the college."

He drove them south of Branson to Point Lookout where the College of the Ozarks was built on a plateau overlooking lower hills and valleys.

This time it was Will who did the introducing. He let her meet several couples, all the time keeping a possessive arm on her shoulder or holding her hand. Several times he steered them away from Dave Robbins, but finally got cornered by his friend, who demanded an introduction.

"So, you're filling in for Anita Jane. She and I are good friends. I've been meaning to drop over and visit with her while she's recuperating. Perhaps you'll be there when I come."

"That would be nice," Lyndsay said politely. Dave looked every inch the college professor from his tweed jacket with leather patches at the elbows to his polished loafers. "How do you know Anita Jane?" she asked.

"She's one of the big contributors to the college. We're a very different college. All our students work their way through school by jobs on campus. Kids who wouldn't be able to afford college, but are dedicated to the pursuit of knowledge, will find a home here."

"An unusual approach," Lyndsay said. She was interested in the college, even if Dave sounded like an ad for the school. Although she'd accused Will of doing the same thing for the Ozarks, somehow it had sounded different coming from him.

"Would you like to see the facilities?" Dave asked. "We have a first-rate restaurant at the gate. We could go there for a cup of coffee, and we have an Ozarks' museum and even a fruitcake department that is a very busy place this time of year." He flashed a charming smile.

"A fruitcake department at a college?" Lyndsay asked.

"It's where all the nutty professors teach," Will said.

"That's Will's favorite joke. He usually adds that I'm the chair of the department, but I'm not," Dave said. "We're famous for our fruitcakes. And our orchids."

"Orchids in the Ozarks?" This place was intriguing. Maybe a little tour would be fun.

Will's pager beeped, and he looked down at the number.

"Sorry, I've got to call the hospital. I'll be right back." Although he'd managed so far to reschedule his on-call time, tonight he'd found no one to take over for him. He didn't want to leave Lyndsay with Dave, but he had no choice.

He found a pay phone in the hall and quickly determined that he'd have to leave.

Lyndsay was still talking to Dave, exactly where he'd left her. She seemed fascinated by what he was saying.

"I'm sorry to interrupt, but I've got to check on a patient." He took Lyndsay's arm.

"I'll be happy to take Lyndsay home," Dave offered, "so she doesn't have to leave the party. You can run along, Will."

Will looked at Lyndsay. He didn't want to leave her, but he had no choice. He didn't have time to take her back to the lodge, but he didn't want her with Dave.

"Thank you, Dave, but I'll go with Will," Lyndsay said, interpreting Will's thunderous look to mean she had come with him and had better leave with him. "I need to be getting back to check on Anita Jane."

"What about a tour tomorrow?" Dave asked. "I'm out of class at one. We could have lunch at the Friendship House, and I could show you around Anita Jane's favorite charity. She'd love for you to see the place."

Lyndsay smiled. Probably Anita Jane would like that since Will had also mentioned she was a big donor.

"That'll be fine. I'll meet you at the restaurant tomorrow," she said. "One o'clock." She turned and left with Will and had to hurry to keep up with his brisk pace.

At the stoplight, Will turned north instead of taking the road south to the lodge.

"I'll find someone to give you a ride home," he said. The hospital was little over a mile away; he could be there in two minutes versus the twenty-five minutes it would take to deliver Lyndsay to her door and get back. "I might not be too long."

"I don't mind waiting," Lyndsay said. "What's the emergency?"

"One of my older patients fell and broke his hip. The surgeon has been called, but Mr. Coble has asked for me. He's scared. And I'm scared for him."

"It's that serious?" A broken hip didn't sound like such a terrible injury.

"Mr. Coble's in his nineties. The kind of immobility we're talking about will limit his recovery. In a lot of cases with the elderly, a broken hip is the beginning of the end."

Will parked the car in the doctors' parking area, and they entered through the emergency room door.

"As soon as I check on him, I'll either come get you or find you a ride," Will said. "Sorry about this."

"It's all right," Lyndsay said, although she wondered why he'd looked so upset when Dave had offered her a ride if he were just going to find her another one. She'd had the impression they were friends.

Will disappeared through a swinging door, leaving Lyndsay in the waiting room. A gray-haired couple sat on one side, and a mother with a crying baby sat facing them, while on the far side an entire family of five alternated walking to the emergency room door and peaking in. Lyndsay walked around, studying the pictures on the walls, and could feel the gazes of the others on her.

She'd left her hair down. There had been no time to

arrange it artfully on top of her head, and she couldn't stick it under a hat to go to the Christmas party. But now everyone recognized her.

"Are you Lyndsay Rose?" A little girl from the family group had wandered over to her.

"Yes, I am. What's your name?"

"Jan Coble. I'm seven just yesterday."

"Happy Birthday, Jan. Has your grandpa been hurt?"

The little girl's mouth dropped open. "Do you know my grandpa? He broke his hip. Did you come to sing to him?"

"Well, if his doctor wants me to," Lyndsay said.

"His doctor wants you to." Will stood holding the swinging door open. "Actually Mr. Coble is a fan of yours. He didn't believe me when I said you were here."

Lyndsay let him usher her back to a curtained-off area where a frail-looking man lay on a hard table. His face was almost as white as the sheet under him, but his eyes became more animated when he saw her.

"Hello, Mr. Coble," Lyndsay said. "I just met your granddaughter Jan in the waiting room."

"That girl don't know a stranger," he said through clenched teeth. "You really been out with Doc? I told him he didn't need to leave some good-looking gal to come see me, and he told me you was with him."

"I'm with him all right."

"Well, I'll be." Although the pallor of his skin didn't change, his eyes seemed to twinkle. "Doc here's been holding out on me. It's time he settled down." He coughed, and his small frame shook, and with it his broken hip. He moaned.

"You're fine, Mr. Coble." Will took his hand. "That pain killer should be taking effect by now." Will studied the drip of the IV. "When the surgeon is ready, we'll take you down and get those bones pinned together. Then you'll be all set."

Lyndsay patted Mr. Coble's other hand. "I'll get out of the way, but I'll check on you tomorrow," she promised.

"I'll be out in a few minutes," Will said, and Lyndsay walked back into the waiting room.

"Did you see Grandpa?" Jan asked immediately. It wasn't Lyndsay's place to talk to the family, but if she were in their position, and she had been when Trevor had been so ill, she'd want to know everything that was going on.

"He's getting ready to go to surgery," Lyndsay addressed the family. "The doctor will pin his bones together, so they'll mend. He seems in good spirits, and that's so important."

Had he actually said Doc needed to settle down? She wished she'd taken in Will's reaction to those words.

Twenty minutes later Will exited the swinging doors. If he didn't know better, he'd say Lyndsay was giving a press conference, but instead of cameras and reporters with notebooks and tape recorders, hospital personnel and people in the waiting room were asking questions.

"I guess my favorite song would be the one I'm working on now," Lyndsay was saying. "Every time I start a new one, my favorite changes." She caught sight of him. "One last question. Jan?"

"Do you like my grandpa?"

"Yes, I do. And I'm going to come see him tomorrow."

Will made his way to her side and helped her with her coat, which she'd tossed in a chair.

"You've been a good audience," Lyndsay said. "My show starts at seven. Hope to see some of you there tomorrow night."

Calls of "Thanks," and "See you then," followed them outside, and Will noticed several people held up complimentary tickets.

"You gave out passes?"

"Anita Jane gave me a stack of them, and I hadn't given out any yet," she answered with a shrug. "How's Mr. Coble?"

"He's in surgery now. I'll check on him after I get you home. Seeing you did him a lot of good. Are you really going to visit him tomorrow?"

"I wouldn't have said I would if I didn't intend to."

She sounded a bit put out. "I know," he said. Anita Jane had told him she was a stickler about lying, and she'd apply that to herself above all others. But he knew that about her without remembering Anita Jane's words. He regretted his question, but a big star like Lyndsay Rose didn't drop in on an old man she'd just met and talked to for five minutes. But Lyndsay Rose was more than a big star. She was a woman who had known tragedy and overcome it, and she would remember how it felt and help others.

"Thanks for a most interesting evening," Lyndsay said a few minutes later at her door.

"The pleasure was mine," Will said. He tenderly kissed her. Then again and again. "Well, good night. I'll see you after your show tomorrow. Oh, have me paged when you come to the hospital."

She nodded. "Good night, Will."

She waltzed into her room and saw the light blinking on her phone. The message was to call Anita Jane.

She dialed the number, knowing what a night owl Anita Jane was, even though she was playing the invalid.

"Honey, I just wanted to make sure you were doing okay today, being the fifth and all," Anita Jane said.

Lyndsay nearly dropped the phone. Since she'd been in Branson, she hadn't been aware of the calendar, just of leaving for the show at five-thirty. Four years ago today Trevor had died.

Seven

"How could I have forgotten my husband's . . . ." Lyndsay trailed off. She couldn't call it his deathday, but that was exactly what it was. The opposite of birthday. She paced Anita Jane's living room. Although it was closing in on midnight, she had walked down to Anita Jane's cabin.

"Honey, is that a day you should remember?" Anita Jane asked. "Would Trevor want you to remember it with pain?"

"No, of course not. I just somehow feel disloyal."

"Nonsense. I think that's a sign of healing." She hummed a few bars of a song.

"Is your voice getting better?" Lyndsay asked as she tried to place the melody. "You don't sound so croaky."

"I'm not ready to sing for an audience, but I'm getting stronger. It's time I got out of here. Cabin fever's going to get me long before pneumonia ever could. How was the party tonight?"

Lyndsay knew Anita Jane was changing the subject for her benefit, and she went along with it, explaining about leaving early with Will for the hospital and about Will returning there now to check on Mr. Coble. "I'm going to meet Dave Robbins at the Friendship House for lunch tomorrow. He's going to give me a tour of the college."

"That college does a lot of good. If I get Will's okay, would you mind if I go with you? I haven't been out there in some time, and you wouldn't be gone too long, would you?"

"No, but are you feeling up to it?" Lyndsay wouldn't mind Anita Jane coming, but knew Will would veto it. They were trying to keep her housebound to teach her a lesson.

"I'm feeling much stronger. You said Will was going back to the hospital?" At Lyndsay's nod, Anita Jane dialed the hospital number and had him paged. "I told you he worked too hard. See what I mean?" She turned her attention to the phone and explained to Will about the next day's outing.

At the other end of the line, Will Hamilton breathed a sigh of relief. He didn't want Lyndsay spending one minute with Dave Robbins. Anita Jane just might be a Christmas angel after all. She was sure helping him out right now.

"Are you ready to tell her the truth?" he asked.

"No. I'm not strong enough to sing yet, but I'd like to

71

get out of this place for an hour or so. We wouldn't be gone long."

This was getting better and better. It would insure that Lyndsay didn't spend much time with Dave.

"Okay, I'll tell her you can go."

Anita Jane handed the phone to Lyndsay.

"I think we'd better let her get out before she does something rash," Will said. "Besides, she might catch on to us if I told her she couldn't go, since it is with you, and since she is pretending to feel better."

"If you think that's wise," Lyndsay said.

"It'll work out fine. Oh, Mr. Coble is in recovery and doing fine."

"Already?"

"The procedure only takes thirty minutes. It was a lag screw and plate job. He was lucky he didn't need a prosthesis. This could have been much worse, but now I'm optimistic for him."

Lyndsay didn't understand what he meant by lag screw or prosthesis, but the important thing was the optimistic part.

"I'm glad," she said. "Are you headed home?"

"Pretty soon. I'll wait until he's awake enough to reassure him. I'll see you tomorrow. Will you drop by after your tour of the school?"

"Yes. Good night." Lyndsay hung up the receiver and looked thoughtfully at Anita Jane, who was humming that tune again. "Well, it's all set. I was going to ask if I could use your driver. Is he someone on call or can I rent a car?"

"Oh, I'll take care of that. Be ready at twelve-thirty, and we'll pick you up. Now I'd better get my beauty sleep. And, honey, I'm glad you're doing all right."

Lyndsay nodded, knowing she was referring to Trevor. She hugged her friend and then walked the narrow road back to the lodge.

It took some time for her to fall asleep. She thought of Trevor. And she thought of Will saying it was all right for Anita Jane to get out. Was he wanting to end this farce? Was he wanting to end their time together?

"Dear God," she prayed aloud. "I feel like I'm at a turning point in my life, and I don't know which way to go. Please direct me. Please."

ॐ

Anita Jane was right on time. Lyndsay had been watching out the window of the lobby, and walked outside before the driver climbed the steps of the lodge. Her friend looked the picture of health in a navy blue wool coat buttoned up against the weather that had turned frigid during the night.

"What happened to warm afternoons?" Lyndsay asked once she was settled in the back seat with Anita Jane.

"They tell me there's an Ozark saying: If you don't like the weather, stick around ten minutes and it'll change. But I don't think it's likely to change back to warm anytime soon."

"It can't be over twenty. With the wind chill it's easily in the single digits. Are you sure you should be out in this?"

Lyndsay wasn't about to let Anita Jane off the hook. "I'm bundled up."

"All right. But if you get tired, say the word and we'll leave. This tour isn't that important. Dave said you would like for me to see the college, and he'd asked to take me home last night, but I wanted to go with Will, and I didn't want to hurt Dave's feelings, but I didn't want to encourage him. Sorry, this isn't making much sense, is it?"

"Perfect sense. This is much safer."

Lyndsay raised her eyebrows. "Exactly."

At the Friendship House, the two women sat at a table and waited for Dave. When he arrived, he glanced at Anita Jane then at Lyndsay.

"You brought a chaperone," he said. "Was this Will's idea?"

Anita Jane grinned. "No, I asked myself along."

"Why would you think Will had anything to do with this?" Lyndsay asked.

"I can read his signs. I've known the boy all my life."

The boy? Never in her wildest imagination would Lyndsay call big Will Hamilton a boy.

"You're wearing a hat," Dave commented.

"Yes. It's cold outside," Lyndsay said with a smile. It was a perfectly good small-brimmed hat that matched her black coat, but she wasn't about to take it off even inside. She had pulled her hair back in a ponytail and stuffed it under the hat. She wanted an easy afternoon, not one where she had to sign autographs.

She steered the conversation back to Will and over lunch Dave entertained them with tales of Will and himself as lifelong friends, fishing Ozark waters and dating the same girls in high school.

After lunch, Dave drove them around to the different buildings. Lyndsay had to admit it was interesting. Seeing seven thousand orchids in the greenhouse stunned her. The fragile flowers seemed out of place. The weaving studio and grain mill were much more in keeping with what she thought of the Ozarks.

Before they ventured into the museum, Anita Jane said she was feeling tired, and they'd better cut their tour a little short. Dave drove them back to the Friendship House where their driver was waiting.

"I'm glad we left early," Lyndsay said as they pulled out of the gate. "It's a fascinating place, but I want to go to the hospital this afternoon. I promised Mr. Coble that I'd visit him today. Remember, the man with the broken hip? Would you mind if I borrowed the car after we drop you off?"

"I'd like to meet him myself. Billy, take us to Skaggs Hospital."

"But if you're tired. . ."

"I'm not that tired. Is Will at the hospital? Maybe he'll take time to listen to my lungs and tell me I'm all right now."

"I'm supposed to page him when I get there."

Anita Jane smiled and hummed that tune again until they arrived at the hospital. What was that song?

At the information desk, Lyndsay asked for Mr. Coble's room.

"Two-fourteen," the receptionist said. "I had instructions to call Dr. Hamilton when you arrived."

"Good. Please tell him we'll be in two-fourteen," Lyndsay said.

Mr. Coble's daughter, whom Lyndsay had met the night before, sat in the only chair in the hospital room. Mr. Coble's eyes were closed.

Lyndsay motioned for the woman not to disturb her father.

"Pappy would never forgive me if I didn't wake him up to see you," she said in a raised voice. "He talked about nothing else all morning. Is that Anita Jane Wells with you? She's his favorite singer. Oh, no offense, Miss Rose."

Lyndsay grinned and looked at Anita Jane. "They're more the same age," she said and winked. "Hello, Mr. Coble." Obviously their conversation had awakened him. She walked to his side and took his hand that wasn't attached to the IV. "I've brought you another visitor."

"Anita Jane Wells! Is that really you?"

Anita Jane laughed. "How are you, Mr. Coble? I heard you had a fall. Are they treating you all right in here?"

"They're not feeding me. I want fried chicken, not this here colored water they call soup."

"You'll be on solid food soon, Mr. Coble," Will said from the doorway. He moved over by Lyndsay. "How'd it go at the college?" he asked in a low voice.

"Very interesting. But we didn't stay long. Anita Jane was tired."

Will nodded. She was earlier than he expected, although he'd been waiting impatiently for the receptionist's call. It had been a good day at the office with patients early and appointments running ahead of schedule. He had two more routine physicals scheduled, and had only fifteen minutes before he should walk back to his office in the building next door.

"Would you pop in and see another patient of mine?" he asked Lyndsay. Anita Jane had settled in the chair the daughter had vacated and was visiting with Mr. Coble about the way the music business had changed and what had become of the old sound, when a fiddle and guitar were the main instruments instead of an orchestra playing behind the singers.

Will led Lyndsay from room to room introducing her to his patients.

"Do you usually make hospital rounds during the afternoon?"

"No. I do it in the morning and again in the evening, around six or so."

"But today is different?"

"Yes. When I saw what you did for Mr. Coble, I

figured you could raise the spirits of my other patients, too. I can see why Princess Di makes hospital visits. And now I have to get back to the office. Thanks for doing this."

"You're welcome," she said as he walked her back to Mr. Coble's room. "Oh, Anita Jane said something about getting you to listen to her lungs. Is that for real or is it part of her plan?"

Will asked Anita Jane to step into an empty room while Lyndsay talked to Mr. Coble. Her lungs were clear, not even a whisper of a wheeze from asthma, but he didn't expect to hear one. She was as healthy as a horse.

"You could be singing."

"Soon."

"Could I have a time table on this? When are you telling her the truth?"

"That depends on her. Her contract ends a week from Saturday. I'll tell her before then, so she can make travel arrangements."

Will frowned. He didn't want to think about Lyndsay leaving. But what could he do? What did he really feel towards her? Last night he'd been afraid to look at Lyndsay for her reaction to Mr. Coble's comment about settling down. He'd known Lyndsay only a few days. He couldn't base a relationship on a few hours spent together. Oh, there was chemistry between them, he couldn't deny that.

"Will?" Anita Jane's voice sounded as if she'd said his

name more than once.

"Yes?"

"I asked where you were taking her tonight?"

"I'm not sure. Going out yourself?" he asked with a wicked grin. "You wouldn't want her to see you. This little outing has worn you out. I'll be sure and tell her so."

"You want me to tell her the truth now?" Anita Jane asked.

"Yes," he said, but his heart cried "no." Lyndsay couldn't leave now. They needed more time together. More time to know each other. More time to share their deepest secrets and their highest goals.

Anita Jane frowned with her mouth and with her eyes and with the line on her forehead.

"Well, I can't yet. I just can't." She stormed off muttering something about hard-headed men.

What was with his old friend? One minute she was as sweet as lemonade on a hot day and the next she was all frowns and anger.

He followed her to Mr. Coble's room and arranged with Lyndsay to take her to dinner after tonight's show and to his office party on Saturday night. Sunday he'd attend her gospel singing show in the morning and take her out afterward for Sunday dinner. Then maybe they could go for a long drive, and he'd show her more of the wonderful area he loved. He wanted her booked up. He wouldn't let Dave weasel his way in again.

Eight

The Friday show went off without a hitch and, like her other performances, was a sell-out. When she walked on stage, Lyndsay waved to the folks from the hospital waiting room who sat in the front row of the side section. She was glad they'd come and felt as if they were family. Odd. She'd only met them the night before, but maybe when people were thrown together in an emergency room, they tended to bond. She called Jan Coble and her cousins up for the "Jingle Bell" sleigh ride number and gave them gifts from under the giant Christmas tree at the end of the song.

After the show, Will took her out to dinner at a small steak house where their booth was at the back. They talked about Will's patients she'd met, and he told her about growing up in Branson and his friendship with Dave.

"Morgan and Callie are leaving tomorrow," Lyndsay told him over dessert. "Did you know Grandma's been forcing that remedy of hers on Anita Jane every day?"

"So I've heard. That's probably been harder on her than staying home."

"Do you think we've taught her a lesson yet?" Lyndsay didn't want to know, yet she had to find out if he wanted out of squiring her around. "Is this one of Anita Jane's favorite places?" It was a romantic little place, but were they there to keep Anita Jane from showing up?

"She loves this place, but I don't think she'll show up tonight. She wants to keep you in the dark awhile longer, and I'm not sure why. She got angry this afternoon when I told her she should tell you."

So, he did want it over. He'd asked Anita Jane to tell her the truth. What a topsy-turvy world she was in. One minute she thought he cared for her, and the next minute he was telling her he wanted to get rid of her. Oh, he hadn't said it in those words, and certainly his kisses didn't communicate that sentiment. What did he want from her?

"Could we go now?" she asked. She smiled, but it was forced. She needed the privacy of her room to evaluate this bit of information. And she needed away from him.

"Sure." He signaled for the bill. "Tired? The hours I've been off work, you've been working."

She smiled instead of answering. Her throat was

filled with the tears she wouldn't let show. What was wrong with her? On the way home, she answered his questions with monosyllabic replies. Her mind whirled with thoughts and emotions. She'd been crazy to think that Will cared about her. She'd been crazy to think of loving again.

She hummed that song that Anita Jane had been humming the last couple of days. It had been in her mind, but now she remembered the name. "Only Love Can Break a Heart; Only Love Can Mend It Again." Gene Pitney. A song from long ago. How ironic that she remembered it now. Well, Gene was wrong. In her case, love broke a heart, and broke a heart again.

When they arrived back at the lodge, Will took the road to Anita Jane's. "Just to make sure she's in," he said.

In the street light Lyndsay could see a wisp of smoke from the cabin's chimney.

"She's burning a fire," she commented. "Pull in, Will."

He glanced at her, but parked the car in the narrow drive.

"I want it over with." Lyndsay opened her door and stepped out before Will could turn the engine off. A few steps before she reached the cabin, Will caught up to her and placed a restraining hand on her arm.

"Why, Lyndsay? Why now? We still have a week together."

Lyndsay looked up at the big man. "I don't like

games, and I don't like deceit," she said in a louder voice than she'd intended.

"Who's out there?"

Lyndsay turned back toward the cabin, even though Will didn't release her arm. "It's Lyndsay."

The door opened, and light spilled out onto the sidewalk, silhouetting Anita Jane's form. She looked at Lyndsay then at Will.

"Are you fighting?"

"No," Lyndsay said.

"Yes," Will said at the same time.

"Come on inside, and we'll straighten this out."

Lyndsay removed Will's hand from her arm and strolled ahead of him into the cabin. She took a seat in a chair opposite Anita Jane's recliner. Will stood by the fireplace.

"Well?" Anita Jane asked.

Now that the game was up, Lyndsay wasn't sure how to start. Attack Anita Jane for being insensitive, not only to her emotions but also for using Will's time, or merely ask for an explanation? They hadn't planned this part. But then this wasn't a mutual decision. For some reason Will wasn't ready, although earlier he'd said. . . It was too confusing.

"I know you're not sick," Lyndsay blurted out.

"Yes, I know you know," Anita Jane said.

"Why did you do this? Why did you bring me down here under false pretenses?" Now that she had started, the going was easier. "Didn't you know how I would feel? Didn't you care that I'd be devastated knowing one more person I loved. . ." She stopped when Anita Jane's answer registered. "You know that I know?"

"Of course. Once Will Hamilton saw you, I knew he'd never let you think I was next to death's door. He has more compassion than that."

"You set me up?" Will asked. He'd been leaning on the mantel, but now he stood straight and tall. "Why?"

"I told you. I'm your Christmas angel."

"Nonsense," Will said. "You have purposely manipulated two lives." His voice was rising with each word.

"Yes, I have," Anita Jane said calmly and with a smile on her face.

"Anita Jane." Lyndsay strove for calmness in her voice. "Please explain your actions. And don't pull that Christmas angel thing. Will told me you wanted me to be with people, but you know I'm not a recluse in December. I'm with people I choose to be with. And I really do write songs in December."

"I know. I did this for Will."

"For me?" he asked.

Lyndsay glanced at Will, who looked as bewildered as she felt.

"Yes, you. All you do is live at that hospital. And fish. That's it. You need more. You deserve more. So, I decided to get it for you."

"I'm the more?" Lyndsay asked. She had never blushed before in her life, but she felt hot and knew she was beet red.

"What about Dave? If you brought her here for me, why did you keep pushing her toward him?" Will asked.

"Oh that." Anita Jane dismissed his question with a wave of her hand. "A decoy. He didn't know anything about my plan, but I knew you wouldn't want him becoming friendly with Lyndsay. And that would make you spend more time with her yourself."

Lyndsay's humiliation was complete. "You've really manipulated Will and me. Why didn't you try honesty?"

"If I'd asked you to come down for a few weeks because I wanted to fix you up with a nice man, would you have come?"

"No."

"That's what I thought," Anita Jane said with a nod.

"But, your plan didn't work. Just tonight Will told me he wanted you to tell me the truth. He wants me to go."

"No, I don't." In two quick strides, Will reached Lyndsay and pulled her out of her chair. "I never said I wanted you to go. I wanted everything to be honest, but I don't want you to leave—ever." He held her shoulders in a tight grip.

Lyndsay looked up at the big man. "Then what do you want?"

"I want time. Lots of time with you. I want to learn all there is to know about you. I want you to learn about me and learn to love me. . . like I love you," he said in a soft voice.

Lyndsay gasped. She'd prayed for God to give her directions for this crossroads in her life. The direction couldn't be any clearer.

Will still held her by the shoulders, and she reached up and placed her hands on his arms. "I do love you. But we've only known each other a few days."

Will smiled and bent down and kissed her.

"Then what we both want is time. Will you stay here in Branson through Christmas? Please?"

"Yes."

"We'll get to know each other—what we like and what we don't like. We'll give our relationship time to grow. A courtship period, that's what we need."

Lyndsay threw her arms around him. "Right now I feel this could be the shortest courtship in history."

Anita Jane cleared her throat. Will and Lyndsay turned toward her.

"Am I to take it this Christmas angel is forgiven for her meddling?"

Headlights coming down the road shined in through a gap in the drapes at the front window, and for an instant the light settled around Anita Jane's head.

Will and Lyndsay glanced at each other.

"Did you see a halo?" Lyndsay whispered in awe.

Will laughed and shook his head to dislodge the image. "If I did, it was a tarnished one."

Veda Boyd Jones is the author of six inspirational romances, including the award-winning *Callie's Mountain* (**Heartsong Presents**). Besides her fiction writing, Veda has authored numerous articles for popular periodicals. A sought-after speaker at writers' conferences, Veda lives with her husband and "three rambunctious boys" in Joplin, Missouri.

Hope you find your own Christmas angel.

Seasons Greetings,

Veda Boyd Jones

Christmas Dream

Tracie Peterson

One

"Would you care for anything to drink?" the dark-haired flight attendant asked Mark Williams. Her brilliant smile and honey-smooth voice caused Mark to look up with a grin.

"I'll take coffee," Mark replied and turned to his wife. "How about you, Texas Rita?" The nickname was born out of his wife's pretended desire to move to the warmth of the south and forget about Alaska.

Rita pushed back her shoulder-length black hair and shook her head. "No, I'm fine."

"Where are you headed?" the flight attendant asked Mark as though she had only him to serve.

"Fairbanks."

"What a coincidence. I live in Fairbanks."

"We live near Tok, actually," Mark told her, taking the coffee.

The woman eyed Rita as though noticing her for the first time. "Oh," was all she said before pressing on to serve the next row of passengers.

"Friendly service," Mark said with a wink at his wife.

She appeared a little too friendly as far as Rita Williams was concerned. Her marriage to Mark, now barely a month old, left her feeling very possessive of the man at her side. "She was a flirt and you know it," Rita said, pretending to read the magazine in front of her.

"Your eyes look like black diamonds when you're angry," he whispered against her ear, then nipped the lobe playfully to make sure he had her attention.

"Mark!" she squealed, without meaning to. The flight attendant glanced back to see what the commotion was, causing Rita to break into a fit of laughter. "Being married to you is so stressful," she teased. "Women are always looking you over."

"Right," Mark said, unconvinced.

"I've seen it with my own eyes," Rita replied, putting the magazine into the seat pocket. "When we were at that kennel outside of Seattle and you were browsing through the sled dog possibilities, you weren't aware of the way those two women proprietors were looking you over. I thought maybe for a minute they were going to ask to see your papers."

Mark laughed. "Yes, but I was checking out the dogs, not the women, so you have no reason to be jealous."

"Jealous! Me?" Rita tried to sound indignant. "I'm not jealous, just annoyed."

Mark reached his hand up to touch her cheek. He

smelled of spicy musk and looked at her with such passionate warmth that Rita instantly felt her face grow hot. "I'm yours, Rita. Nobody else matters. No one else is of any interest," he whispered low and seductively against her ear.

Rita melted against him and sighed. This was the man she loved and had pledged to spend the rest of her life with. She mentally pictured the home that awaited them outside of Tok, Alaska. A lovely cabin built by Rita's father, August Eriksson, and Mark, and decorated by Rita and her mother, Beth. A lovely home. Her home. Hers and Mark's.

"You mean the world to me, Rita," Mark, said, then took a long drink of his coffee before adding, "besides, who else will help me with the dogs when it's forty below?"

"Mark!" Rita exclaimed with a sharp jab to his ribs. Coffee threatened to spill on them both, but Mark mastered the cup quickly. "What a thing to say!"

"Well, a hundred dogs take a lot of work."

Rita thought of their kennel. Her father and Mark had raised and cared for the dogs when they held a partnership in the kennel. Upon Mark's marriage to Rita, August had presented his share of the kennel to them as a wedding gift. While much appreciated by the newlyweds, August's gift demanded a great deal of attention. Sled dogs needed to be constantly worked in order to stay happy and healthy.

"I hope Daddy found someone to help him," Rita

thought aloud, sobering at the thought of her aging father out working in the icy north cold.

"I'm sure he did."

"You should have let me call them," Rita said. "I'm sure other people phone home on their honeymoons. What if they needed us?"

"Rita, you have nine other brothers and sisters. If there had been an emergency, they would have had a small nation of people to call to their rescue."

"I know, and there was a time not long ago that it wouldn't have mattered to me whether they needed me or not," Rita said, remembering her rebellious youth.

Born the youngest of ten children, Rita had struggled to feel a part of the massive brood. The age differences were so diverse, as were the lifestyles and interests of her siblings, that there was never any one thread that held them all together. True, there were the threads of Christianity and two rock-solid parents who loved their children more than life itself, but until Rita had put her life in God's hands the previous March, she'd completely ignored these valid treasures.

"So do you want to stop by the folks on our way home, or shall we go to the cabin first?"

Rita heard Mark's question above the drone of jet engines and passenger chatter, but it startled her for a moment. "We're really going to keep house together," she said.

Mark laughed. "Guess so, unless you'd like to move back in with your parents and visit on the weekends."

Rita wrapped her arms around his. "No way. I'm very possessive of what's mine, and you, Mark Williams, belong to me." She grinned up at him and met his loving gaze. "I think I would just as soon go on home and call Mom and Daddy from there."

"Christmas is really going to be different for us," he said thoughtfully.

"Definitely. I've never known a time when I cherished the thought of being in the middle of all my brothers and sisters and their kids. But this year, I do. I keep thinking that they'll all be there when we get home, and it makes me so anxious. I haven't even seen some of them in years."

"It's too bad they couldn't have all come for the wedding," Mark commented.

"Yeah," Rita agreed, "but you know, I like this better. It was a trade-off, the wedding or Christmas. But I'm glad Christmas won out. Mom and Dad aren't getting any younger, and this will be a very important celebration for them. Just imagine it, Mark: all the children you'd brought into the world gathered around you with their children and, in some cases, their children's children."

"So you want to have ten kids?" he questioned.

Rita rolled her eyes. "No, I most certainly do not. Let Mom and Dad hold that record. I just want us to have a nice-sized family that you can seat around one table when you go out to eat."

"We could just request big tables."

"We could just leave you at home," she teased.

He ignored her. "So what do we do first? I mean when we get home."

Rita paused a moment to consider their options. "Well, I thought it would be a lot of fun to sled out and cut our own Christmas tree."

"Naturally. The dogs will be half crazy for a run."

Rita and Mark were avid dog sled racers, and anything connected to dogs and sleds had become a major part of their lives. Even though Rita had a job in Tok at one of the local doctor's offices, she was seriously considering giving it up to help Mark with the kennel. It was either that or hire on someone to work part time.

"So then what?" Mark asked.

"We decorate the tree of course," she replied. "I thought maybe tomorrow on Christmas Eve you and I could spend a quiet, romantic evening together. We could decorate the tree, drink hot chocolate, and exchange our gifts to each other."

"Didn't you get enough of that romance stuff on our honeymoon?" He sounded annoyed, but there was a twinkle in his eye.

"I'll never get enough of that romance stuff, Mark, so you'd better just get used to the fact here and now. I expect to be—"

The annoying bong of the airline's intercom system demanded their attention. "Ladies and gentlemen, this is your captain. A medical emergency has made it necessary for us to divert to Juneau. Please assist the flight attendants by returning your trays and chairs to their upright and locked positions. We'll try to be back up and running just as soon as possible, so please be patient with us. Thank you."

"A medical emergency?" Rita questioned. "I wonder if they need any help."

Mark reached up to signal the attendant. When she appeared, looking a bit harried, Mark offered her a smile. "My wife is a registered nurse. Do you need any additional assistance?"

The woman relaxed a bit. "No, we have it under control, but thank you." She gave Rita an appreciative nod.

Thick white clouds engulfed the plane as they descended. Rita felt a bit hemmed in by the sudden loss of open skies. "Seems so cold and frightening," she whispered.

Mark glanced out the window. "We'll be through it before you know and then—"

The captain's voice again interrupted. "The National Weather Service reports a major storm has moved into the area, leaving visibility dangerously low. Another massive system has moved down from the north where it dumped two feet of new snow and ice on Fairbanks, closing the airport there. We'll try to keep you posted with any news of the situation, but for now we'll be grounded in Juneau until further notice. Attendants, please prepare the cabin for landing."

"I don't believe this!" Rita tried not to raise her voice.

"Mark, we have to get home. It's nearly Christmas."

Mark quickly drained the last of his coffee. "I just hope they have a good restaurant. I'm starved."

"How can you think of food at a time like this? All of our plans are in shambles. Why can't we just fly over the storm?"

"Where are you going to land, even if they do?" Mark tried to reason.

"May I take that for you, sir?" the flight attendant asked. She was all business.

"Thanks." Mark handed her the cup and turned back to talk to Rita.

"Sir, you'll have to return your tray to its upright and locked position," the flight attendant told him before he could comfort his wife.

Doing as he was directed, Mark smiled at the woman. There was no return smile for Rita to object to, but she was concerned by the woman's preoccupied manner. Were they actually in more danger than the captain had let on? Was the medical situation just an excuse?

"Excuse me, miss," Rita said, causing the flight attendant to halt. "What's the condition of the airport at Juneau?"

The woman's gaze seemed to dart from one side of the cabin to the other, as if trying to determine whether she should answer the question.

"Yeah," an older businessman chimed in from across the aisle. "What is the condition? Am I going to be able to get a cab into town?"

"I'm sure the captain can better advise us," the flight attendant said. "I'll relay your questions to him and have him check on the airport conditions." She quickly made her way to the front of the plane, leaving Mark and Rita staring after her.

The businessman had already returned his attention to a computer printout on his lap. "It's just like I thought," he muttered. "Juneau must be nearly snowed in already."

"What?" Rita questioned, leaning across Mark. "Do you think we're in any real danger?"

"We're twenty thousand feet in the air and planning to land in high winds on what is probably an ice-covered runway. What do you think?" the man asked gruffly.

Rita was taken back, but Mark was angered by the man's attitude.

"There's no need to be that way with her. She asked a simple question."

The man looked up at Mark and the tightness in his expression relaxed a bit. "No, there was no need, and I do apologize. I'm not going to make it home for Christmas at this rate, and I promised this year would be different. Three kids are sitting in Fairbanks, expecting me to be there on Christmas Eve for their church program, and it'll be just one more year that business came between us. I shouldn't have taken it out on you, ma'am, and I do apologize."

Rita's heart went out to the man. "I understand. I feel the same way. My family is expecting me home for Christmas as well."

The man went back to his report with a shrug that said it all as far as Rita was concerned. They were up against something bigger than they could control.

"We should pray, Rita."

Mark's words broke through her self-pity. Together they held hands, and Mark murmured petitions to God, while Rita begged forgiveness for her selfish focus.

Two

Juneau's airport was filled with disgruntled travelers, most of whom were arguing with airport officials and demanding information about their flights.

Lugging their carry-on baggage with them, Rita and Mark found a spot to sit and discuss their situation.

"I can't stand this," Rita said, plopping down beside her husband. "It isn't fair. I had such plans."

"Just be glad we're on the ground safely and not flying around trying to navigate this weather. Look out there and tell me you wouldn't rather be here safe and sound."

Rita glanced out the window. It was impossible to see anything but white. "I'd rather be almost anywhere but here!" She crossed her arms defiantly against her chest and pouted.

"Look, I'm going to brave the crowd and see if I can learn anything about our situation," Mark said, getting

101

to his feet. "You want me to bring you back anything?"

"No," Rita replied curtly.

Shaking his head, Mark turned and trudged toward a ticket agent.

The look on Mark's face when he returned told Rita everything she needed to know. Clearly disappointed, Mark took the seat beside her and slouched down, sticking his hands deep into his pockets. "We're not going anywhere for a good long while. This storm has no intention of letting up, and there isn't any transportation in or out of town. Too dangerous."

"So we're to just sit here? Is that it?"

"That's it. Look, Rita, I know you wanted to hear better news. So did I."

Rita shook her head. "This is our first Christmas together. I had such great plans, and now everything is ruined."

"It's not ruined," Mark protested. "So we celebrate late if need be."

Rita narrowed her eyes. "You just don't get it, do you? I've planned this for months. I've given our first Christmas celebration almost as much planning as I did our wedding."

"And a lovely wedding it was, as I recall," he added, grinning from ear to ear.

Rita knew it was his attempt to lighten her mood, but she'd have no part of it. "Don't! Don't even try to make a joke about this."

"Well, what do you suggest I do? Lose my temper

like you?" Mark lowered his voice to a whisper and added, "I can't see where getting angry about it is going to get us out of here any faster. You can go up there and make a spectacle of yourself by raging at the airline personnel, but I don't think it's going to change a thing."

"You just don't care," Rita said in a voice that mingled hurt and angry accusation. "If you really cared, you wouldn't talk like that."

"Well, tell me what you want to hear, Rita, and I'll say it. But my words won't change the fact that the National Weather Service has issued winter storm warnings and we're grounded hundreds of miles short of our objective."

"It's not our objective, it's home. We can't get home, and it's almost Christmas!" Rita declared, not caring that her raised voice was attracting attention.

"Rita, calm down." Mark reached out to take hold of her hand, but she'd have no part of it. "There is a time and place for everything. This is neither the time, nor the place."

"I'm angry, Mark. I'm angry about this storm and the complications to my plans, but most of all I'm angry at you for not understanding how important this was to me. I thought you knew me so well."

Mark eased back in his chair and replaced his hands in his pockets. "I understand you well enough to know there isn't any reasoning with you when you're like this. You're being childish and misjudging me. I care a great deal about what's important to you, and believe me, blizzard or no blizzard, if I had a sled team at my disposal, I'd put you on it. But I don't, so you're stuck here with me and all the rest of these disappointed people, and if you'd stop feeling sorry for yourself, you'd see that everyone here is in the same position you are."

"Fine!" Rita got to her feet, grabbed her purse, and stomped off without looking back once to gauge Mark's reaction. She wanted him to come after her and assure her that everything would be all right and that her Christmas dream would still come true. But he didn't.

After stomping around the terminal for about fifteen minutes, Rita was a little calmer, but no less upset. *This isn't the way I want it to be, God.* She leaned against the wall outside the ladies' restroom and looked to the ceiling.

I had such plans and hopes, she continued. *I wanted to share this Christmas with all my family. I wanted to have a romantic Christmas Eve with Mark, just the two of us in our new home with our own tree and decorations.* Tears filled her eyes. *I won't be a cry baby about this,* she thought, putting an abrupt end to her prayer.

Glancing around her for the first time, Rita noticed other travelers. Concern and disappointment lined their faces and mirrored the hurt inside her soul. Dreams were supposed to be fun, hopeful things, not painful reminders of what you couldn't have, Rita thought. At least, that was the way she figured it should be.

"You look like you're carrying the weight of the world, deary," an aged female voice called from the right.

Rita looked over to find an elderly woman sitting not five feet away, crocheting with a huge ball of white thread. The woman's gray head remained bent over her project even as she continued. "This is a sorry time to be stranded in an airport. Do you have far to go?"

"Fairbanks, and then we were going to take a hop to Tok. How about you?"

The woman looked up and smiled. "I was headed home to Fairbanks after visiting my grandchildren in Seattle."

Rita nodded but remained fixed to her spot.

"Why don't you come sit a spell with me. I'm Abbey," the woman said and cleared off the seat beside her. "Abbey Strom."

"I'm Rita Eriks. . . ," she paused, shook her head, and began again. "Rita Williams. I'm returning from my honeymoon, but I'm still not used to the name."

Abbey smiled again and put down her handwork. "How wonderful! And where's your young man?"

Rita grimaced. "I'm afraid I ditched him at the other end of the terminal. We had a difference of opinion."

"Ah," Abbey said with a knowing nod. "Is this your first fight?"

Rita laughed, breaking her melancholy mood. "Good grief, no. We fight all the time. Well, not really fight. I'm just opinionated and he's, well. . .he's opinionated too."

Abbey nodded again. "Sounds like my Herman. Goodness, but that man could argue up a storm to rival the blizzard outside. Will you forgive your young man right away or make him sweat it out?"

Rita shrugged. "I don't see anything to be gained by holding a grudge. I just wish he better understood me and why it was so important to me to be home for Christmas."

"Had big plans, did you?" Abbey picked up her crocheting and resumed her work.

"The biggest," Rita replied, surprised that she could open up so easily to this stranger. "See, this was our first Christmas, but there was more to it than that. I come from a big family. There's ten of us kids, and we span a score of years and well. . . , I've not always felt very close to any of them. In fact, until recently, I wasn't on the best of terms with my mom or dad, either."

"What changed to make things better?"

"I did. I got right with God," Rita said without thought, then quickly added, "I don't mean that to sound flippant. I really did set things right with God. It wasn't like some grandiose religious experience—I grew up in church and my folks had always taught me about the Bible. It's just that I finally came to see the truth for myself."

Rita paused to take a deep breath and realized that

Abbey was staring at her blankly. "Sorry," Rita offered. "I got a bit carried away."

Abbey chuckled. "In this day and age, we feel a little compelled to justify and explain the acceptance of Christ in our lives. Faith in God seems too insignificant a thing when held up against the video game machine and virtual reality."

Rita laughed. "Where in the world did you learn about virtual reality?"

"Grandkids. I wanted to take them shopping at a local mall. You know, Grandma stuff."

Rita nodded, although she'd never known her grandmothers.

"Anyway, they insisted I come with them to the video arcade. The next thing I know, they've got me shooting and dodging everything from alien life forms to characters from the Wild West. With entertainment like that to occupy and—if you don't mind my saying so—fry their brains, listening to Grandmother talk about God is just a little on the boring side."

"Did your husband travel with you?"

Abbey's eyes glossed over, and she put down her crocheting for a second time. "Only in spirit. He died earlier this year. This is my first Christmas without him."

"I'm so sorry. I didn't mean to bring up something unpleasant."

Abbey smiled behind her tears. "Herman, unpleasant? Never!" Her mild declaration touched Rita deeply. "My Herman was a joyful man in life, and I'll not remember him any other way. He was fun to argue with, fun to work and play with, and a blessing to love and live with." Abbey rummaged around in a bag at her feet and brought out a well-worn handkerchief. After dabbing her eyes, she drew a deep breath. "Tell me about your plans for Christmas. The plans you and your young man had."

Rita was still unnerved by her blunder about Herman. "I, well, that is," she stammered and finally stopped all together.

Abbey patted her hand. "Tell me."

Rita opened her mouth and found herself relaying every imaginable detail about the plans she'd had for the holidays. "I wanted us to dog sled out. We do that, you know? Well, of course you didn't know, but we do. Mark and I both love to dog sled, and we own over a hundred dogs."

"How interesting. I've always wanted to know more about that kind of thing, but I've never known anyone, until now, who actually operated dogs and sleds."

Rita continued. "Mark and I both love to race. That's actually how we met. My father and Mark were partners in the kennel business, and when I came home from college to race in the Iditarod, there was Mark."

"The Iditarod? You don't mean that monstrous race they have every spring? The one from Anchorage to Nome?" Abbey questioned in disbelief.

"The very same. I raced it for the first time last year, and I plan to race it again. I didn't do too bad, but

Mark beat me out. In fact, he saved my life on the trail, and that was when I realized how much I needed God in my life."

Abbey was a captive audience, so Rita continued. "I got caught in a storm like this one. I lost track of my dogs and found myself stranded there without my supplies or any hope of finding them. But God and Mark were watching out for my foolish attempts at independence. Mark found me and cared for me, and I saw for the first time in my life that I was no good on my own."

" 'Two are better than one; because they have a good reward for their labor. For if they fall, the one will lift up his fellow; but woe to him that is alone when he falleth; for he hath not another to help him up.' " Abbey's voice broke, and tears fell.

"That's from Ecclesiastes," Rita said, reaching out to touch the old woman's hand. "I know those verses very well. Chapter four, verses nine and ten. Mark and I had them read at our wedding, and they are very special to me."

"They were special to us as well. I hope you'll forgive this old lady's tears. I know I'm not alone and God is watching most tenderly after me. I feel His presence even now, especially now, but sometimes it's a bit much."

Rita nodded but said nothing. She continued to hold tight to Abbey's hand, and the old woman spoke on.

"I remember one of our first Christmases. We still lived in the lower forty-eight and we'd gone to one of those tree lots to find a Christmas tree. Well, what we could afford with our meager earnings and what they had there were two entirely different things. So Herman gets the idea that we should go cut our own tree down by the lake and save the money.

"Well, if ever an operation was doomed to fail, it was this one. First we couldn't find a decent tree even remotely related to the pine family, and when we finally managed to find a pitiful example of one, Herman nearly cut his foot off trying to axe the thing."

"No!" Rita exclaimed, completely caught up in the story.

"I'm afraid the money we saved cutting our own tree went to buying Herman a new pair of boots and paying a nearby farmer to pull our car out of the ditch."

Rita grinned. "Best laid plans, eh?"

"Only we hadn't laid any at all, and that was half the trouble. When we got that scrappy tree home, we realized we had to figure out how to get it to stand up in the living room. I found a bucket, Herman filled it part way with dirt, and then we put the tree in it and filled it the rest of the way with dirt and water. Then we stood back and the thing collapsed, spilling mud all over the only rug we owned."

Rita was now laughing in earnest. "What did you do?"

"I think we finally just leaned it against the wall," Abbey said, laughing with her. "Oh, it was a sorry sight to be sure, but it was one of the very best times we had together, and I will always remember that Christmas. We didn't have much money, we'd made a mess of the tree and Herman's boots, but we were so in love. You know, when you love someone, the little things have a way of not being quite so important."

Rita sobered and nodded. She couldn't begin to imagine what it would be like to celebrate Christmas without the man she loved more than life itself. "I think I'm just learning that lesson. I guess I owe my husband an apology."

Abbey reached down again into the bag at her feet and pulled up a white crocheted snowflake. "I've been working to make enough of these ornaments to hand out to the kids at church tomorrow night, but I want you to have one for your tree."

Rita took the gift and held it up to study. "It's beautiful, Abbey. I wish I could do things like this, but I'm afraid the only sewing I'm able to do is with a suture needle and thread. I'm a registered nurse, but that's where my sewing talents begin and end."

"I guess we both have our talents, eh?"

Rita got to her feet and tucked the snowflake carefully into her purse. "Thanks, Abbey. I think I'm going to go talk to my husband. Maybe I'll get back to introduce you two."

"I'd like that," Abbey said. "If not, I'll be praying for you."

"Me, too," Rita replied. "I mean, I'll be praying for

you. I appreciate what you told me tonight. I've been a pretty hard case most all of my life, and I guess it's time for me to soften up a bit and admit I need to make some changes in my attitude."

Three

Mark felt rather proud of his ingenuity. After being told by one of the ticket agents that they'd most likely be spending the night at the airport, Mark started looking for ways to make their situation a little more comfortable. First he'd gone to the lost and found and procured from the airport personnel two long-forgotten sleeping bags. They were in pretty good order and would make an overnight airport stay a lot more comfortable.

Next he'd surveyed the airport waiting areas and found a nice, out-of-the-way corner where he unrolled the bags and made himself at home. It wasn't much, and no doubt it would do very little to change Rita's attitude. He sat down with a sigh. She had a right to be disappointed, he told himself. It was just hard to imagine that she couldn't see how disappointed he was, as well. Married life definitely took some getting used to.

When he was a single man, an interruption of this type would have been inconvenient, but little more. It wasn't because he didn't enjoy making special holiday plans or that he couldn't appreciate coming together with family. Mark knew how important such things could be, and he knew how important this Christmas celebration was to his wife. Rita had so long been at odds with the world that now, after coming to terms with so many things, she wanted to make up for lost time. All at once.

"Ahem."

Looking up, Mark met Rita's dark apologetic eyes. With a lop-sided grin, he lifted his hand to her. "Our own private utopia."

Rita tossed her purse to the ground and joined Mark on the sleeping bag pallet. "Where did you dig these up?"

Mark shrugged. "I have my ways. Like it?"

Rita nodded. "I suppose I'll like it even better in the middle of the night when I'm trying to get warm and comfortable."

"So you heard," Mark said, testing the waters.

"Of course. You know me—I asked. I thought maybe there was a chance the weather had changed in the last ten minutes and that we'd soon be on our way. You sure you don't want to get a hotel?"

"Security advised everybody to stay put. The roads are impassable, the blizzard is blinding, and the temperature has dropped twenty degrees in the last hour.

I don't think we'd be wise to try it. Besides, we aren't the only plane grounded. I'm not sure the hotels can take the load. You and I are used to roughing it though, and I figured we could sleep here a lot better than some."

"True," Rita said, sounding absentminded. "Look, Mark, I was wrong, and I apologize. It was just so disappointing to have this all happen. I wanted things to be perfect, and now everything is out of my control and. . ." She paused, smiling broadly. "That's where it always begins, isn't it?"

"What?"

"I lose control over the situation and then I get ugly." Rita pulled the crocheted snowflake out of her purse. "I met the neatest old woman, and she gave me this. She was crocheting these for some children." Rita laughed. "Maybe my childish attitude reminded her of them—I don't know. Anyway, I don't know why, but it seemed as if I'd known her all my life. Pretty soon I was telling her everything. I mean, I just poured out my heart to her."

"Did it help?" he asked sympathetically.

Rita nodded. "It did more than that. It humbled me."

"Humbled you?"

"Yeah. There I was complaining about how I couldn't have the Christmas I wanted and how I'd made all these plans for you and me to do things together." Rita's voice dropped. "I told her it was our first Christmas."

"And what did she say?"

Rita's expression softened. "She told me this was her first Christmas without her husband. He died earlier this year. Oh, Mark," her voice cracked and she snuggled into his arms. "I felt so badly for her. The pain was so clear in her eyes, like when I'm working on a patient who's in sheer agony but who's trying hard to tolerate it. Abbey, that was the woman's name, she was so sweet. She said she was going to remember all the good times and how much fun they had together. She told me stories about their lives together, and it made me sad to think she's going to spend Christmas alone."

"Where's she going? Maybe she's spending the holidays with her kids."

"She's on her way home. She's already seen her kids in the lower forty-eight. Now she's going home to Fairbanks. I guess God used Abbey to show me how selfish I was being. I kept listening to her and thinking how lame it was for me to complain about my problems when she was facing this terrible thing. Oh, Mark," Rita said sitting up. "I can't bear to think about losing you."

"Then don't," Mark said, pulling her tightly against him. "I'm not going anywhere. You and I will have a good long time together, and if anything happens to prove it to be otherwise, God will see us through."

"I know, but it really made me think," Rita said. "I'm disappointed by having my plans changed for a day or two, but Abbey's entire future has been rewritten. When I think of it from that perspective, I feel very childish and stupid."

"You aren't stupid, Rita."

She eased away, laughing. "But I am childish."

Mark laughed. "This is one of those questions I should answer by saying, 'Of course not.' "

"What are you talking about? One of those questions?"

"You know, like when a woman asks you if you think she looks nice. What she really wants is for you to compliment her. Or if she asks you if you think she's fat, she wants you to convince her that she looks thin."

Rita frowned in concentration. "So you think I'm fat?"

Mark's howl of laughter brought stares from other travelers. "That's exactly why I should never have answered you."

Rita shook her head. "No, really. If you think I'm fat . . ."

Mark took her face in his hands and kissed her soundly. Pulling away he whispered, "You are not fat, but yes, you do act childish at times. Now, explode and rage at me if you must."

Rita shook her head. "I'm sorry I got so angry, Mark. I should never have taken it out on you. Of course, you must be just as disappointed as I am, but I didn't think about your feelings and that was wrong. I assumed that because you were trying to handle things in a positive manner, it wasn't important to you. I guess I wanted you to tear your clothes and weep with me over the loss."

Mark breathed a sigh of relief. "I just figured getting angry about it wouldn't change things. It doesn't mean I'm not angry or that I'm not annoyed to find my plans disrupted."

"Would you like some peanuts?" the voice of a woman sounded from behind Mark.

"I beg your pardon?" Mark questioned, turning.

"The airline realizes the inconvenience to your travel plans, and we thought we'd show our regret by offering some snacks."

"I'd rather you put us in the air again," Mark said flatly.

"Or accommodate us with a hotel room," Rita added.

"Really," the attendant said defensively, "the airline isn't responsible for what happens because of the weather. We'll happily see you to your destination when the snow clears, but we can't be held accountable for things out of our control."

Mark took the offered foil packages and smiled. "I wasn't trying to blame you, personally. It is Christmas, after all, and you probably have somewhere you'd rather be as well."

The woman nodded. "That's for sure. I hate this northern route, but I have family in Fairbanks and that makes it convenient. But I do get tired of the fog, snow, and ice delaying flights and causing people to miss out on important things. They always seem to blame the first airline person they come in contact with."

"I'm sure that's true," Rita offered sympathetically.

"If it's any consolation, we don't blame you."

The woman nodded and moved on, leaving Mark with the distinct impression that she'd squared her shoulders to do battle with the next traveler.

"That's not a job I'd want just now," he said, opening a package of peanuts and handing them to Rita.

"Thanks. I suppose it's a bit like nursing. People are always looking for someone to blame for their ills." She ate a couple peanuts and continued. "I remember one mother in Anchorage when I was still in training. She'd just been told her daughter had cancer and the first question out of her mouth was, 'How did this happen? Who could have given it to her?' I felt sorry for her. She just wanted someone to be responsible for the problem and solve it."

"Yeah." Mark finished a bag of nuts and opened a second. When he'd finished those as well, he started toying with the foil wrappers. "Well, one thing's for certain, Texas Rita, we've got no one to blame but ourselves for traveling in Alaska during the winter."

"I suppose you're right. We even discussed the possibility of bad weather when we were planning the wedding. I seem to remember Mom pointing out that maybe we should come back sooner from our honeymoon to avoid the possibility of missing Christmas at home."

"Maybe one of these days we should start listening to that woman," Mark replied.

"I'm going to," Rita agreed. "She always seems to give

good advise. She's the one who told me before we got married that my temper was going to get me into trouble if I didn't learn to control my mouth."

She paused. "Look Mark, I know this isn't going to be easy for me. I'm too inclined to react to what's going on instead of thinking it through. I do love you, though. I hope you believe me and know that I will try to do better."

Mark held up his creation. It was a foil wrapper ring he'd devised. "Our love for each other is like this ring. Like the rings on our fingers. It has no beginning and no end. I know you love me, Rita. I'd never have thought it to be conditional or I'd never have married you. And just as your love isn't conditional, neither is mine. I love you with all my heart—and I knew your stubborn temper all too well when I married you. Now I'm not saying don't work on it. I think you should. Just like I need to work on my know-it-all attitude."

Rita looked surprised and Mark laughed. "Don't tell me that little confession surprises you."

"I suppose it does. I didn't think you knew. . .Well, I mean. . ."

"Didn't think I knew how oppressive I could be about how to do things and when and where to do them?" Mark laughed. "How could I not? Look, these are things we can help each other through as long as we remember our love for each other."

Rita took the foil ring and put it with the crocheted snowflake. Tucking her purse safely between them, she snuggled down on the sleeping bag, and Mark immediately joined her. Wrapping her in his arms, he heard her sigh and knew that all was well.

"I love you, Mark."

"I know you do," he said, inhaling the sweet flowery fragrance of her hair. "And I love you."

"Maybe we could have a code word," Rita suggested.

"A code word?"

"Yeah, you know, a word we could say when we hear the other one starting to lose control in our problem areas."

"What kind of code word?" Mark tried hard to keep from smiling when he added, "Something like, 'Knock-It-Off'?"

Rita laughed. "Something like that, only just between you and me. Something personal to us. Hey, I've got it! 'Iditarod.' "

"Iditarod?"

"Sure. If I start to get out of control with my temper, you could just say, 'Rita, Iditarod!' Then walk away or wait for me to acknowledge what you've said. When I hear that word, I'll know that I need to rethink the way I'm acting and what I'm saying."

"And you won't get even madder because I pointed out that you were losing your temper?"

"Are you going to get mad if I point out that you're being a know-it-all?"

Mark laughed. "Probably, but I'll give it a try. Iditarod it is."

Four

Mark eased out of Rita's arms and thrust off the sleeping bag. More than a little anxious to know what the weather was doing, he didn't have to go far to realize nothing had changed. The windows were still thickly covered in ice and little light shone through.

"The storm is as strong as ever," an airport maintenance man told him. The man was decked out in heavy coveralls and a beaver cap and looked anxious to be on his way.

"There's no news at all?" Mark questioned before the man could leave.

"Only thing I know is that everything north and west of here is covered in a good three feet of new snow. The windchill is pushing minus sixty, and nothing and nobody is moving out there," the man said gesturing to the window.

Mark watched the man exit through a doorway marked Airport Personnel Only, and felt hopelessness wash through him. He'd have to go back and tell Rita that they were snowbound for at least another day. By the looks of it, they were snowbound for another night as well.

"Lord," he whispered, "I believe You have all of this under control, and as much as I'd like to be home right now and as disappointed as I am that we're stuck here on the eve of Your Son's birth celebration, I believe nothing happens by chance. If there is something here for me to learn or someone I'm to help, then open my eyes to it. Show me how to get through this thing, in Jesus' name, Amen."

He glanced up to find Rita coming toward him. Her bleary-eyed expression and yawn made him wonder if she'd had a hard time sleeping.

Rita glanced first to the ice-covered window and then back to Mark. "I suppose you're going to tell me it's still snowing."

"Yup. Airport maintenance said we might as well get used to this place."

"Oh goody." The sarcasm was clear in her voice as she continued, "Maybe we could start picking out wallpaper and carpet."

Mark laughed. "Wouldn't do any good. He also told me nothing is moving out there. All of Juneau is shut down tight."

They walked arm in arm back to their things. "You

got any food in those bags?" Mark asked hopefully.

"Not even a candy bar. Why don't we try the restaurant? Surely they aren't out of food yet."

"Let's get a locker then and put all this stuff inside. I'd hate to have to hunt it down in case someone decided to get greedy," Mark said, rolling up the bags.

Rita followed suit. When everything was safely stashed, Mark turned and kissed her lovingly. With wide eyes, Rita looked up in surprise. Mark kissed her nose and pulled her hand into his.

"Merry Christmas Eve," he said softly. "I only wish it could have been the way we dreamed of it."

Rita said nothing until they'd reached the restaurant. It was crowded, but they agreed to take the only table remaining—in a small corner of the smoking section. When they were finally seated and had been handed menus by a woman who's name badge read "Nell"— and whose attitude clearly showed her dismay at the weather—Rita turned to Mark with some questions.

"So if things had worked out, what plans did you have for today?"

Mark considered his answer. "Are you sure it wouldn't just make us more depressed to talk about it?"

"I want to know," she insisted. "If I can't live it in full, at least I can imagine it."

"Well, I suppose I can get into that," Mark replied. "I guess the first thing I wanted was to wake up in each other's arms."

"We did that."

"True, but I had other things in mind as well." The mischievous thoughts he had must have been reflected in his eyes, for Rita blushed attractively and lowered her eyes.

"Yes. . .well. . ." She kept her head down. "What else?"

"I guess I thought like you that we might hike out with the dogs and get a tree. Then we could build a great big fire and brew some of our special coffee blend and decorate the tree."

"Sounds identical to my dream day," Rita said, finally able to look him in the eyes again.

"Then after we made the appropriate phone calls to wish everyone a good day and finalize plans for the Christmas morning celebration, we could plan a special dinner, and I could give you an early Christmas present."

"Really?" Rita questioned. "A present? What kind of present?"

"Oh, no you don't. I'm not giving you even a hint of what it is, although. . ." He paused as if trying to decide whether to reconsider. "No, I won't do it. You have to wait."

"But you were going to give it to me on Christmas Eve, and this is Christmas Eve."

Mark laughed at her child-like persistence. "I had planned to do it in a special way. You know," he sobered, "I wanted candlelight and music."

"Well, there's something playing on the restaurant

intercom," she said with a smile.

"No, Rita, and that's final." He smiled and got up. "I'm going to find a restroom. When and if the waitress makes it back, let her know I want coffee and the breakfast special."

"Yes, sir!" she exclaimed with a pout.

"Iditarod, Rita dear, Iditarod."

Rita laughed as Mark walked away. He grew more special to her with each day. She couldn't imagine what life would be like without him, nor did she want to try.

"Have you decided what you want?" demanded the irritated voice of the waitress Nell.

Rita glanced up. The woman, tall, thin, and very blonde, acted not the least bit concerned about her surly attitude. "Yes, we'll both have coffee and the breakfast special."

"How do you want the eggs?"

"Scrambled on both," Rita said, trying her best to sound sweet. Coals of kindness, her mother would have said, often turn around the sourest disposition.

"We're out of wheat bread, so you'll have to have white toast or pancakes."

"The toast is fine."

"The special comes with your choice of orange, apple, or grapefruit juice." Nell looked down at Rita, expecting an instant answer.

"Well," Rita considered the matter. "I guess we'll both take orange juice."

"We're out of orange juice."

"All right, then apple." The woman wrote furiously on the pad and started to leave.

"Oh, and if it wouldn't be too much trouble," Rita added, "I'd like some cream for my coffee." The woman glared but nodded and went off in the direction of the kitchen.

Poor woman, Rita thought. *No doubt she's missing out on a special time with her family too.* The thought made Rita take a look around, and as if seeing the situation for the first time, she suddenly realized that all these people were missing out on something. As she studied the people at the various tables, Rita happened to notice a row of candles and holders on a shelf above the water glasses. Mark had thought of having candlelight and music for their Christmas Eve dinner. Maybe he'd enjoy it for his Christmas Eve breakfast instead.

Nell returned with the coffee and juice, wearing the same harried expression. Digging into her pocket, she produced several containers of cream and deposited them.

"I was wondering," Rita began, hoping she wasn't going to further irritate the woman.

"Yeah?" The woman stuck her pencil behind one ear and waited for Rita to speak.

"Well, I suppose in the middle of this mess, the last thing you need is someone with a special request, but," Rita paused, trying to determine how Nell was taking this approach. The woman's expression was unchanged, however, so Rita continued quickly. "Well, I noticed you have some candles over there." Rita pointed and smiled weakly. "My husband and I are newlyweds and . . .well. . .we, I mean I'd like to surprise him with a candle this morning. Could I buy one?"

Tears of pain filled Nell's eyes.

"I'm sorry, did I say something wrong?"

Nell shook her head. "No, I'm afraid this weather has gotten to me. I'm not myself, not at all. I'm sorry."

Rita put her hand out to touch Nell's arm. "I'll bet you had big plans for Christmas Eve too."

"I sure did. But it's not going to happen now."

Rita noticed some customers not far away who were trying to catch Nell's eye. "I shouldn't have kept you so long. I see some of the other customers are waiting for you."

"Let 'em wait. You're the first person today who's showed me any kindness."

"Everyone is so focused on their own disappointments," Rita offered. "I have to admit, I wasn't feeling too kindly myself last night."

"What changed your mind?" Nell asked, suddenly seeming to need answers to unspoken questions.

"I realized that being mad about the situation wouldn't change it. I also met a wonderful old woman who reminded me to be thankful for what I had instead of mourning what I didn't."

"It's just that I was sure my boyfriend was going to propose tonight. His sister told me he'd been making plans for a big dinner out, and that he'd made several trips to the jeweler's. I was sure this was it."

"I'm sorry. I know this must be very hard for you. Not only are you stuck in a place where you can't get to him, but you have to serve all these angry customers. I'll say a prayer and ask God to help you through it."

Nell's face contorted several times as though she was trying to keep from crying. "Thank you." She snuffed back her tears and hurried to where the candles were. Bringing one back, she inserted it into the holder and put it on the table.

"I don't have any matches," she said before offering Rita a smile and leaving.

Rita pulled a lighter out of her purse. Thanks to her backwoods habit of keeping the tools for starting a fire close at hand, Rita quickly had the candle lit.

"What's all this?" Mark asked, taking his seat.

"You wanted candlelight and music. I begged the waitress, and she brought it to me."

"Our waitress performed an act of generosity?"

"Oh, Mark, it's so sad. I started talking to her, and she told me how her boyfriend was supposed to propose tonight. Now she's stranded here working instead of getting a diamond."

"That is too bad, no wonder she's—"

"Two breakfast specials," Nell said in decidedly lighter spirits. She smiled and winked at Rita. "If I can get you two anything else, just let me know."

Mark's amazement registered on his face, and Rita burst out laughing. "See where a little kindness will get you?"

"You must have given a great deal of kindness to get a smile out of that woman!"

"Iditarod, Mark Williams," Rita said with a knowing look.

"Okay, okay." Mark tried hard to sound oppressed, but he reached out and touched Rita's hand. "Let's pray." Mark blessed the food and prayed for an end to the storm before giving Rita's hand a squeeze. "The candle's a nice touch, Texas Rita."

"So do I get my present?" Rita asked with a forkful of eggs halfway to her mouth.

"No, but you do get my undying devotion, love, and admiration."

Rita held the fork suspended in air and thought for a moment. "I suppose that will have to do," she said with a sigh and ate the eggs.

"I love you, Rita. You're something else, you know?"

"Why do you say that?"

"You changed that woman's whole day, all because you took time to extend some Christian love."

Rita blushed under Mark's scrutiny and raised her coffee mug to give a toast. "To us and the others who are stuck here. Happy Christmases for everyone. . ."

"And may they all know the real meaning of the season," Mark added.

"Amen," Rita breathed, touching her cup to Mark's.

Five

The day wore on in absolute lethargy. There was no break in the weather and no hope of getting beyond the closed confines of the airport walls. Feeling a little hemmed in, Rita went in search of something to eat, while Mark decided to stretch his legs.

"That's my ball!" one child exclaimed to another, and a tug of war ensued not three feet from where Mark stood.

"Mom! Danny won't let me have my ball."

"It's my ball. I brought it on the airplane!"

Mark chuckled to himself, but the old man sitting nearby did not. The scowl on his face and his low-pitched grumbling made it clear that the man was unhappy.

"They sure have a lot of energy," Mark commented to the man.

"They ought to be taught some manners," the

stranger replied as three children ran willy-nilly past them. The argument for the coveted ball had not yet reached its peak.

"I want it!" the smallest of the three kids yelled.

"They're just excited," Mark said, laughing as the group went by in a whirlwind of colors and flailing arms.

"They're unruly and out of control," the aging man grunted.

Mark eyed him for a moment, then not knowing what else to do, extended his hand. "I'm Mark Williams."

The man eyed him suspiciously and, without accepting Mark's hand, harumphed his displeasure with the whole situation.

Mark thought the expression in the man's eyes was nearly one of pain. "I have some aspirin in my carry-on bag if you need some."

This caught the man's attention, but he shook his head. "What I need is for those young hooligans to be seen and not heard."

Mark smiled at the man's old-fashioned notions. "They are kids, and they've been confined to an airport for some time now. Besides, it's Christmas Eve. No doubt they're excited about celebrating and seeing what kind of presents are under the tree."

"That's all anyone really cares about this time of year. The greed is outrageous," the man said, drawn almost unwillingly into conversation.

"I think that's true of a lot of folks." Mark took a seat beside him and noticed the intricately carved cane at the man's side. "May I?" he asked, motioning to the cane. The man shrugged indifference, and Mark continued to speak while inspecting the object. "Oak, right?"

The man nodded.

The head of the cane was carved with a remarkable likeness of an eagle's head. "This is some beautiful work. Did you purchase it here in Alaska, Mr. . .?"

The man's anger seemed to abate slightly. "Bart Thomas is the name. Got it near Sitka several years ago."

"I've seen others that were similar, but none so well crafted."

The sound of a screeching child followed by a motherly reprimand caught the man's attention. "It's about time!"

"Well, Mr. Thomas, I remember being a kid at this time of year. The excitement and fun blotted out everything else. I knew the season was about the birth of Jesus, but it was a lot of fun to imagine what I was getting for Christmas and to keep secrets about what I was going to give."

The man's defensive walls seemed to go up. "They don't care about the season or what it costs their elders. They only care about getting the latest advertised gadget or whatnot."

"Seems kind of harsh to lump all kids into one

package. They could just as easily lump all older people into the stereotype of being senile." Mark handed the man his cane.

"Kids these days are given too much, too soon. They expect it to just keep getting bigger and better. Why I remember being perfectly entertained with wooden blocks at their age, but now it has to be computerized or electronic to be of interest to them."

"That is a growing problem. Especially in commercial areas. I still see a lot of simplicity in the small towns, however. Although," Mark said with a smile, "they have plenty of commercialism and name-brand products there, as well."

The kids raced by again, this time intent on battling for first place to the drinking fountain.

"I beat you!" a voice cried out.

The taller of the three shoved aside the winner. "I'm oldest so I get to go first."

"Mom!"

"See what I mean? Greed. Pure and simple," Bart said, thumping his cane on the floor.

Mark eyed the balding man for a moment. He looked to be in his seventies, maybe older. Then again, maybe his negative attitude made him look older.

"Are you from Alaska, Mr. Thomas?" Mark questioned softly.

"No," the man replied, then turned steely blue eyes on Mark, "and if you're going to insist on calling me by name, then you might as well call me Bart."

"I'd like that," Mark said, extending his hand once again. This time the old man hesitantly shook it. Mark was careful not to squeeze the gnarled hand too tightly. "You can call me Mark. Are you traveling alone?"

"As usual," Bart answered, sounding bitter. "I offered to bring my youngest son, but he was too busy making the almighty dollar to take a little time off to help me out."

"Are you up here to see family?" Mark asked, trying desperately to draw the man's glowering expression from the children. They were only an arm's reach away, shoving each other and bickering about who got to play with what first.

"Go sit down with your mother and be quiet!" Bart suddenly demanded. The kids immediately fell silent and looked at Bart in surprise. The youngest broke into tears and ran to his mother's waiting arms.

Mark could see that the woman had watched the entire scene. She seemed to understand and, at Mark's apologetic expression, smiled slightly and patted the back of her crying child.

Bart thumped the cane a couple times as if it helped to calm his nerves. "Should have never made this trip. Nobody appreciates it anyway."

"Why do you say that? Wasn't your family happy to see you?"

Bart grunted. "I suppose my daughter was happy enough. She complained the whole time about her finances and how expensive it is to live in Alaska.

135

When I told her she ought to come back to the lower forty-eight, you would have thought I'd suggested she move to Siberia."

Mark chuckled. "Sounds like she has some fire to her."

"Oh, that's nothing," Bart said, temporarily forgetting the kids who were now racing up and down the aisle. "She quit four jobs in two months. Told me they didn't appreciate her style of doing things. In other words," Bart paused and leaned closer to Mark, "she didn't want to do what she was told. When I mentioned this possibility, she told me I didn't understand her generation. Told me I was too old to appreciate what she was up against in this day and age, especially as the wife of an air force captain who was gone more than he was home."

"She probably feels very isolated. Where does she live?"

"Fairbanks. I've never cared for the town, and I'm glad to be headed home."

"Did you just go up for Christmas?"

"Yeah, but I went early so I could be with my other three kids and their families for Christmas Day. Not that any of them will miss me now."

Mark frowned. "Why do you say that?"

Bart's expression contorted, passing looks of anger, pain, and finally, resolve. "I'm old, and I don't have anything to offer. I don't know the latest crazes, and if I give anything other than cold hard cash for gifts, the kids just take it back and exchange it for whatever it is they want anyway. My grandkids are as greedy as their parents, and the whole lot disgust me."

"Surely something keeps you going back?"

Bart shrugged and glared at the still-racing children. "I keep hoping something will change."

"But it doesn't?"

"Nope. I'm just an old man who isn't in tune with the times and who doesn't have anything to give that anybody wants."

"I find that difficult to believe. You seem to be quite intelligent. I'll bet you have a lifetime of stories to share," Mark commented.

"Hah! The day those hoodlums want to sit and listen to stories is the day I'll fall over dead!"

"I beg your pardon?" Mark was genuinely surprised by Bart's response.

"They don't care, I tell you." Bart thumped the cane nervously. "I've tried to share all sorts of things with them. Gave my daughter her mother's depression glass and she said, 'Well thanks, but I don't know where I'll ever find a place for it.' Gave my son a collection of commemorative coins from the World's Fairs his mother and I had attended. We used to do that every year, you know."

Lost in his memories, Bart didn't wait for Mark's reply. "Liddy, that was my wife, wanted to see as much of the United States as possible. We went to the World's Fair celebrations, tourist attractions, museums, all the capitals—wherever she wanted to go, we went."

Mark noted the loneliness in Bart's voice. He suspected the old man wasn't nearly as angry as he was lonely and displaced. "And your wife is gone now?"

Bart nodded. "Nigh on ten years. She turned sixty and just up and died." The cane thumped twice, then fell silent. "My son said the coins could probably be sold for quite a tidy sum since we had so many consecutive issues. I got mad and told him if that's the way he felt, I'd just take them back."

Mark nodded. "They didn't hold the memories for him that they did for you, I take it?"

Bart shook his head. "Guess not. Greed, that's what holds my children's interest."

Mark was compelled to say something, but hard-pressed to figure out what it was. He could address the issue of loneliness and how the holidays were always difficult to face without the one you loved, although he was no real expert on that subject. He could imagine, remembering Rita's story about Abbey, that living without a lifetime mate was at best, difficult, and at worst, unbearably painful.

"My kids see dollar signs, and old Dad has never been with the times enough to know what's what."

"It's mine!" The boys were back, and all three were scuffling to take control of a toy car. It would have turned into an outright brawl, but Mark interceded.

"Hey, you want to take this wrestling match somewhere else?" His voice was non-threatening, almost jovial. The boys stopped what they were doing and froze in place. "I like Christmas," Mark continued, "but I don't like fighting."

Just then the boy's harried mother came up, toting an infant on her hip. "I'm sorry," she offered Mark and Bart. "They're a real handful and well. . ." She pulled the three boys to her side.

"If you can't control them, you should make them sit with their father," Bart grumbled.

"They don't have a father," she snapped. "At least not one that wants to be a father."

Bart was clearly taken back, but he didn't say anything. Mark tried a sympathetic approach. "Sorry. Look, they aren't being that much of a bother. I was just afraid they might get hurt."

The woman nodded, seeming to take Mark's kindness hesitantly. "I'll try to keep them out of your way." She herded the boys back to where their things were, and Mark watched as she shook her finger at them and whispered reprimands.

Bart was strangely silent for several minutes, and Mark glanced around for Rita. She had gone off to find them something to eat, and he was beginning to feel pretty hungry. Mark remembered Rita's gesture with the candles, and his heart warmed at the thought of her.

"Why are you smiling now?" Bart questioned, shaking Mark out of his thoughts. "I suppose it's more of that Christmas cheer and goodwill you're so fond of."

"I am fond of it," Mark agreed. "I love Christmas. I love what it represents and the joy it brings me."

"Commercialism is what it represents, and it brings a lot of overspending and disappointment."

"No," Mark replied seriously. "It doesn't at my house." Bart's eyes narrowed, but he said nothing and Mark went on. "Christmas at my house is a celebration of Christ's birth. It's a season to remember that God loved us so much, He held nothing back, He gave the very best as a gift to an unworthy world. He gave us Jesus, a Savior. Christmas is a time to remember that gift, and even though I accepted Christ as my Lord and Savior some time back, I like to remember that He didn't come as an overbearing dictator, or as a demanding Father, but as little baby. A baby who was despised by some, worshipped by others, but nevertheless, was and is the Son of God.

"Don't get me wrong," Mark added, seeing some skepticism in Bart's expression, "we still exchange gifts, but the focus isn't on what the gift is, but on the heart of the person who offers it."

"Religious mumbo-jumbo," Bart finally said.

Mark shrugged. "To some, I suppose it seems that way. But," he smiled confidently, "I know no better way to celebrate Christmas."

Bart seemed completely unreceptive, so Mark fell silent, choosing instead to offer up a prayer for the old man. He was deep in thought and prayer when a tug came on his sleeve. Mark looked down to find one of the three boys who'd so plagued Bart.

"My mama thought you might be hungry. She made these to take to my grandma's house in Seattle, but she says we might as well eat them now."

Mark took the offered homemade pretzel. It was soft and huge, and his stomach growled loudly at the thought of eating it. "Thank you, I'll just share this with my wife when she gets back." The boy beamed and held up another pretzel to Bart.

"Sorry we were so loud," he said, his expression sincere.

Bart stared uncomfortably at the boy for a moment, then took the offered pretzel. He murmured his thanks and watched the boy scamper back to his mother.

Mark wrapped his pretzel in a handkerchief and stuffed it in his pocket. He saw Rita approaching and got to his feet. "Bart, it's been nice talking to you. If you should need anything or if you just want some company, my wife and I will be over there in that corner."

Mark pointed, but Bart's eyes were focused on the mother with her little family. The old man said nothing, but something in his expression told Mark that his heart had been softened toward the entourage of children.

Plant seeds, Mark thought. Even in the icy cold of a heart that had been frozen by greed and avarice, seeds of hope and love could be scattered. By offering up a simple pretzel and an apology, a little boy had warmed the spot on which Mark's seeds had fallen. Who knew, maybe in time, the ice would thaw.

Six

"Well you certainly look pleased with yourself," Mark commented as Rita motioned him to their corner of the airport.

"I am. Look what I managed to get. Tuna salad sandwiches, potato chips, and ta-da!" She held up a can of apple juice. "I knew you were sick of soda, and this seemed a logical substitute."

"Hey, this is great. How did you manage it all?"

"Nell."

"Nell?"

"The woman in the restaurant," Rita answered, biting into her sandwich. "The variety of food is falling off, but there's still plenty of food to eat, and if you aren't too picky you can eat rather well."

Mark started to dig in, then held up the pretzel. "Look here, I have a contribution as well."

Rita smile and broke off a piece of the twisted bread.

"Ummm," was all she muttered before stuffing it in her mouth.

The ear-splitting cry of a child in pain brought both Rita and Mark to their feet. Trained eyes darted back and forth trying to size up the emergency. Rita's short career as a nurse made her ready to spring into action, and by nature of her training, she was already cleaning off her hands and looking for how she might help.

Mark caught sight of the child and pointed as he grabbed Rita's hand and pulled her along with him. The boy was the same one who had offered him the pretzel. The worried mother had placed her infant on a blanket on the floor and instructed the other two boys to watch the baby while she tended her bleeding child.

"I'm a nurse. Can I help?" Rita asked softly, taking hold of the boy's arm without waiting for an answer from his mother.

"He fell!" The woman's voice was raised in near hysteria. "They were running. I told them not to, but they are just kids."

"Yes, and active kids will have accidents. What's your name, son?" Rita questioned the boy as she took him from his mother's arms and placed him in the chair beside her.

"His name is Timmy," the woman sobbed, and Mark put his arm around her.

"It'll be all right," he offered. "My wife is one great nurse!"

"You're a real nurse?" the woman questioned.

"Yes." Rita examined the bleeding head wound and wiped at the blood with a crisp, clean handkerchief that someone offered. "The cut isn't all that deep, but it is a bleeder." She placed direct pressure on the wound and turned to the mother. "I think he'll be just fine in a little bit. He won't need stitches or anything so traumatic. You will, however, Mr. Timmy, need to sit still for a while and take it easy. Do you have a coloring book or something to read?"

The boy nodded tearfully while his brothers stared up in awe from where they held vigil over their baby sister.

"Is Timmy's brains gonna come out?" the youngest asked, and even their mother laughed.

"If they did, Timmy wouldn't miss them," she rebuked. "If you'd been using your brains, you might have thought to mind what I said and not run up and down this terminal."

"I'm sorry, Mama," the bleeding boy said earnestly. "I'll be good. I promise."

"Oh baby, you are good. You just did a naughty thing," his mother said with tears in her eyes.

Rita pulled the cloth away and grimaced. "Mark, this bleeding isn't even slowing."

"What can we do?" the worried mother questioned before Mark could answer.

"Well," Rita said and smiled up at her husband, "I have an old herbal remedy my mother taught me. Are you game?"

145

"Of course, if it will help Timmy."

By now a circle of the curious had gathered, and Rita was beginning to feel rather hemmed in. "First, it would be nice if everyone would step back or go back to what they were doing. We're a bit crowded here. Then Mark, if you would go find Nell in the restaurant and ask her for some cayenne pepper." Mark nodded and went off in the direction of the eatery.

"Cayenne pepper? Whatever will you do with that?" one woman questioned from the crowd.

By this time, Bart Thomas had managed to put himself beside the still crying Timmy. "Cayenne is an old pioneer trick for stopping the blood flow. I know it works because my pappy used it when he came up here during the gold rush."

"That's right," Rita confirmed. "A few grains, and I mean only a few—otherwise it burns the wound—will stop the heaviest flow. People even use it for internal bleeding when they're in the middle of nowhere and can't get to help. Like on the Iditarod."

"You know about the Iditarod?" Timmy questioned suddenly. "I love the dog sled races."

His mother laughed behind her tears. "That he does. It's all he talks about. He wants to ride on a sled some day and lead his own team."

"Well," Rita laughed, "it just so happens that my husband, Mark, and I raced in the Iditarod last year. We raise dogs and race whenever we can."

"You do?" the boy enthusiastically cried out, forgetting his plight. "Tell me about the race. How cold was it and how far did you go?"

"I made the full race," Rita replied, ignoring the way the circle of people pressed back in to hear her tale. "I came in seventeenth, but one of these days I'm going to win it."

"What was it like?" Timmy asked.

"Cold, tiring, and. . ." She paused, looking into the faces of the crowd. "Wonderful!"

Smiles greeted her, along with knowing nods. Soon she found herself telling the story of her race to Nome from Anchorage. She told how the race commemorated the old mail trails through Alaska during a time when there were no roads and the mail had to be mushed through on sleds. It was also symbolic, she told them, of the desperate race to take diphtheria serum to Nome earlier in the century when an epidemic had threatened thousands.

"Even though they took the serum by train from Anchorage to Nenana," she told Timmy and the attentive audience, "most folks think the Iditarod is only in memory of that race to heal folks."

Mark returned with the cayenne. Nell hurried along right behind him.

"Is the little boy okay?" Nell questioned as Rita instructed Mark to sprinkle a bit on Timmy's wound.

"He's fine," Rita said, then turned her attention back to the boy. "Just a few grains, Mark." She knew Mark was well acquainted with this method to stop bleeding, so she relaxed her grip on Timmy and watched the wound cautiously.

Mark barely dotted the cut with pepper and waited for Rita to let him know if it was enough. Everyone held their breath, and when the flow of blood seemed to miraculously stop, a cheer went up in unison.

"Praise be to God!" the mother cried out and several "Amens" echoed from the crowd.

Just then an airport worker came up with a first-aid kit in hand. "Will this help?" he asked, and Rita nodded enthusiastically.

"Exactly what I needed."

She rummaged around in the metal box and pulled out sterile gauze, peroxide, antibiotic ointment, and tape. "Now if I can just find some. . .ah, here they are." She held up a small strip of unrecognizable paper. "Butterfly closures. This will hold the wound together and act like stitches."

"Stitches!" Timmy cried out, but Rita patted him reassuringly.

"Like stitches but without any needles." The boy relaxed and let Rita go to work.

"Is he up to date on his shots?" Rita questioned his mother while she worked. "You know, DPT and such?"

"Oh, yes. I'm very careful about such things," the mother replied.

"Good." Rita had Mark tear strips of tape while she cleaned around the wound with peroxide. Seeing that this caused it to start bleeding again, Rita reused the cayenne, then smiled up at Nell. "Thanks for the help."

Nell beamed, happy to have been of use to someone.

Timmy started fussing and fidgeting when Rita took too long, so Bart took it upon himself to start telling the boy a story of when his father had panned for gold in Dawson, hoping to find enough gold to fill his boots before going home.

"Did he really find a nugget as big as his shoe?" Timmy asked.

Bart chuckled. "Naw. He did find my mother, though." The crowd laughed and began to disperse a bit. "My mother was a native to the Yukon. She was very beautiful, and she knew a bit about gold."

Timmy's eyes were wide with wonderment, and Rita finished her bandaging task without further complications. Standing to join Mark, she left the boy completely engulfed in Bart's tales of the wild Yukon and dark, frozen nights of eerie mystery.

"That old man is great!" Rita exclaimed as they went back to their corner.

"He sure is. You couldn't tell by watching him now, but just fifteen minutes ago he was cursing those kids."

"You're kidding, right?"

"Not at all," Mark watched the man, and Rita's gaze followed his. "He was a lonely old man, hurt by some things done to him in the past—things that made Christmas seem humbug and unpleasant. Now I think things will be different for him."

"Why do you say that?" Rita asked, watching her

husband with tender love. His dark eyes were fairly shining, and the smile on his face held a mystery that she wanted to understand.

"Oh, I'll tell you later tonight when we're all snuggled down and you need a bedtime story," he teased, pulling her into his arms. "You did a good thing there, Texas Rita."

She accepted his kiss with abandonment, wrapping her arms around her husband's neck. Never mind that they were in the middle of the Juneau airport. Never mind that it was Christmas Eve and they should have been home. They were together, and that was all that mattered.

Seven

"The weather advisory is for all non-emergency personnel to stay off the streets," the television news anchor stated seriously. Rita and Mark stood with half of the people stranded in the airport, watching and waiting for some sign that the blizzard would abate.

"Looks like we were lucky to set down when we did," one woman in the crowd said to her companion.

"Yeah, did you hear them say there's three feet of new snow in Anchorage?" someone else commented.

"I heard them say Fairbanks is completely buried and has a temperature of minus fifty."

The crowd was alive with speculation and rumors. Rita leaned close to Mark and whispered. "Fifty below? Kid's play. Harness up the dogs, and I'll take it on."

Mark chuckled and pulled her closer. "Harness your own dogs at fifty below. I may be gallant and a wonderful husband, but I think a warm bed, crackling fire, and a hot cup of soup sound better."

"Who said you were a wonderful husband?" Rita teased, poking him playfully in the ribs.

Mark eyed her with a raised brow and a bit of a smirk. "As I recall, you did."

Rita felt herself grow flush under his impassioned stare. He was a wonderful husband. Attentive, loving, giving, but also hot-headed and know-it-all when he wanted to be. She thought to tease him with some smart retort but instead leaned up to kiss his cheek.

"Yes, you are a wonderful husband, and I wouldn't trade you for the best sled dogs in Alaska."

Mark laughed and hugged his wife. The crowd was dispersing to various corners of the terminal. Retrieving their things from the locker, Rita was beginning to feel a bit like a turtle carrying her home on her back. It seemed like the terminal grew smaller by the hour, but she knew it must just be her imagination. When enough of a path had been cleared between her and the windows, Rita purposefully wandered over and stared out through the icy covering.

Mark was instantly behind her, pulling her pack off and putting it on the floor beside his own things before wrapping his arms around Rita. She eased back against his chest and let him envelop her with his warmth.

"I tried to call home again, but all the lines are either busy or down," Mark said softly against her ear.

"I hope they aren't too worried," Rita replied. "I

know how my mother can fret about little things."

"Little things like jumbo jets crashing in blizzards or skidding into the ocean off icy runways?"

"Okay, okay. I get your point," Rita said, grinning up over her shoulder. Mark squeezed her more tightly to him. "Still, I wish we could reassure them," she continued. "I know they care, and now with it being Christmas Eve and all the family except us gathered together, they'll be—"

"They'll be offering up prayers on our behalf. We're probably so covered in prayer right now," Mark said lightly, "that we'll be blessed and protected for years to come."

Rita chuckled and shifted in his arms to face him. "Oh Mark, I know we're all right, but just look at all these people. Some of them are really hurting. And some of them are completely alone."

"Like Bart." Mark's gaze traveled to where the old man sat alone.

"And Abbey," Rita said, nodding toward where the old woman worked with her crochet hook. Suddenly an idea came to her. "Mark!"

He looked down at her with a bit of a surprised expression.

"Let's get them all together and have our own celebration. All the people we ran into could use a good party. We could get Abbey, Bart, Nell, and that sweet mother with her children."

"Might just as well include anybody else who wants

to participate," Mark suggested.

"Sure. We can give each person a task. I'll go talk to Abbey right now. You talk to Bart, and we'll go together to see the woman with her kids. I need to check on Timmy's head anyway. After we've decided on a time and place, I'll find Nell and see what we can do about refreshments."

Some time later, Rita came to find Mark and relate the positive reaction she'd received from Nell. "She told me she can bring us some cookies and hot cocoa. Isn't that perfect!"

"You'll have the whole terminal wanting to celebrate with us." Mark laughed and gave her a quick peck on the check. "You did good, sweetheart."

Rita beamed and began rummaging in her purse. "Timmy is doing great. He doesn't even have a headache. Elaine, that's Timmy's mom, told me he has an iron constitution and always has." Pulling out a small travel Bible, Rita thrust it at Mark. "I thought it would be nice if you read the Christmas story out of Luke. You know, kind of dramatic-like and with plenty of feeling."

Mark pushed back the Bible. "I don't need it. I memorized it when I was six. My grandmother paid me five dollars, which in those days was a mint, to memorize the entire second chapter of Luke. She said it was important to know about the birth of our Savior."

Rita put the Bible back in her purse. "I'm going to lead them in some Christmas songs. Oh, Mark, this is going to be great!"

"No one felt midnight was too late to celebrate?" he asked seriously. Both he and Rita had thought midnight to be a rather special time.

"Not at all," she answered. "It is Christmas, after all. So at the stroke of midnight, we'll gather over there," she pointed and eased back against the wall.

Mark joined her with a sigh. "It seems strange not to be rushing around for last-minute preparations."

"It's wonderful. I never thought about it before, but even in the days when I wasn't focused on Christ at Christmas, I was always hurrying through the season. There were gifts to buy and decorating and trees and such. My college roommate was real big on the party aspect of Christmas, and we must have celebrated every night for two or three weeks."

"The twelve days of Christmas, eh?"

"More like the thirty-one days of December," she said, laughing. "You don't even want to know about New Year's Eve."

"I think New Year's is a great time. Renewal, reflection, restoration, and rebuilding."

"With our group it was the party scene all the way. There was no stopping to renew or reflect. That would have forced us to see how empty our lives were. I wasn't the only person brought up in a Christian home who was ignoring God's truth. There were several of us. It was probably what attracted us to each other. We were just this side of being able to throw off our spiritual understanding and give in to wild abandonment."

Rita paused thoughtfully. "We drew unspoken, unwritten lines of agreement, however. No drinking, no smoking, no sex. We all knew the truth of God's Word and will for us; we just hoped it would be something we could put off until we were old and frumpy and had nothing else to live for."

Mark nodded. "I know a lot of folks who feel that way. Kind of deathbed Christians, if you would."

"Why is it so hard to see the immediate rewards of trusting in Christ as our Savior? Why does it take getting hit over the head by some folks in order to see what a precious gift we're wasting?"

"I don't honestly know, Rita." Mark scooted closer and pulled her against him. "Maybe it's like being snow-blind. The light is so intense that we can no longer see. The brilliance of it is blinding, so instead of basking in the warmth, feeling completely surrounded by the purity of it, we avoid it, turn away, look for something dark to hold up against it."

Rita drew a deep breath and sighed. "The light can be pretty intimidating when you're the example of darkness held up to it."

"Yeah," Mark agreed. "I know."

At midnight, Rita and Mark joined Abbey and the others for their private celebration. There was a small amount of hubbub going on throughout the terminal, but for the most part, things had quieted down for the night.

The kids were quite excited about what was to take place, and Timmy immediately chose to sit by Bart, who had become a grandfather figure to the boy.

"I thought we might sing some Christmas songs," Rita announced. "We all know certain songs from school or church. Does everyone know 'Away in a Manager'?" Everyone nodded, so Rita began the song.

The kids seemed extremely pleased to be able to participate, and after the song had finished, Timmy piped up, "We sang that song in our church Christmas pageant!"

"Yeah," one of his brothers added, "we had to recite a poem and everything."

"But we got candy after it was over," the last one added, not to be outdone.

"That's wonderful," Rita commented. "You can help with our celebration by reciting for us tonight." The boys suddenly seemed a bit shy, so Rita quickly hurried on. "You know, that song is probably one of the first Christmas songs we learn. And there's a little story I thought I'd tell that goes along with the idea of the manger scene." All eyes brightened and turned to her for the tale.

"A long time ago, a man named St. Francis was worried that common people like you and me might have trouble understanding the sweetness of Christmas. People always heard the routine message, 'Jesus was born to save our souls,' " she said in a deep, austere

157

voice. With a smile, she softened. "Which of course He was, but in the year 1223 with so much hardship around them and not much to help them along their way, people thought of God and heaven as a faraway kind of thing."

The kids were captivated, and even Mark appeared surprised by this turn of events.

"Anyway," Rita continued, "St. Francis wanted to do something that would help the people keep Christmas in their hearts and minds. He wanted to give them something to remember, and realized that words, no matter how wondrous or special, would soon be forgotten. You see, there were no Bibles for the common people, and even if there had been, most folks couldn't read. St. Francis knew that sayings and teachings from the church were things that most people soon forget, except when threatened with their very lives for not remembering.

"St. Francis thought and thought on this matter and decided it might be nice to dramatize the Christmas story. He found a manger and brought it into the church. This was in Graecia, Italy, and he knew everybody in town would be in church on Christmas Eve for the special services to celebrate Christ's birth. He filled the manger with straw, wrapped a bundle to look like a baby, and placed it in the manger, then had some of the church workers dress as Mary and Joseph.

"When the townspeople came to church that night, they found the nativity scene at the front of their church. It made them cry for joy because they felt they were actually a part of the birth of Jesus. Since then, people have found it comforting to have the nativity as part of their Christmas celebration. And we should remember that we are much like Mary and Joseph on that special night so long ago. We are travelers, and there is no place for us to stay. We are bedded down here at the airport without even a pillow for our heads, but God is watching over us and He sees our need."

The children's eyes were wide with wonder, and Rita noticed Abbey wiping tears from her eyes. Bart seemed strangely silent, but his face radiated a tranquility that had not been there earlier.

"I think now would be a good time for your poem, boys," Rita said to the children. Timmy motioned his brothers, Mike and Danny, to stand with him.

"I have a special Christmas gift, that might be hard to see," Timmy began. "But if you listen closely, you'll hear what it might be."

Mike took his place, looking sober and thoughtful. "It isn't wrapped in paper with tinsel, tape, or bow." He paused and looked at his mother, who was mouthing the words along with him for encouragement. "But it's a gift which everyone really ought to know."

Danny stepped forward, grinned broadly at Rita and then at the rest of the audience around him. "The gift," he shouted in his best four-year-old voice, "is something special, sent from God above. The gift He gave is Jesus—" Danny's special emphasis on the word Jesus made everyone chuckle. "From God to us with love!"

Everyone cheered and clapped. The three boys bowed several times and smiled proudly. Elaine hugged them all, while their baby sister slept soundly.

"That was perfectly wonderful," Rita said, clapping every bit as loudly as their mother.

"It's my turn," Abbey announced. She held up crocheted snowflakes. "These are for you boys and your sister, and here's one for you, Mr. Thomas." She handed old Bart the snowflake and turned to give each of the boys theirs. Only Rita saw Bart wipe a single tear from his eye and tuck the snowflake lovingly between the pages of the book he held.

"Now, I will share something else with you. My grandmother came to America from Denmark. That's very far away," she said for the boy's benefit. "In that country they speak a different language, but they still love Jesus, and they still celebrate Christmas. My grandmother taught me a song, and I thought I would share it with you for our celebration."

"Oh, yes! Please!" the small group exclaimed in unison.

"It's called, 'Her Kommer Dine Arme Smaa.'"

"That sounds funny," Timmy said with a giggle.

Abbey smiled. "The English name is, 'Thy Little Ones, Dear Lord, Are We,' and it was written in 1732 by a great Danish hymn writer named Hans Brorson. When he published it, the song appeared in a book called *A Little Hymn For Children*, and with it was the

Bible verse Matthew 21:16: 'Have ye never read, Out of the mouth of babes and sucklings thou has perfected praise?' "

Abbey ruffled Danny's hair gently. "Brorson wrote a great many hymns, and he is very well loved in my grandmother's country."

"Please sing it for us, Abbey," Rita encouraged and stepped back to find herself wrapped in Mark's arms. She relished the feeling of security and love.

"Her kommer dine arme smaa, O Jesus, i din stald at gaa; Oplys enhver i sjael og sind, At finde veien til dig ind!" Abbey sang, then laughing aloud at the puzzled expression on the faces of the boys, she repeated the verse in English. "Thy little ones, dear Lord, are we, And come Thy lowly bed to see; Enlighten every soul and mind, That we the way to Thee may find."

"Amen," Mark said softly against Rita's ear.

"Amen," Rita echoed.

"That was so cool!" Timmy exclaimed. "I never heard someone sing in that language."

Abbey was pleased with her contribution. "Merry Christmas to you all, and may you find the Christ child in your heart always."

Nell appeared with refreshments, and after everyone was seated with cookies and cocoa in hand, Mark left Rita's side for his part of the celebration. Rita's eyes grew moist as she watched him. Her heart swelled with pride at the commanding figure he made. How different things were from just a year ago! She hadn't even liked Mark, much less loved him. Well, maybe she liked him just a little, she mused.

"I'll share with you from the second chapter of Luke," Mark commented, "and retell the story of our Lord's birth." He cleared his voice and began, " 'And it came to pass in those days. . .' "

Rita heard the words she'd heard a hundred times before. How many Christmases had those special verses been quoted, only to have Rita ignore them. She'd done a great deal of ignoring in her life. She'd ignored the love her parents had offered her and the friendship of others. She'd ignored the wonderful security of a family and home. She'd ignored God too, only He refused to take it as well as the others had.

" 'And so it was, that, while they were there, the days were accomplished that she should be delivered. And she brought forth her firstborn son, and wrapped him in swaddling clothes, and laid him in a manger; because there was no room for them in the inn.' "

No room in the inn and no room in the hearts of man, Rita thought. Mark's tender baritone rang out, and glancing around her, Rita could see that others had gathered to listen. Perhaps they, too, had ignored the baby who had come so long ago to save them. Perhaps they were even now searching for some tiny spot in which to let the Savior take rest.

" 'And the angel said unto them, Fear not: for, behold, I bring you good tidings of great joy, which shall be to all people.' "

Rita saw the children completely taken in by Mark's animated recitation. They were his captive audience, as were the others: Nell, Bart, Abbey, and Elaine with her tiny daughter—all were immersed in this unplanned airport celebration.

" 'And suddenly there was with the angel a multitude of the heavenly host praising God, and saying—' "

Bart's gravely voice inserted, " 'Glory to God in the highest, and on earth peace, good will toward men.' "

Everyone fell silent, but Mark nodded to Bart and the old man smiled in such a way that Rita was sure he'd finally found something very precious. Mark walked back to where Rita had taken a seat.

"You know," Elaine said softly, "I was actually dreading this holiday. I had so much anger inside me. Resentment, bitterness—you name it. I just want you all to know that this night has changed me." Her eyes reflected the truth of her statement.

"Me, too," Abbey said with a glance to Rita. "I know for sure that I never have to be alone. No matter where I am, God is there, and if I'm with His people, I have my family around me."

Nell sobbed softly and tried to hide her sniffling behind sips of cocoa, while Bart opened and shut the book in his hand to look at the snowflake Abbey had given him. Even the boys remained quietly fixed on their goodies.

The airport terminal was strangely silent, but in the distance, almost unheard, a single voice began to sing

"Silent Night." Then another voice joined in. Then ten. Then twenty, and soon, everyone was singing the haunting melody.

"Sleep in heavenly peace, Sleep in heavenly peace."

The chorus faded, and everyone nodded knowingly to one another. Mark and Rita made their way to their pallet, while Elaine bedded down with her children, kissing each one lovingly and holding them for what seemed an extra long time. When she took the baby into her arms, Rita was reminded of Mary and the wonder of that night so long ago.

"Maybe that will be us next year," Mark whispered, pulling Rita into his arms.

"I'd like that very much, Mr. Williams," she murmured against his lips. "You know," she said, pulling away and surprising him, "I really do love you."

Mark laughed. "Just now figuring that out?"

Rita sat down and motioned him to do the same. She pulled the sleeping bag over their legs and leaned back against the wall and Mark's comfortable shoulder. Sighing deeply, she sought the right words.

"It's just that I'm overwhelmed with how much God must have loved us, still loves us," she said softly. "And I'm overwhelmed at how much I love you and how wrong I was to suggest we couldn't have a fantastic Christmas, even if it wasn't the one I had planned."

She sat up and searched Mark's brown eyes. What she saw reflected was the unconditional love she'd come to count on, but there was something else as well.

Could it be admiration?

"Christmas is a matter of heart," she said and reached out her hand to touch Mark's bristly cheek. "It doesn't matter where you celebrate or if there's a tree or gifts. It only matters that you see the real meaning. It only matters that you understand that Christmas is all about love. God's love for us, our love for Him and each other, and love for those yet to cross our paths who are lonely and rejected for whatever reason.

"It's understanding that God gave us the very best He had, and even though we didn't understand the sacrifice and could hardly appreciate His love, He gave it anyway because He knew without it, we would die— lonely and rejected."

Mark pulled her back into his arms and kissed her forehead. "You're quite a woman, Texas Rita. I'm glad I married you, and I wouldn't have missed this part of our honeymoon for anything in the world. There will always be celebrations with our family at home, but this family of strangers will probably never again cross our paths. We made a difference here today. I know it and feel it, just as surely as I feel your love for me."

"The real gift is that God has opened our hearts and minds," Rita said, lifting her face to his. "The real gift is understanding that He never meant for us to be lonely or separated from Him."

Mark kissed her with the same enthusiastic passion that had thrilled her a hundred times before. But this time there was something more, Rita thought. This time there was a bond of spiritual understanding that they'd not soon forget.

Sliding down to the floor of the airport, Mark pulled the bag close around them. "Merry Christmas, Rita," he whispered, his breath warm and sweet against her cheek.

"Merry Christmas," she replied. "And sweet dreams."

"Christmas dreams," Mark murmured sleepily. Neither one noticed that outside the snow had stopped and the wind had calmed. Beyond the icy windows of the airport, the north star shone brightly and pointed the way home.

Tracie Peterson has written over eleven inspirational romances including some under the pen name Janelle Jamison. Known mostly for her historical romances, Tracie was pleasantly surprised when *Iditarod Dream*, a contemporary romance, was voted "Best Inspirational" by *Affaire de Coeur* magazine in their annual readers' poll in 1994. Tracie, who is currently writing an historical series with Judith Pella for Bethany House Publishers, lives with her husband and three children in Topeka, Kansas.

Merry Christmas

Tracie J. Peterson

Joshua 1:9

Winterlude

Colleen L. Reece

One

I t started with a single snowflake, as out of place on the windshield of Emmet Carey's ostentatious Pierce Silver Arrow as a date palm in Alaska.

Alaska! Emmet shuddered and pinched his aristocratic nostrils with well-cared-for fingers. Nothing about that frozen wasteland—a place he fervently hoped never to see—could remotely touch his life. Except, he conceded, the birth there twenty-four years ago of the girl who sat beside him.

Emmet's tight lips relaxed, and the brown eyes that matched his hair held an appraising look. How different she looked from the first time he saw her! And yet—he relived the moment from the previous spring. He was accustomed to the endless parade of girls and women interested in his tall, attractive self and his fortune, but not one of them had attracted him as did

Ariel Dixon, fresh from her birthplace of Ketchikan. His jaded blood had stirred at the freshness of her sparkling gray-green eyes, naturally pink lips, and pale blond hair. Parted on the side, carelessly pulled back, and anchored with a ribbon at the nape of her neck, the severe hairstyle suited her. It gave Ariel a madonna-like look when her face was in repose, made her a sea sprite when she laughed.

"Outdoorsy," Emmet murmured, mentally disparaging Ariel's boyish, ivory flannel shirt modestly buttoned to show only a small vee of her creamy neck. Yet he had to admit the color enhanced her matching skin with its healthy pink cheeks that neither tanned nor needed cosmetics.

A light turned red on the busy San Diego street. Emmet braked and took advantage of the pause to glance at Ariel. Her slim five-foot, seven-inch body brought the top of her shining head just past his shoulder. A skirt and sweater of her favorite ivory brought out the green in eyes that had opened wide in delight. Her rosy lips parted in a little "o."

"What is it, darling?" He dropped his right hand over her shapely fingers and stroked the oversized diamond she had been wearing for the last month.

"A snowflake." She glanced at him, wonder in her gaze. "Imagine! A snowflake in San Diego, the first week of November."

"Trust you to get excited over a snowflake, little Eskimo," he indulgently told her. "I'd think you had scen enough snow to last a lifetime." He quickly laughed to cover the disdain in his voice. "Or at least, I'd hope so. We seldom get snow here and it never lasts long."

The awe in Ariel's eyes faded. Their sunny green took on a grayish hue. "I know." She turned back to the window but the small miracle had melted. A sigh escaped her lips.

Was she homesick? Emmet resented the idea. As his wife, she would have everything: wealth, power, prestige. A far cry from her status as a fisherman's daughter, even though her father was the uncrowned king of the mighty salmon industry in Alaska.

Don't be foolish, Emmet told himself. One of the things he admired most in Ariel was her adaptability and eagerness to please him. All he ever needed to do was make a suggestion. "You do love me, don't you, Ariel?" he asked.

"Of course." She squeezed his hand, then released it when the traffic light turned green. Yet Emmet felt that while her body remained beside him, her elusive spirit had fled far away, to a land he secretly and jealously despised.

≈

The sight of the single snowflake had entranced Ariel. Yet just as one ill-placed boulder can break loose and trigger an avalanche, so the tiny, crystalline flake set off a storm of rebellion in her heart. She could usually forgive Emmet's amused patronage because of his charm, but today it grated on her nerves. For the hundredth time she wished he showed as much appreciation for her heritage as for his own.

Ariel leaned her head back against the seat and closed her eyes. A feeling of needing to evaluate Emmet, herself, and their engagement crept into her heart. Why? a little voice demanded. He's a fine young man as well as being the sole heir to the holdings of the house of Carey. Holdings second to none, Ariel silently added. The crash of 1929 had barely dented the Carey fortune. Neither had the depression during these early 1930s. Emmet and his family carried on their usual gracious life, undisturbed by the despair that gripped the nation.

Ariel unconsciously lifted her chin. Thirty-year-old Emmet shone brightly in San Diego and southern California, but would he ever have the respect accorded her father?

A tender smile curved her lips. Her father—Big Tom Dixon, as he was known by the small and the great— inherited nothing but had built an empire. He fought and won success by sweat, fair play, and a shrewd knowledge of the fishing industry. When the fish were running, the cannery at Dixon Cove, fifty miles down the coast from Ketchikan, worked twenty-four hours a day. Natives and whites labored side by side, silver knives flashing against a backdrop of clanking machinery. "Get the fish, put up the pack, meet or beat competition from other canneries," drummed in their ears.

A small pack meant hardship for all. Ariel thought of '27, a year of fish famine so bad thirty canneries went broke. Her father held on. He sent men far afield. If the fish did not come to him, then he would go to them. His daring plan kept the Dixon Industries afloat, literally.

A wave of homesickness hurled itself against her heart; she felt sick. Could she turn her back on her own, even for Emmet, whom she adored? Could she abandon Alaska, the thrill and challenge of facing and conquering wilderness and weather? How would she feel, never again to know a swaying deck beneath her planted feet? Or never again to hear her tawny father bellowing fishermen's songs at the top of his lungs one moment, the next bowing his head to the God he had taught his daughter to love and honor?

Doubt dropped into Ariel's churning mind, like the single crystal snowflake. She dismissed the doubt as unworthy, but it came again, a veritable snowstorm this time. For the past seven months she had lived Emmet's life, frankly enjoying the luxury of her wealthy aunt's estate that bordered the vast Carey property. Every waking moment had been spent with Emmet, ever since she met him at the ball her aunt gave to introduce Ariel to the richest cream San Diego society had to offer.

"I've waited for years for this moment," her aunt had

said when Ariel came down the curving stairs wearing a misty green evening dress. More than ever, she resembled some lovely sea creature.

At her aunt's insistence, Ariel's father had granted her a year to introduce Ariel to another way of life. At first, Ariel had felt frustrated, eager for the year to be over so she could return home to Alaska, but the lovely dress had erased some of her impatience. She could not help but look forward to the ball.

When she had met Emmet later that evening, she had been impressed by how proper and observant of social conventions he was. She had thought she sensed warmth beneath his meticulous properness—but in truth was there more beneath his surface than the good companion he had always seemed? She knew he could sometimes be overbearing—certainly he had methodically gone about acquiring her love with the same dogged determination he showed on golf and tennis court—but she had always thought his charm to be as genuine as his love. Now she wondered.

Ariel returned to the present when Emmet said, "Would you like to come in with me or wait in the car?"

She glanced at the discreet display in the jewelry store where Emmet had left his favorite watch to be cleaned. "I'll wait, thank you."

He smiled and slid out of the car. "I won't be long."

Ariel watched him stride down the sidewalk, imposing and attractive in his tailored clothing. She was filled with a passionate longing for something. "I'd like to get you away from civilization and find out what kind of man you really are," she told his retreating back. "Dad always says you find out what's important about people when you pit them against a squall at sea or a blinding snowstorm."

A daring idea attacked Ariel's mind. What if she. . . no. . .he would never agree, but why not? In all the time since she'd met and learned to love him, not once had she asked special consideration. Of course everything they did was worthwhile; they simply did it Emmet's way. His choice of sports. His schedule. The church he and his ancestors had attended since having it built and supplying its minister.

"It isn't all Emmet's fault." Ariel frowned. "Whenever he suggests something I either agree or say, 'whatever you wish.'" She pulled a tiny mirror from her handbag and stared at her reflection. "Good heavens, am I becoming a spineless jellyfish? What would Dad say?"

He hadn't said much in answer to her ecstatic letter, she remembered. Just a telegram stating she should be old enough to choose for herself and he would respect that choice.

Ariel squirmed. Should be old enough could mean anything. The tepid words little resembled the man who had been father and mother both since his wife died when Ariel was small. She brushed mist from her eyes, remembering.

"It's just you and me now, mate," Tom Dixon told his

daughter after the funeral. "We'll have to carry on without our skipper. It's what she'd want. When things get tough, our Father in heaven will see us through. He knows what it's like to lose someone He loved."

"Aye, aye, captain." Ariel still remembered her smart salute, her attempt to be brave for his sake. "Is Mother with Jesus?"

"Yes."

"Will He take good care of her, so she won't feel sad?" Echoes of the childish voice rang in Ariel's soul. So did her father's answer.

"Ariel, child of my heart, God loved all the people in the world enough to send Jesus to die so those who believe on Him can live forever. Now, don't you think He's going to make sure your mother's happy?" She saw the glisten of tears in his craggy face. "You know, before God sent you to us, we had a little brother who only lived a few days. He's been waiting in heaven all this time, just as they'll be waiting for us to come someday."

"Daddy, when will we go?" She crept into his arms and laid her head on his massive chest. She heard his heart pound like a cannery engine, making a dull thud-thud noise.

"When it is the right time, we will go," Tom Dixon promised and held her close. "Always remember, Ariel. Mother cannot come back. We must keep our faith in Jesus so we can go to her." Not until years afterward did Ariel realize her father spoke as much to comfort himself as her.

Now she whispered, "I want to go home and take Emmet with me." All the pent-up emotion she hadn't known existed came together in an overwhelming desire. If only he. . . She could barely wait until he returned to the car.

As soon as he got in and started the motor, she said, "Emmet, I've never asked you for anything, although you've given me much. Now there's something I want more than I've ever wanted anything."

"Of course, darling." He smiled at her. "What is it?"

She plunged in, thrilled at his quick response. "Must we wait until spring to get married? I want us to have our wedding now." Heart glowing with anticipation, she rushed on. "We can fly to Ketchikan, better yet, fly to Seattle and take a steamer to Ketchikan. The Inside Passage is gorgeous. We can spend Christmas with Dad. You love sports. I can offer you skiing, snowshoeing, a hundred exciting things to do and see." She spread her arms in an embracing gesture. The prospect of going home sent flags of crimson into her lovely face. "What a glorious place for a honeymoon!"

Disapproval oozed from his every pore. "You expect me to spend my honeymoon in an Alaskan fishing village?" Outrage darkened his eyes. "I can't think of a worse place on earth than your frozen, uncivilized north, especially in winter."

"Your honeymoon?" Ariel blinked. "I thought it was ours."

"It is." He flashed her a quick smile. "But Mother would die of mortification if we changed the plans. Careys don't hurry up their weddings. We'll be married on Valentine's Day, as scheduled. That should be romantic enough for you."

"Whose wedding is this, ours or your mother's?" Ariel quietly asked. To her amazement, he laughed.

"When you're in my position. . ." A shrug of his shoulders finished the sentence. "Besides, people would think it odd."

A dangerous glint came to Ariel's eyes, deepening them to twilight gray. "Odder than a man becoming engaged to a girl her father hasn't even met?" she asked in a deceptively mild voice.

"How old-fashioned you are!" Emmet put the car in gear and swung into the street. "He isn't making trouble, is he?" Impatience colored his question.

"I haven't heard from him since the telegram."

Relief showed in Emmet's face, but at the next red light he turned his most beguiling little-boy look on her. "We can certainly add Switzerland to our itinerary, if you wish. Mountains are mountains and I dare say you'll forget anything around Ketchikan when you see the Alps." He went on with his plans.

Ariel shut her ears. She had been so sure he would grant her wishes. Instead, he had overridden them with Carey traditions, Carey arrogance, Carey certainty that whatever they chose was best. She put one hand to her throat, feeling suffocated. Could she stand the life that yawned before her like a crevasse in a snow field?

Ten minutes ago, she would have considered such thoughts disloyal. Now she did not. She turned her face toward the side window. Her heart felt frozen, as though her love had shattered into icy splinters. They lay in a glittering pile at her feet, jagged as the Alaskan glaciers that tear free and plunge into raging streams to be carried far from their birthplace.

With sudden insight, Ariel realized that even if she attempted to explain, Emmet would never understand. Careys could honestly not believe that any intelligent person would ever question the things they revered.

Ariel turned to her Source of help. *God*, she wordlessly prayed, *is what I'm feeling of You?* She waited, but no answer came. She took a long breath, held and released it. Had God sent the snowflake to warn her, as one snowflake often heralded a blizzard in her beloved homeland? Pain laced through her. If she married Emmet, she must renounce Alaska, Ketchikan, even her father. Today's revelations showed the folly of believing Emmet would permit anything else.

Two

A riel jumped when Emmet asked, "Why the sudden yen for Ketchikan?" She bit her lip and didn't reply, knowing and dreading the amused look he would give her if she told the truth. Something deep inside, buried by the gaiety and excitement of being pursued by the most eligible bachelor in southern California, had responded to a lone, misplaced snowflake.

He didn't push for an answer but expertly guided the Pierce Silver Arrow through San Diego's wide streets and avenues. At last he turned into the long and winding drive, bordered with palm trees and a high fence smothered in bougainvillea, that separated the Carey estate from the home of Ariel's aunt. For the first time since arriving in California, the girl failed to thrill at the brilliant profusion of blooms surrounded by rich red and purple bracts.

Neither did she feel the usual sense of awe that always came when she saw the sprawling Spanish-style mansion with red-tiled roof and climbing bougainvillea on the porch columns. All the Carey magnificence could not erase the hurt Emmet had inflicted by refusing her single request.

"Don't mention any of this to Mother," Emmet warned. "No sense upsetting her with your whim, now that we've settled it." He reached to open his door.

His unfortunate choice of words broke another silken thread that bound Ariel to him. "Wait, Emmet. This is not a whim. I want to go home."

"You are home, darling." He'd never been more appealing. "Come." He stepped from the car, opened the door on her side, and held out his hand.

Ariel reluctantly took it, but the rebellion in her heart remained.

Swinging her hand, Emmet led her across green velvet lawns that looked as if they had been trimmed with fingernail scissors. Choice roses perfumed the air. A choir of birds sang from a nearby hedge. At the edge of the lawn, he paused. "All this is yours once you marry me."

In spite of her determination not to give in, Ariel felt the pull of the spot. Sheer beauty surrounded her as far as she could see. On one side, the Pacific Ocean sported lazy, silver-crested waves. On the other, orange and lemon groves stretched like a citrus carpet until they gave way to rolling hills.

"I always give thanks when I stand here," Emmet said huskily. He put one arm around her shoulders and kissed her brow. "Especially since you came."

A rush of love swept through Ariel. This was the man she loved, not the heir to millions. If only she could forget the other side of him, the part that continually strove to mold her into a woman worthy of the position his wife must occupy!

"Emmet," she abruptly asked. "Why did you choose me from all the girls and women you know?" Ariel felt the entire world held its collective breath waiting for an answer so important it would affect their lives forever.

Emmet's handsome face took on a rueful smile. "I've asked myself that a hundred times. I'm still not really sure." He laughed uncomfortably. "You're beautiful and will bear me lovely children—"

"So would several dozen California socialites," she reminded him.

"You're strong and have lovely hands and manners—"

"So do they." Her heart sank as he enumerated her points in much the way she had seen him do when examining a choice vase or fine animal.

"Confound it, Ariel, I suppose because the first time I saw you, you looked—different. Even now, in that ridiculous shirt—" He shifted weight from one foot to the other and released her.

That ridiculous shirt. Ariel winced. She had fashioned the garment from ivory flannel her father gave her because it looked like pale winter sun on a snow-topped mountain. Her shoulders drooped. "If I attracted you because I was different, why do you try to make me like everyone else?" She gestured at her skirt and sweater. "You even chose the rest of my outfit."

"You may remember I asked you to get it in pink," he reminded.

Pink! She inwardly shuddered. Pink was for lovely ladies who sipped tea and endlessly prattled. Although she admired it on others, she refused to wear a color she loved most in sunrises, twilight, and roses.

Emmet turned to face her. "You'll have to admit my taste is exquisite. Ivory flannel hardly fits the Carey lifestyle. Of course, if we go to Yosemite, it will be appropriate. As for making you like everyone else, it isn't your fault your father short-sightedly kept you in a fishing village for most of your life. Your aunt tells me she wanted to take you after your mother died. Too bad she didn't."

Ariel stepped back, stricken at the words that rained on her like ice pellets. Did Emmet notice? Perhaps, for he hastily added, "I'm sure your father did what he felt was right." He smiled warmly at her. "Actually, it's amazing how cultured you are in spite of—"

"Don't say it." Blood drained from her face and she held out a shaking hand to ward him off. "You don't know me at all." She stared at him, eyes grayer than a blanket of fog. "You must come with me to Alaska or we can never be happy. You cannot marry the girl you think I am before seeing me in my native habitat." Ariel shifted her body and faced the ocean.

"I cannot deny the beauty of your home." She spoke quietly, wondering how she could sound so in control while struggling with disillusionment, even as she fought for her freedom. "Mine is rough by comparison, a comfortable, weathered house on a hundred-foot cliff that overlooks Ketchikan and the water. We have no bougainvillea, but wild roses, bluebells, and columbine nod in the breeze. The aspens' leaves whisper secrets in summer, and forget-me-nots grow everywhere, bluer than the sky." She broke off and caught her lower lip between her teeth. A long-ago event gnawed at her mind. Forget-me-nots. A summer day. Young laughter, replaced by pain, loss. Ariel felt tears crowd behind her eyes.

"You sound like an advertisement to lure tourists." Emmet's comment rudely interrupted her attempts to recapture the memory that brought both joy and sadness. Ariel dragged her attention back to him. "I'm simply saying you must know all I am, if we are to be happy. Can't you see?" She spread her hands appealingly. "As your wife, I enter a new world. Even when we go back to visit, it will never be the same." She failed to catch the stubborn set of her fiancé's chin, the denial in his eyes when she mentioned visiting Ketchikan. Gaze fixed on the sweeping Pacific, she fumbled to make herself clear. "Emmet, I need a bridge to span the chasm between the two chapters of my life." She searched for just the right description. "An interlude back in Alaska before I go forward into my new life."

"You mean a 'winterlude,' don't you?" Emmet laughed at his new word.

"If you want to call it that." Ariel swung back toward him, eyes glowing. Placing her hands on his arms she pleaded, "Come with me, Emmet. We don't have to be married now. Keep the wedding on Valentine's Day, but spend Thanksgiving and Christmas in Alaska. It can be my wedding present."

The heir to the Carey fortune didn't even consider it. "Impossible! I couldn't be gone so long. I'm taking three months for my honeymoon, remember?"

His honeymoon? Ariel set her lips, burning to remind him that his father had offered six months leave if Emmet wanted it. She refrained, stubbornly raised her chin, folded her arms across her chest, and issued her own little declaration of independence. "Then I'll go alone."

His mouth dropped open. He had never seen Ariel like this. Big Tom Dixon had. His normally tractable daughter seldom opposed him, but once she got that look on her face, all the rain in Ketchikan couldn't drown out the fires of her determination.

Emmet's usually calm demeanor deserted him. "Have you taken leave of your senses?" A tiny muscle twitched in his left cheek, a sure sign of inner distress. His brown eyes flashed with unaccustomed sparks of anger. "You will do no such thing. How can you even think of ignoring your obligations? You have fittings and teas, a half-dozen dinner dances, excursions and fêtes planned by the finest families in California."

He paused for breath, then announced in a voice that cut, "Marrying a Carey isn't like standing up before some itinerant, northern preacher with an uncivilized fisherman. If you can't see that, then you'll have to respect my authority as your future husband, Ariel." He gave her a reproachful look. "I can't imagine what's come over you. You've always been so cooperative." He shrugged. "I can't allow my fiancée to go kiting off to Alaska. That's final." Emmet held out his hand and smiled. "We'll forget all this unpleasantness and go on up to the house." He laughed carelessly. "You know how the cook gets if we're late for luncheon."

His comment pushed Ariel past the limits of endurance. What kind of man had more concern for offending the family cook than meeting the father of the girl he loved? Rage such as Ariel hadn't experienced since coming to the States exploded within her. Emmet's slur against hard-working men unafraid to face the elements and wrest a living from them for their families was also a slur against the father she adored. She tore the sparkling diamond ring from her engagement finger and thrust it into his hand. "Your fiancée may not go, Emmet. I shall."

Emmet's mouth opened and closed like a salmon out of water. Shock and disbelief warred in his face. "You don't mean that! You know I'm only doing what is best."

"For whom? You? Your mother? The cook?"

"Stop this nonsense immediately," he ordered. "Put your ring back where it belongs. I'm not impressed with histrionics, Ariel." Only once had she heard him speak in that steely tone of voice. A stray dog on the street had dared plant muddy feet on a Carey's immaculate white trousers.

"No."

At her uncompromising reply, he changed tactics. "Surely you won't let such a trivial matter as this come between us. Please, Ariel, put your ring back on." He sent a hasty glance toward the house. "What if a servant should overhear?"

Thank You, God, for showing me the real Emmet, Ariel silently prayed. She fancied she heard the sound of shackles breaking, crashing to the ground with a mighty clanking sound. Her anger fled. Pity for the man who had so much, yet possessed so little of real value filled her and gentled her voice. "I'm sorry, Emmet. We are of two different worlds. Remember the expression, 'ne'er the twain shall meet?' I hope someday we may be able to look back and remember the good times." She saw his bewilderment, his utter lack of recognition of his offense. "You need someone who will accept your will as law. I can't do that and I can't marry you. Not for all this—" She waved a hand from horizon to horizon. "I'm going home where I belong." A tide of joy and freedom rose in her.

"And just what am I supposed to tell people, especially Mother? She always said—" He had the grace to bite off the sentence.

"Don't apologize for her. I know she had someone picked out for you long before I came to San Diego."

"Apologize for Mother? Her conduct is always beyond reproach. It is you who should apologize, Ariel. When you do, your ring will be waiting." He pocketed it. "In the meantime, what shall I say?"

A flash of insight told her that her defection would hurt Emmet's ego far more than his heart. The last of Ariel's guilt vanished. Joyous laughter came in its place. "Tell your mother and your friends and the cook—" She clutched her sides and laughed until tears rained. "Tell them your fisherman's daughter turned into a mermaid and went back to live in the sea." Ashamed of her flippancy but unable to hold back merriment, she finally subsided, then broke the stony silence Emmet had maintained during her outburst. "Whatever you decide to say is all right with me."

He haughtily accompanied her back to the house. "I shall tell them you feel you need to see your father, that he isn't well. No one need know you have foolishly taken off the Carey betrothal ring."

Hysteria threatened. "I won't stay for luncheon."

"Just as well. Mother would surely notice the absence of your ring. Do you want me to escort you, or would you rather have the chauffeur drive you home?"

"I'll walk," Ariel decided. "Good-bye, Emmet." She waited while he opened an intricately carved gate in the flower-covered fence separating the estates.

"This isn't the end, you know. Careys always get what they want." His voice followed her, bringing a curious chill down her spine. She didn't answer. Once she arrived safely home in Alaska, neither Emmet nor his influential family could touch her.

Thirty minutes of brisk walking later, Ariel reached her aunt's home, a slightly smaller replica of the Carey place built by the husband whose death left his wife the sole possessor of his estate and iron-clad securities. "Madam would like to see you in the library," the solemn-faced butler announced after he had unbolted the heavy front door to admit her.

She smiled at him, thinking how in Ketchikan people lived behind unlocked doors. "Very well, but I'll freshen up first."

"Madam said you were to come the moment you arrived, miss. She seemed dreadfully upset." The man's bump of curiosity overrode his usual discreet manner for a moment.

"Really?" Ariel's heart pounded. What if it were bad news from home? Fear lent wings to her feet and she raced the length of the great hall and burst into the book-lined room. "What's wrong, Auntie? It's not Dad, is it?"

Adelaide Patten, who still showed traces of the beauty that had captured her wealthy husband, shook her head. Her dark eyes flashed. "No. Now what's all this about you throwing a tantrum and threatening to break your engagement just because Emmet Carey refused to let you browbeat him into giving you your own way?" Her lips quirked unexpectedly and she added, "I quote. I just spoke to him on the telephone."

Ariel hadn't counted on Emmet's beginning a reclamation campaign so soon. She seated herself in a chair more stylish than comfortable and confessed, "I didn't threaten. I meant it when I gave back the ring."

Her aunt slumped, defeat in her face. "Perhaps I've been selfish, but it was all so perfect, knowing you'd be right next door. It isn't like you to be rash, Ariel. What's the real reason? His mother?" She snorted a most unladylike snort. "Mrs. Carey's the biggest liability Emmet has."

"Not only his mother. Emmet and his cook and—"

"His cook! Ariel Dixon, you broke your engagement on account of an overpaid cook?" A chuckle followed. Then another, until the elegant little lady rocked back and forth.

That laughter did what all Emmet's raging hadn't accomplished. Ariel bolted from her chair, knelt beside her aunt, and buried her face in the satin-clad lap. Hot tears squeezed out. The touch of her aunt's soft hand on her hair brought another freshet. "H-he was more c-concerned about offending the c-cook by being late to l-luncheon than c-caring about meeting D-dad," she choked out. "He r-reminded me I wasn't marrying a f-fisherman." Between giggles and sobs she managed to tell the story.

"Pompous donkey," Adelaide promptly said. "Go wash your face and blow your nose. I can't abide a sodden niece."

"Thank you, Auntie." Ariel impulsively dropped a kiss on the beautifully arranged hair. Her heart kept time with her feet as she skipped from the library, up the stairs, and to her luxurious room. In a short time, she returned and told the story again, starting with the transient snowflake.

"It was so lovely while it lasted. Then the city absorbed it, as it has me." She met her aunt's dark gaze squarely. "I know Dad promised me to you for a year, and I appreciate everything you've done for me. You opened your heart and lovely home. I've been treated like your own daughter." She swallowed hard and her gray-green eyes shone like a rainbow through a waterfall. "I'll never forget it, Auntie, but I want to go home." Yearning spilled into the costly room and beat time with the well-modulated clock marking off life's hours in soft, but inexorable ticks.

Three

"Will you release me from Dad's promise?" Ariel asked. "I'll stay if you insist but it will be awkward for everyone, with the Careys just next door."

"Are you sure you don't just need a winterlude, as Emmet so disrespectfully labeled it?" Adelaide probed, keen eyes steady.

"No. Today I saw the real Emmet Carey. Not the popular, sought-after man, but a man who chose me to transform into a worthy Carey wife. I don't doubt that he loves me, as much as he's capable of loving anyone who isn't a Carey. It isn't enough, Auntie. Emmet doesn't care enough to let me be myself."

After a moment she added in a low voice, "I don't think he wants to acknowledge the part of me that belongs to Alaska. He acts afraid of meeting that girl,

I suppose for fear she won't fit into his life. I know now he planned to wean me from my past so in time San Diego would forget I was ever anyone but a Carey." She pounded a knee with one fist. "As if I'd forget! In time I'd grow to despise myself and hate Emmet for forcing me into his pattern."

The older woman leaned forward. "So your love is not strong enough to accept Emmet with all his power and influence?"

Ariel considered well before she said, "Not unless there is more to him than what he showed today. Perhaps if he had been the person I believed him to be when we met. . ." Her voice trailed off. "That's probably why I wanted him to go north with me. To see him in surroundings where he can't get what he wants by buying it. There is no obstacle in Emmet's world money can't overcome. Alaska's different. People are judged by what they are, not what they have."

"Do you honestly think Emmet could pass the test, even if he agreed to go?" Doubt crept into Adelaide's face. "You can't very well confess you're taking your fiancé north to see if he's a real man."

"No." Ariel brought the heart of the problem into the quiet room and faced it squarely. "I did want to give him a chance. I suppose love, or infatuation if that's what it was, dies hard. I can't respect someone who tramples me, who refuses to allow me the right to choose." She considered the thought for a long time. "Maybe I just wanted Emmet to see me as more than a mass of soft clay pliable enough for him to create into his ideal woman." A mischievous laugh bubbled out. "I'll wager the end result would be a younger replica of his mother."

"It wouldn't surprise me," her aunt grimly said. "Ariel, if you feel like that, you must not marry Emmet, for his sake as well as yours." Late afternoon light seeped through the casement windows and set the diamonds in her wedding and engagement rings gleaming. "All the riches in the world can't bring happiness unless you know Emmet's failings and love him in spite of them." She set her mouth in a thin line. "Too bad the Careys never see they have failings. My husband used to say they raised Emmet to believe he was understudy to God."

"Really? I wish I could have met your husband. He sounds like quite a man."

"He was." Her smooth hands clasped. "I married for love. Others doubted it; Frederick never did. We had a perfect blending, as God intended. Not that our life together was smooth as a trotting park. No marriage is. Heartache comes in spite of riches and possessions. We longed for children and none came. Instead of tearing us asunder, as is often the case, it strengthened our love. After he died, life seemed endless. Then you came."

Ariel listened intently, realizing her aunt had never before opened her heart like this. So might Ariel's own mother have spoken to her, if she had lived. Until this moment Big Tom Dixon had been all-sufficient. Now Ariel realized in spite of his tender care, she had missed much in not having a mother during her years from childhood and youth to womanhood.

The older woman leaned back in her chair, shadows deepening around her. "When the time comes, someone will ask you to go to the ends of the earth with him—and you'll be not only willing but eager. And even then, ask your Heavenly Father if it be right. You can trust Him to guide you. If you feel His blessing, let nothing stop you. Seize happiness with both hands. Set your course and steer straight ahead, guided by the Master Pilot and knowing you are in His and your beloved's care. Never marry until this comes." She hesitated. "I don't mean to pry, Ariel, but have you ever felt this way about Emmet?"

"Never." A warm blush rushed to paint the girl's ivory skin. "I've been thrilled and excited, proud he chose me. He has kept me busy with plans and compliments and promises of how happy we'll be." She wrinkled her smooth forehead. "My goodness, what I felt for him is nothing like what you describe!" She sighed deeply. "I shouldn't condemn him so harshly, should I? My reasons for marrying him were no more valid than his for me. The fact he came into my life like some knight in shining armor and swept me off my feet is no excuse, especially when I had the example of Dad and Mother's love."

"How can that be?" Adelaide protested. "You were

little more than a tot when she died."

"Mother's spirit has never left him, as far as Dad is concerned." Ariel's voice dropped to a whisper. "She's as alive and real in memory as she was in life. Dad once told me each time he stands at the wheel of a ship and sails into the sunset or sees a sunrise, he feels her presence. He said even after all these years, when he comes home at the end of a weary day, he half-expects her to come running to meet him at the gate." Ariel drew a ragged breath. "That's why he never remarried, even to provide a mother for me."

A wave of revulsion went through her. "Oh, how could I have been so blinded by riches and attention I didn't see I was prepared to accept a substitute love, simply because I've never experienced the real thing?"

"Any girl would be flattered," came the quick response. "Forgive me, my dear, but were there sweethearts in Alaska? Did you have anyone with whom to compare when you met Emmet?"

Ariel shook her head. "Not really, although I had a horde of friends." Her eyes grew dreamy. "Only one touched my heart and that was years ago, a playmate with whom I grew up. In the way of childhood, we vowed to always be together. When I was twelve and he was fifteen, the family went away. No one seemed to know why or where. I haven't thought of Jean for a long time. Then today while describing Ketchikan to Emmet, I mentioned forget-me-nots." A poignant feeling of regret and loss went through her. "The day before we parted, Jean picked a single forget-me-not. He said someday he would come back to me, but I never heard from him again. I pressed the tiny blue flower between the cover and flyleaf of my Bible. I cried when it crumbled to nothing." She dabbed at her tear-wet eyes with a filmy handkerchief. "Isn't it silly how old memories still have the power to bring tears?"

"Was your childhood friend like Emmet?"

"Oh, no." Melancholy beat a hasty retreat. Her misty eyes glistened. "Jean Thoreau was slim and dark, as are many French-Canadians. He could leap like a mountain goat and run like a deer. Dad taught both of us to swim, all about boats, to shoot—rifle, pistol, bow and arrow. He insisted we learn how to survive if caught in a blizzard or storm at sea." Memories softened her voice. "Those skills wouldn't mean much to the Careys, except perhaps my expertise in archery. Yet Dad gave us everything anyone needs to survive in a land that is both magnificent and cruel."

Dusk lurked outside the windows and thrust dark fingers into the room. Neither occupant made an effort to turn on the soft lights designed to send shadows flying. At last Adelaide said, "I fully intend for us to be together for the full promised year."

The heart that longed for home sank, but Ariel would not break her father's word.

A moment later, her indomitable aunt sat up straight and announced, "Ariel, your winterlude makes me want to see Ketchikan and as much of your Alaska as I can handle in winter. Do you think your father will forgive the unwarranted interference of a meddling sister-in-law? A well-meaning but misguided old woman who bullied him into lending his most precious belonging, because I told him you deserved the chance to see a world outside the far north?"

Speechless, Ariel could only stare.

"Well?" Adelaide snapped, an unreadable expression in her dark eyes.

Her answer came in the form of a flying figure that detached itself from the chair and flung strong arms around her. "You wonderful aunt! You aren't old at all. As for Dad, when he hears we're coming, he will roll red carpet through the streets of Ketchikan and have the shingle—seashore to you—swept clean. He'll kill the fatted calf, and—"

"That's quite enough of your foolishness," came the sharp rejoinder. "For the love of heaven, don't smother me. Turn on the lights, please. It's darker than an igloo in here."

Ariel chortled. "As if you know about igloos!" Her arms drew back. She flipped a switch and set recessed lights glowing, then spun into a dance that could have been inspired by a zephyr. Suddenly she stopped. All the joy drained from her expressive face and unfettered heart. "I-you-Auntie—?"

"What is it? Second thoughts?"

"No. It's only, I hate to mention it, but how will your maid feel about leaving sunny San Diego? She may hate it and find our log home uncomfortable."

Adelaide threw her hands into the air, but a pleased expression belied her exasperation. "Thanks for implying I'll be comfortable, even if my maid isn't." Sarcasm dripped from her tongue. "I hope I have sense enough to leave the trappings of society behind and when in Ketchikan do as the Ketchikanites do."

"Ketchikanites! Auntie, you're the best sport in the world." Ariel sank to the floor in an ivory heap. She stroked the rug with one hand. "Just think. Soon you'll be walking on a bear skin rug instead of a priceless Persian carpet."

"Forget carpets and bear skins and help me plan. Now, about leaving—"

"Give me fifteen minutes to pack and another five to leave a note for Emmet. I suppose I owe him that, since he didn't take me seriously."

"Not so fast. What's the best way to get there? By aeroplane? People have gone flying mad lately, ever since the thirties began."

Ariel ached with eagerness to say yes, to arrive in Ketchikan as soon as possible, but she shook her head. "That's one way, but you'll see more if we take passage from Seattle. You'll see some of the most beautiful scenery on earth."

"As if you know all about the earth and its beauty," her aunt teased.

Ariel was undaunted. She dropped back to her position on the rug and half closed her eyes. "The Inland or Inside Passage, as it's sometimes called, stretches more than a thousand miles, from Seattle to Skagway, north of Juneau. Other than one short stretch of open sea, we'll steam with the mainland on one side, the coastline so rugged in places it's said to resemble the fjords of Scandinavia. Forested islands dot the open water on the other. If we're lucky, we'll see whales, maybe bears or other wild animals."

Her pulse quickened with anticipation. "It's by no means a straight stretch." She laughed, bringing a smile of sympathy to her aunt's lips. "Ship captains often rely on the echo of the ship's whistle to help them steer a safe course."

"Really? Why should they do that?"

"Smothering fog, as well as sharp turns to catch the unwary off guard." Ariel fell silent. "Auntie, there's no way I can describe Alaska to you. You'll just have to see it for yourself." She again buried her face in the welcoming lap. "I am so glad you're going. I just wish you'd stay with us forever."

"Nonsense! I'm a bossy old woman who'll drive your father to distraction and unless he's chivalrous enough to put up with it, he's likely to throw me out long before forever comes!" Wistfulness crept into Adelaide's voice, like the fog Ariel had said stole over the Pacific. "No, my dear, I can't leave San Diego permanently. My husband is buried here. If you ever want to come back—I hope you will—I'll be here." She laughed, a bit shakily. "That doesn't mean I won't pay other visits to Alaska. If it's as grand as you say, I'll want to see it in summer, as well as winter."

Hours later, Ariel lay sleepless in the canopied bed she might not occupy again for years. She smiled into the darkness. Once her aunt made up her mind, Adelaide wasted no time. Through business connections of her late husband she chartered a private plane to take them to Seattle the next day. Another acquaintance recommended and made reservations at a Seattle hotel. A third secured passage for the travelers a few days later.

Money certainly had a way of smoothing out bumps in the road! A hasty note to a favorite reporter ensured that the next edition of the evening paper would carry news of their departure. A carefully worded report would follow the blazing headline: ADELAIDE PATTEN HEADS NORTH. Ariel chuckled, remembering her aunt's face when she read aloud what she had written in fine Spencerian script.

"Mrs. Adelaide Patten, widow of Frederick Patten, well-known financier, disclosed today in an exclusive interview her plans to leave San Diego in the height of the winter season for an extended visit to Alaska. Accompanying her is her niece Ariel Dixon, whose beauty and charm has taken our fair city by storm. Miss Dixon is the daughter of Thomas Dixon of Ketchikan, who was largely responsible for turning Ketchikan into the Salmon Capital of the World and is well known and highly respected throughout Canada and the entire northwest."

"The Careys aren't going to like this," Ariel warned uneasily.

"Who cares? We won't be here." A mischievous smile changed Adelaide from a society woman into a middle-aged elf.

"You fraud," Ariel cried. "You're absolutely gloating over the storm that's going to break when they discover we're gone, aren't you?" Her gray-green eyes widened when a guilty flush reddened her aunt's face. "All these years, I'll bet you've just been itching to kick over the traces."

"I have. For Frederick's sake, I held myself in. Not that he would have cared. He never kowtowed to anyone." She shifted restlessly and turned somber. "I don't think I realized how much I wanted to break free after he died until you came, fresh and unspoiled as your homeland."

"Auntie, why didn't you let us know? Why didn't you come to Ketchikan?"

"I was never invited."

The desolation in the quiet words broke Ariel's tender heart. She choked, "If we'd ever dreamed you felt this way, Dad and I—why, we'd have seen to it you came if we had to kidnap you."

A quick clasp of hands spoke volumes and the delicate moment forged an unbreakable bond between them. Adelaide broke the silence by ordering, "Go write your note to Emmet. It's only fair that he gets it before the paper comes out." She cocked her head to one side and her dark eyes twinkled. "Why don't you simply write, 'I meant everything I said. Good-bye, Emmet,' and leave it at that." After a moment she added, "If I know Emmet, and I do—a lot better since you told me what happened, by the way—he will punish you by refusing to call for a day or two. That gives us time to make our getaway."

"Getaway!" A trill of laughter lightened the atmosphere. "I didn't realize how informed you are about gangster jargon. You sound like a heavy in a mystery motion picture."

"There's a whole lot about me you don't know—but will probably find out," Adelaide Patten retorted. "Go write your farewell note and get some sleep, if you can." She rose from her costly chair, marched toward the library door, and turned, the elfin look back on her attractive face. "I know I can't. I haven't been this excited since I was a child waiting for Christmas. One thing. I prefer not to remain and shop here. We can purchase gifts in Seattle, can't we?"

"Of course. What a wonderful Christmas this will be! One of the hardest things when Dad agreed to have me come for a year was knowing I'd have to go through the holiday season in a warm, sunny place, without a flake of snow."

"You got your flake of snow and look what happened!"

"I know. Isn't it wonderful?" Ariel looked at her bare

ring finger. "I didn't realized how heavy that ring was until I removed it."

"Carey traditions can weigh one down, all right," her aunt said cryptically. A curious expression crossed her face. "What and how much are you planning to say in your telegram to your father, besides announcing our day of arrival?"

"It's been running through my mind," Ariel admitted. "I think I'll ignore the engagement entirely. I need to sit down with Dad, start at the beginning, and go from there." Laughter danced in her eyes. "It's a family tradition. As far back as I remember, we ended each day by relating in sequence everything interesting that had happened, then we thanked our Heavenly Father for His loving care."

"He may be a fisherman, Ariel, but Tom Dixon is a wise man." Her aunt walked out, head high and body erect.

"A very wise man," Ariel whispered to herself in the seclusion of her room. She yawned, plumped her pillow, and turned on her side. Her last waking thought was of home—and a dark-eyed boy who gave her a blue flower and then went away.

Four

A few short weeks after Big Tom Dixon sent his daughter into temporary exile with her aunt, a slim, dark-haired young man paused on the wide veranda of the salmon king's residence. Long and spacious, with weathered shingles of silvery gray, the house blended into a background of ferns and aspens as if it had been there forever. Climbing roses showed promise of a thousand blooms once the sun stopped sulking behind the heavy clouds and condescended to cast its rays on the sodden earth. A forested slope rose behind the house. A hundred feet down the steep cliff from the veranda, Ketchikan's Front Street bustled with fishermen and women, native and white, all waiting for the fish run when the canneries would open and offer work to all. Curio shops and stores, with heavy concentration on fishing supplies, flanked both sides of the street.

The man's pulse quickened. Fish—life's blood of Ketchikan.

His mouth firmed. A shadow crossed his expressive face. Would he be welcome here where he had spent so many happy childhood hours? With a resolute movement that yet held grace, he raised a slim, strong hand and knocked on the partly open door, hand-hewn from a single mighty tree slab.

"Come in, come in," came an answering roar.

What poignant memories that voice held! Merry laughter. The mingled aroma of furniture polish and wood smoke from the stone fireplace built to accept a six-foot length of log. Warm, spicy fragrance floated from a kitchen he knew was in back of the massive living room that ran the length of the house. Mischief danced in his black eyes and brightened the somber cast that had settled over his usually laughing face. If he had a dollar for every cookie he'd begged from Molly, the Dixon's cook, he'd have a cache richer than most of the sourdoughs in the Klondike gold rush.

"Are you coming in or not?" A heavy tread accompanied the demand. The door opened, revealing a man to match the footsteps. Disheveled, fair hair topped a ruddy face etched with hard but clean living, a keen gaze that changed from surprise to welcome. Giant paws reached out, grabbed the younger man in a grizzly-bear hug, and hauled him inside. "Praises be, if it isn't Jean Thoreau and just when I'm needing him most. God is good." He raised his voice in a shout.

"Molly, bring this prodigal son some coffee and those cookies you're baking."

Any lingering doubts about his reception vanished. Jean's laugh rang out with the clear sound of a sharp ax splitting a tree trunk. "I'd travel a lot farther than from Nova Scotia for Molly's cookies."

"Nova Scotia? For the love of Mike, what were you doing in Nova Scotia?" Dixon motioned Jean to a comfortable chair, intricately carved. "You can't get much farther from Ketchikan than that and still be in North America. Son, why in all these years have you never sent a word to your old friends?" The gruff voice betrayed bewilderment and hurt.

Jean winced. "It's a long story." Before he could continue, Molly appeared with a tray bearing huge mugs of steaming coffee and a plate of what the master of the house always called "Alaska-sized cookies."

Now he rumbled, "Good. Never could stand those dainty little things some of the packers' wives serve. What doesn't stick in your teeth, falls down your front in crumbs!" He took an enormous bite of spice cookie and grinned.

Molly's wrinkled brown face wreathed in smiles. Jet-black eyes twinkled and her thick silver braid bounced when she trotted away after she first patted Jean's arm and said, "It's good to have our boy back."

Jean choked on his coffee. "Twenty-seven years old and still a boy to Molly."

Furtively, Dixon looked both ways, then whispered,

"I'm more than twice your age and she still calls me a boy, too!" He shouted with laughter, then shot Jean a curious glance. "You said you had a story, but let me speak first, if you will. Thanking God for your coming wasn't just idle talk." His craggy face darkened. He set his coffee mug down on a hand-made table nearby with such force a few dark drops splashed onto his hand. Dixon idly rubbed the red spots they left but never looked away from Jean's face.

"There's dirty work going on. I need you to help me fight it." Great cords stood out on his neck. "Here we are on the eve of what could be the biggest haul in years and my cannery superintendent walks out on me! I'd take it on myself but I need to be out with the fleet. What concerns me most is being betrayed. Olson's gone over to my biggest competitor."

"Thad Olson? I'd have staked my life on his loyalty!"

"So would I." Dixon gritted his teeth. "They say every man has his price. Evidently Thad did." He spread his arms wide. "What do you say, Jean? Will you run my cannery and help me put up a record pack?"

"Will I!" Jean's blood leaped. Was this God's answer to the prayer of longing he'd silently uttered all the way across Canada? His right hand shot out to seal the bargain, then drew back. "I'd give anything to accept but before I do, there are things you need to know about me." Pain crept into his voice.

Something flickered deep in the watching gray-green eyes so like his daughter's. Doubt? Dread? Disappointment? A combination of all three? "The offer stands. Whatever has happened or whatever you've been in the last twelve years is your business." He extended his hand.

Jean's eyes stung but he shook his head. "Hear me out. Then if you still want me, I'm yours."

"Fair enough."

"Remember when Ariel and I were kids and you taught us God hated anything except the truth? I never forgot." Memories surged through him. "I've never sailed under false colors and I won't start now." He took a deep breath, held it, then released it and squared his shoulders. "Tom, I came back because I've been in love with your daughter as long as I can remember."

Dixon sprang to his feet, face working. "Do you mean that?"

"I never meant anything more in my entire life." Graceful as an Indian slipping through the forest, Jean rose and faced the old friend whose height topped his own sapling-like body by a good four inches.

"Why didn't you come sooner? Before. . ." Dixon dropped back into his chair.

"Before what?" A chill colder than the runoff from a glacier trickled down Jean's spine and he clenched his fists. "Ariel—she—she's not dead, is she?"

"No, but she's gone." Life drained from the older man's face.

"Gone? Left Ketchikan?" Jean felt the same way he

had when hit in the stomach with a lacrosse stick during a heated game years before.

"Yes. I sent her."

Jean weakly sat back down, brain spinning. "Why? Did she want to go?"

"No. Her only aunt, her mother's sister, convinced me Ariel needed to see the Outside, to know something other than Alaska." The monotone words fell like hailstones on Jean's heart. "She's to stay in San Diego for a year. Adelaide Patten is wealthy and Ariel will have every advantage." He spoke as if trying to convince himself more than Jean Thoreau.

"When did she go?"

"Less than a month ago." Dixon turned haunted eyes toward his guest. "Jean, when I saw the ship steam out of sight, I had the feeling she'd never come back."

"Are you crazy?" Jean bit his lip. "Forgive me, but Ariel would die away from Alaska." Even as he said it, though, he wondered. Much could happen between the ages of twelve and twenty-four. How did he know what his playmate had become? Would the glitter of the world lure and hold her? No! Warmth stole through him. The faith instilled in them as children would protect Ariel Dixon, no matter how far away she might be.

"That's what I told myself, at first." Dixon sighed and his brow furrowed. "Now I'm not so sure. She's met someone, a rich neighbor." The succinct statement refroze Jean's heart. "I think she may marry him. Seems

Emmet Carey is San Diego's best catch."

"Is he a man of faith?"

"I hear he's a faithful church attender, beyond reproach. Who knows how deep beyond that it goes?" The two men exchanged significant glances. In their world God was Father, and Jesus was not only Savior but Companion, Guide, and Friend. "I trust my daughter, but she's lived a simple life here. God forgive me if I've sent her to a world that may attract her by its very difference! San Diego society is evidently falling all over itself to entertain and honor her."

Jean stretched and placed both hands behind his dark head. "She may be dazzled for a time, but if she's anything like the Ariel I knew, it won't last." The confidence in his voice brought hope to Dixon's eyes.

"If you'd been here, I wouldn't have given in to Adelaide's pleadings. I always—" He broke off and restlessly moved in his chair, a tawny mountain lion of a man. "Was that all you wanted to tell me—that you had designs on my daughter? If so, what took you so long?" A smile lurked at the corners of his mouth and robbed the questions of any sting.

"I thought you—she—didn't care about me any longer."

"What?" Dixon's massive frame jerked erect.

Jean bowed his head until his words grew muffled. "I wrote a dozen letters but never got an answer."

"A dozen letters? We never received even one!"

"I only learned that a few weeks ago." The young

French-Canadian raised an anguished gaze. "Over the years, sickness took all of my immediate family. Mother was the last. Before she died, she gave me the letters I had written."

"I don't understand."

"I'm still trying to understand it myself," Jean admitted, feeling anew the shock he'd experienced at his mother's confession. "She knew she was dying but she held on until she told me the truth." He paused and Dixon silently waited, sympathy in his softened face. "The story in the simplest of terms is: back when we still lived here, Mother saw I'd learned to care for Ariel. She and my father respected you greatly, but feared you might feel a trapper's son wasn't good enough for your daughter. They couldn't bear to have my heart broken and so they prayed, asking God what to do. About that time a letter came from friends who wanted us to go to Nova Scotia. My parents saw it as an answer from God. We moved immediately; they didn't even tell me where we were going until after we had left. They didn't want me to tell Ariel where we were going."

"And so you went."

"Oui. I didn't want to leave." Jean stared out a shining window at a bird busily building its nest. "I promised Ariel one day I would come back. She cried and I turned away to hide my feelings. When she did not answer my letters, I wrote to you, fearing her to be sick, even dead." His face twisted. "I finally accepted what Mother and Father said: that I should be glad God had given me a wonderful childhood friendship but now that I had become a man, I must move on."

"Did you find another love?" A strange note crept into Dixon's voice.

"No. Deep inside I clung to the hope there must be a reason neither of you wrote. Perhaps you had moved away and my letters did not find you." He shrugged. "A boy's hope dies hard, but in time, the years together seemed like a dream, except for my promise." His black eyes glowed. "You yourself had taught me promises must be kept, so I vowed one day to return."

A pool of silence fell, broken only by a whisper of breeze that sprang up and danced through the still-open front door. Jean leaned forward. "Today I'm keeping that promise." He sighed. "Even if Father and Mother were wrong, it is too late for me to hope I might make Ariel care. Especially now she may have fallen in love with another man." Desolation surged over him. "However, I could not accept your offer without you knowing the truth about me."

"Blast the Thoreau pride!" Dixon angrily slammed his fist on the table again. "I know your parents did what they felt they could to keep you from heartache. I honor them for that, but how wrong they were! For years I watched Ariel turn toward the rising sun, the way you had gone, with a look in her eyes I could do nothing to erase. I saw her lips tremble when no message came. She never spoke of it. Dixon pride, I suppose." After a moment's silence he fiercely added, "I used to pray for your return. You're the son I never had, the only man I'd trust completely with Ariel's life and happiness. The fact you have traveled thousands of miles to keep a promise to one who seemed to have forgotten you confirms what I knew long ago. Jean Thoreau, you will stand true in the face of any temptation to be less than the person God asks you to be. Now, may I shake hands with my new cannery superintendent?"

Jean wordlessly held out his slender, steel-muscled hand, sealing the agreement.

"I'll shoot a telegram off to Ariel right away," Dixon exulted. "If only we could see her face when she gets it!" He clasped his hands in a victory signal.

"I'd rather you didn't tell her," Jean slowly said.

"Are you being quixotic?"

"No. It's just that I'd like to make good on the job here first."

"You don't have to prove yourself to me," Dixon's eyes flashed fire.

Jean chose his words well. "I know." Blood rushed into his lean face and his eyes darkened with yearning. "Good friend, it is I who must know I am worthy, whether or not God in His mercy ever entrusts Ariel to my care."

Five

"Getting up before dawn and standing at the rail won't get us to Ketchikan any faster," Adelaide Patten acidly observed from her comfortable shipboard berth. The sparkle in her eyes belied her complaint.

Ariel cocked her shining head to one side. Back in the ivory flannel shirt she loved, the jubilant girl radiated health, vitality, and anticipation. "It might get us there faster." She planted her hands on her slim, ivory-clad hips and flashed a smile that brought a twitch to her aunt's lips. "Lazybones people miss the best part of the day."

Her aunt scowled. "Lazybones! My dear niece, it isn't yet five o'clock. Even the sun's asleep. I don't remember you rising this early in California."

"That's because I stayed up until all hours." Ariel

secured her hair at the nape of her neck. "Auntie, when we left San Diego, I felt like I'd dropped my burdens in the bay. I'm free as a sea sprite." She whirled on tiptoe, then dropped to the berth in the best accommodations the ship afforded. "How do you like it so far? Isn't Puget Sound grand?"

"I didn't realize it offered such glorious scenery," Adelaide admitted. "All those islands huddled in the water like giant tortoises."

"You haven't seen anything yet," Ariel promised.

"Then get on your way and let me get dressed." Adelaide stretched and yawned again. "You're the only person on earth I'd tell this, but it's a relief not to have a maid simpering around. I never told Frederick how I hated it. Poor dear, he thought not having to do for myself would make me happy. He should have known I never needed anyone but him."

Ariel slipped into a warmly lined parka of silvery-green that matched her eyes, went into the passageway and onto the deck, remembering how Adelaide had spotted the parka in one of Seattle's finest department stores. She'd exclaimed, "You have to have this coat. It's you." She'd insisted on buying it as an early Christmas present. Under Ariel's tutelage, she also selected a complete winter outfit for herself. "I see what you mean about California clothes being for California," she had commented. "I've been cold ever since we landed."

"You won't be in that seal coat." Ariel had turned

pensive. "In San Diego I hated seeing women wear fur. I believe God created animals for our use, but waste is wickedness in the law of the North. The entire time I was in California, no occasion was cold enough to warrant the life of one of God's creatures."

"Tell it to Mrs. Carey," Adelaide had said grimly. "She bragged on one occasion she had seventeen fur coats, four of which she'd worn only one time. I agree with you. Killing animals for the sake of fashion is wrong." She stroked the silky fur. "Believe it or not, this is the first fur coat I've ever owned."

Ariel had hugged her, feeling again the kinship steadily growing between them.

Now at the rail of the liner that steadily plowed forward, Ariel faced north and reveled in the pre-dawn chill. She could hardly believe now that she had ever considered sacrificing the land of her birth for a land of sunshine, even with Emmet. It would be worth it, if you loved him in the right way, her conscience reminded.

"It might, but I don't," she told the friendly stars, glittering white against the night-dark sky. "All it took was getting away from the glamour to see how little we really have in common." Ariel turned toward the east that had swallowed her playmate twelve long years ago. Sadness dampened her joy. The Jean Thoreau she'd known never broke a promise. He must be dead.

A long time later, she roused from her reverie. Time to join her aunt for breakfast. A quick trip to the stateroom showed her bunkmate had gone. Ariel smoothed her hair, exchanged the parka for a heavy hand-knit ivory fishermen's sweater, and ran lightly to the dining room. She joined Adelaide, who sat in solitary state at a table set for five.

"My goodness, you're all alone," Ariel said as she seated herself.

"What do you expect? Other passengers eat at a more civilized hour. The Captain was called away. Some minor problem, I presume." Adelaide unfolded her spotless linen napkin and signaled a hovering, white-jacketed waiter. "Ariel, what will you have?"

"Flannel cakes, a beefsteak—medium rare, fried potatoes, orange juice and coffee," she promptly said.

"I'll have the same."

After the waiter had gone, Ariel continued to stare at her aunt in open-mouthed surprise.

"Close your mouth, child. I told you when in Ketchikan I intended to do as the Ketchikanites do." She further surprised Ariel by announcing, "I do hope this ship is democratic enough to have open seating, at least for breakfast and lunch. I want to sit with fishermen, sourdoughs, what have you. If I'm required to put up with some society woman for anything more than a few dinners, I'll throw something, preferably something that squashes!"

Ariel dissolved into smothered laughter. Trying to keep it inside and not attract attention, she choked and blindly reached for her water glass but only succeeded in overturning it.

"May I?" An amused voice accompanied a slim, tanned hand that vainly tried to stop the flow of water before it could cascade from the table onto her skirt.

Ariel pushed her chair back and mopped at the stream that eluded the napkin. "Thank you, waiter, but I'll have to change. Will you hold my order, please?"

A snicker from Adelaide brought the girl's attention from her soaked skirt to the man who stood beside the table. Ariel dropped her napkin in a sodden heap. Her eyes widened and she felt the blood drain from her face. She sprang to her feet. "Who—why—Jean? Jean Thoreau?"

"Hello, Ariel."

The sound of his voice broke the trance into which she had gone. Ignoring her wet skirt, she held out both hands. "I thought you were dead!"

"No. Very much alive and superintendent of your father's cannery at Dixon Cove." Velvety black eyes gazed into gray-green. Slim, strong hands pressed Ariel's clutching fingers. "I promised to come back, you know."

A sharp voice cut between them like the claw of an aroused mountain lion. Hands that clung dropped to their sides. "Ariel, will you be so good as to introduce me to your—friend?" Not a line in her patrician face showed she recognized the name Jean Thoreau.

"Auntie, this is the boy with whom I played years ago. Jean, this is my aunt, Mrs. Adelaide Patten." She noted the easy grace with which he bowed and took the other's extended hand.

"Forgive me, Mrs. Patten. Tom Dixon said you were sailing on this ship. He had some special errands he wanted done in Seattle but couldn't get away so suggested I come in his place." His musical voice matched his warm smile. "I've been so busy since boarding, I couldn't make my presence known until now."

Adelaide responded with far more graciousness than Ariel would expect under the awkward circumstances. "Will you join us, Mr. Thoreau?" He nodded and she turned her attention to Ariel. "Are you going to stand there dripping all day or make yourself presentable? I'm hungry and I'll wager your friend is as well."

Ariel's sense of humor came to her rescue. "This isn't the first time Jean's seen me soaked, Auntie. Ask him how many times I fell overboard when Dad taught us canoeing." She hurried out, heart thumping, unwilling to miss a single moment of the conversation. Thank goodness her shirt and sweater had escaped the deluge. All she had to change was her skirt.

In the stateroom, hasty fingers snatched a blue serge skirt and fumbled with the buttons. Ten minutes later she reached the table and found her aunt wearing a smug expression. It reminded Ariel of a cat she once had. Puss had needed every one of her nine lives to avoid death at Molly's hands for licking the meringue off a lemon pie meant for company dinner.

"Mr. Thoreau has quite a story," Adelaide wickedly

said. "Since I've heard it, I'll ask you to wait until after breakfast." She applied herself to the enormous steak the waiter placed before her.

Ariel wanted to throttle her aunt. A thousand questions hovered on her tongue, all of them ending with the plaintive cry, *Why did you forget me?* She restrained herself only because of something deep in Jean's eyes when he looked her way. It told her whatever created the long silence between them had not been of his making. She forced her attention to her breakfast. Even the wonder and thrill of Jean's presence could not deter the healthy appetite whetted by her early-morning vigil on deck.

The dining room soon rang with laughter. Adelaide had gotten her wish. Two of the Dixon fishermen who had taken a brief excursion to the States during the winter layoff unselfconsciously seated themselves at Ariel's table.

"What's this about you packing it in and leaving us?" Carl, a mackinaw-clad giant, demanded. "Is this fee-ann-see too good for the likes of us?"

"Naw," Swen asserted between enormous bites of flannel cakes. "We heard you were getting yourself hitched, but I figger it was just old lady gossipers. No Dixon'd pick some rich pup for a mate, now would they?" He gave her a keen glance between bites.

Ariel felt her face flame. She cast an appealing glance at her aunt, wondering what she thought of the free and easy way these men talked; her aunt couldn't be expected to know that these two men had dandled Ariel on their knees since babyhood. She couldn't very well announce her broken engagement to them before she told her father.

Adelaide raised one eyebrow. "You can trust Ariel's judgment," she quietly said. "I can't imagine her turning her back on either old friends or her home."

"Course she wouldn't. Carl's a dunderhead," Swen affirmed.

"Never said she would," Carl quickly put in. His keen gaze fastened on her bare ring finger. "The way I figger it, if a gal ain't tagged, it's open season."

Two pairs of blue eyes twinkled and Swen said, "If me and my pard weren't old enough to be your daddy—and fishermen to boot—I reckon we'd be camping on your doorstep, Ariel."

The hearty approval made her blink. "Don't forget Dad's a fisherman, too."

"Not hardly. He's the hard-workin'est, slave-drivin'est man in the north. Fair, though. Treats everyone the same." Carl savored the last bite of his giant stack of cakes, then grinned across the table at Jean, who had remained silent during the raillery. "Here's another just like him. We put up a bigger pack this year with Jean Thoreau running the cannery than Thad Olson ever did."

Jean laughed and smile wrinkles creased the corners of his eyes. "I can't take all the credit. We not only had a fantastic fish run but Olson's going over to the competition gave us an added incentive. These men and dozens more like them kept the fish coming so fast that if Tom hadn't been far-sighted enough to stock up on cans, we'd have run out halfway through the season!" His eyes gleamed, then he laughed. "Mrs. Patten, I hope all this talk of fish isn't boring you."

"Not at all." She looked at him with frank liking. "In fact, I want to hear more. Why don't you and Ariel go catch up on the last twelve years? Carl and Swen can entertain me. You do have some exciting fish tales, don't you?"

Carl let out a war whoop. "Lady, we'll tell you stories to make your hair curl!"

"Good. See you later, Ariel. Nice to meet you, Jean." She waved them away.

"She called you J-Jean," Ariel stuttered when they started out.

"It's my name," he reminded.

Her clear laugh rang out, bringing looks of approval from the three at the table. "You don't understand," Ariel explained after collecting her parka from the stateroom and preceding him up the companionway to the deck. "In all the time I was with her in California, I never heard her call someone she had just met by his first name." Curiosity overcame her unwillingness to pry. "What did you talk about while I was gone, anyway?"

Jean dramatically laid one hand over his heart. "Ah, that must remain a secret." He bowed and crooked his elbow. "Does mademoiselle wish to take a constitutional?"

She nodded, took his arm, then spoke in a voice so low Jean had to bend close to hear her above the mournful scree of a dozen low-flying gulls. "Why? Jean?"

He didn't pretend to misunderstand, but led her to a sheltered spot near a lifeboat. His face whitened with pain. For a single instant, Ariel saw not the man, but a ten-year-old boy with a wicked fishhook imbedded in his hand. His face had paled then, too, but he made no outcry when Tom pressed the hook deeper to release its cruel clutch, then removed it with his knife. Ariel had cried, hot tears that dripped on the wounded hand. Now those tears gushed again: for the children they had been; the long separation; even for their reunion.

Jean repeated the same words he'd spoken years before. "Don't cry, Ariel. It will be all right." In a few broken sentences, he told her what the elder Thoreaus had done. He added by saying, "I cannot hate them for it. They did what they felt was right, what they felt would protect the son they loved from hurt." He gently turned her to face him. "I have come back, ma chère, as I promised. Is it too late?"

She could only shake her head. She felt him tremble when he gathered her into his arms. She heard him whisper, "Thank You, God." His lips, cool and slightly salty from ocean spray, touched hers in their first kiss.

Hundreds of miles still lay between them and Ketchikan. Yet Ariel felt she had come home to a familiar, safe harbor after a long and stormy journey.

Six

The tossing waves, ravines, silver threads of waterfalls Ariel and Jean had loved since childhood took on new beauty in the wonder of a dormant love that had sprung to full bloom. No longer did Ariel impatiently wish to reach Ketchikan. From the shelter of her beloved's encircling arm, she beheld again the land of her birth, the land holding her future in its ever-changing grasp. Whatever storm winds blew, God and Jean would be there to protect her. No wonder the excitement of being chosen by Emmet Carey had not equated to her aunt's description of love! A prayer of thankfulness for being delivered winged up to heaven from her overflowing heart.

Adelaide Patten heartily approved of Jean. "A real man," she announced after their first meeting. Her dark eyes twinkled; she drew her fur coat close and leaned against the ship's rail, watching a spectacular sunset over the water. Jean had considerately disappeared to give Ariel time to inform her aunt of the change in nephews. "I hope you have sense to see it."

"I do." A tremulous smile touched Ariel's lips. "The minute I saw Jean, I realized how narrowly I escaped settling for second best."

"Good for you! I can't wait to see your father's face when you tell him." She grinned mischievously. "It would be even more satisfying to see Emmet and his mother when they discover you threw away the chance to really be someone for love of a French Canadian fish cannery superintendent!"

Ariel's musical laugh chimed out. A thrill went through her. "I already am someone, a special someone loved by God, Dad, Jean—" A poignant light crept into her lovely face.

"Don't forget me," Adelaide gruffly reminded.

"As if I could." Ariel rushed to her aunt and hugged her. When she saw moisture fill the older woman's eyes, she realized how deeply Adelaide cared and tactfully changed the subject. "So what do you think of our voyage?"

"Like stepping back in time. It's so—so unspoiled." A shadow crossed her face. "I only regret that Frederick and I never came. He would have loved it." She sighed, then a faraway look softened her countenance. One gloved hand pointed to brilliant star clusters hanging low in the settling dusk. "It's hard to believe even heaven can be lovelier than this. Yet the apostle Paul reminds us in his first letter to the Corinthians that the things God has prepared for those who love Him have not even entered the heart of man." She turned toward Ariel. "Ariel, I believe Frederick is in that place, waiting for me to come." Her voice broke and she walked away.

Ariel didn't immediately follow. Sacred moments such as this could only be partially shared. Some must remain in the locked chambers of the heart.

ã

The day their ship steamed into Ketchikan, the heavens smiled, marvelously free of their legendary rain. "Instruments recorded nearly fifty-four inches for the record month of November 1917," Ariel explained. "We usually manage to have a little less than that."

Excitement, anticipation, and the crisp, northern air whipped crimson streamers into her cheeks. She shaded her eyes against sun sparkles on the water. "There's Dad." Her hands flew to her mouth to make a megaphone. "Dad!" She waved her parka-clad arm, unaware she looked like the figurehead on an ancient Viking ship.

"So you've come home," Tom Dixon exclaimed, when they finally docked and Ariel threw herself into his embrace, to the delight of Carl and Swen, who cheered lustily.

Ariel saw their mouths open, each eager to beat the other in telling their boss she had come home to stay. She hastily whispered in his ear, "I changed canoes in mid-stream, Dad. Emmet stays in California. It's Jean

229

for me from now on. He said he told you . . ." She tilted her head back to look into her father's face.

Wonder, relief, and delight played tag over the rugged features. "Thank God!" His mighty paw shot out, gripped Jean's much as it had the day months ago when the young man first came home. "She's yours, son."

Ariel couldn't help laughing at the chagrined expression on the two fishermen's faces. "Aw, it was Thoreau all along?" Carl expostulated.

Swen's jaw dropped, but he quickly made an attempt to hide his amazement. "Of course it was, dunderhead. Anybody'd know that."

"You didn't, you old barnacle," Carl informed him, but Swen maintained his air of superiority. They were still arguing when the other four climbed into the Dixon family car.

"We have close to four hundred automobiles in Ketchikan," Tom proudly said. "Also fourteen miles of road." He laughed his powerful, contagious laugh. "Of course, each road just stops where the wilderness begins!"

Never had Adelaide seen such variance. The short, wide road along Tongass Narrows' silver curves wound through hemlocks. Intriguing houses clung to the side of the mountain above. "No flowers now, but wait until summer," Tom promised. "Adelaide, you'll stay, won't you?"

Her dark eyes showed gratitude for his instant, unquestioning welcome. "Not that long, but I'll come back if I may." She craned her neck to see better and showed no nervousness when the big car climbed steep, narrow streets. At last they arrived at the Dixon home. "It's perfect," she breathed.

From her position behind her father, Ariel's gaze met his in the rear view mirror. Rich and renowned she might be, but Adelaide Carey was a woman after their own hearts. She settled into the pleasant room they assigned her, became part of the family, and immediately won Molly's friendship. Perched on a high stool in the well-provisioned kitchen, the cream of San Diego society confessed she'd longed to cook for years but was afraid of offending her servants!

"Frederick inherited them along with the family mansion," Adelaide explained. "They depended on us for their incomes. I couldn't take their livelihoods away from them, no matter how much I might have enjoyed doing things for myself. But I always wished someone would teach me how to cook."

Molly's brown face glowed with pleasure. She produced an enveloping apron, handed Adelaide a pan of vegetables, and set her to peeling and cubing for a venison stew flavored as much with love and acceptance as the cook's special, secret spices.

Rain inevitably came, but nothing dampened Ariel and Jean's spirits. When he was busy with Dixon Industry affairs, she scooted about in her small cabin cruiser, the *Sea Witch*. Except for the fact of Adelaide being in Ketchikan, Ariel's California odyssey seemed unreal, with Emmet a cardboard character in a meaningless long-ago play. Every day her love for Jean grew stronger. She gazed down the pathway of years ahead and smiled.

One day she picked up a book of poetry she had cherished since childhood days. A small frown wrinkled her brow. Only once had she shyly quoted poetry to Emmet, a gem of verse her father taught her long before.

Emmet had smiled indulgently and raised one eyebrow. "You surprise me, little Eskimo. Isn't Robert Service the only poet Alaskans quote? I'd think 'The Shooting of Dan McGrew' and 'The Cremation of Sam McGee' more to your father's taste." He gave a contemptuous little cough that let her know he thought Service's poetry to be pure doggerel.

"Service worked as a bank clerk in Whitehorse and Dawson and found material for his poetry," Ariel told him. "We appreciate those ballads for what they are. So would you if you'd experienced the hardship and violence of the gold rush to the Yukon in the late 1890s"

"Deliver me." Emmet yawned, frankly bored. "Glad to find out your tastes also include something a bit higher." Emmet went on to discuss an upcoming tennis match.

Ariel had subsided, knowing the man she had chosen—actually he had chosen her—would never understand. Now she berated herself for appearing acquiescent when inwardly she had seethed. How easy to see it here in this untamed land, how impossible in the midst of dazzling pomp and ceremony.

One morning, lazy white flakes drifted from a leaden sky. Others followed. Ariel donned her parka and ran outside to catch snowflakes on her tongue as she had done when a child. She waved to Adelaide, who stood just inside the shining clean window, smiling and shaking her head. Supreme happiness filled the girl. God had been good indeed.

The snow continued just long enough to winter-coat trees and shrubs, gate-posts and streets. By the next morning it had melted. "Too bad." Adelaide sighed audibly at the breakfast table. Sunlight glinted on the nicely laid table and turned Ariel's hair to spun gold. "I wish it had snowed a lot more."

"We may have to take you to Juneau for that," Jean teased from the doorway. With the ease of one who knows himself welcome at any hour, he took silver and china from a nearby cupboard and pulled a chair up beside Ariel. "Ketchikan normally gets less than three feet of snow per winter."

"Maybe this one will be different," Adelaide hopefully replied. "As long as I'm in Alaska, I'd like to get snowed in at least once!" She sternly asked Jean, "Well, if we can't have a blizzard, how about a wedding? You're going to marry this girl of yours while I'm still here, aren't you?"

Ariel felt herself redden, but Jean's strong fingers laced with hers under cover of the starched tablecloth. "Christmas Eve, if it's all right with my girl." He smiled at Ariel and her heart gave a little leap.

"No better time," Tom approved. He placed both wool-covered wrists on the table and leaned forward. "Have you two decided about a honeymoon?"

Ariel hesitated. "N-not really."

"Want to go to California?" Adelaide innocently asked and covered her mouth with a napkin.

Tom's haw haw almost drowned out the emphatic, unanimous, "No!" that greeted her sally. He laughed until tears came. "So what do you want?"

Did she dare speak out, say what lay deep in her heart? A quick nod from Jean encouraged Ariel. "Dixon Cove."

"The cannery?" Tom stroked his chin. "Hmm. Might not be a bad idea at that. No one's there this time of year. You'd have peace and privacy. The shack's not so bad—" Little motes danced in the eyes so like his daughter's.

Adelaide gasped. "They're spending their honeymoon in a shack?"

"Don't let him plague you, Auntie." Ariel patted Adelaide's arm with her free hand. "We have a smaller version of this place for use during the canning season. Two bedrooms. Fully equipped and away from the cannery. Huge fireplace and a magnificent view." She grinned, taking on an uncanny resemblance to her father.

Her aunt snorted. "How do you know it's fit for human occupation?"

"We check periodically," Tom assured her. "It's a good idea, though, to take a run down and make sure

234

everything's in order. It's only fifty miles and I can spare you tomorrow. Better go while the weather permits." He grunted. "Should Adelaide's blizzard come, you may have to change your plans." He took a final sip of steaming coffee and stood.

"Good idea. Aunt Adelaide, you can go with us," Jean promised. "You'll love Dixon Cove, cannery and all." His eyes gleamed. "We'll make a Ketchikanite, as you call us, out of you yet."

To that worthy woman's disgust, she awakened the next morning with a sore throat. "Fine thing," she raged. "I don't have time to get sick."

"I'll fix." Molly nodded wisely, trotted to the kitchen, and returned with a steaming cup of honey-lemon water.

Adelaide drank it but confessed even a trip to Dixon Cove didn't appeal as much as a day curled up on the comfortable couch with Molly in attendance. "Don't wait for me," she ordered. "I can go another time. If not now, when I come back next summer. Staying here means I'll have to stop this before it develops."

At her insistence, they agreed to go and prepared for their run to the cove with all the precaution drilled into them since babyhood. Tom checked the cabin cruiser to see what was already on board. Jean and Ariel added an ample supply of food and fresh water, two extra blankets, and medical supplies. Adelaide watched and exclaimed, "My goodness! Are you heading for Seattle?"

"No, but this country demands that we be prepared,"

Ariel solemnly told her.

"You wouldn't go if you thought there was danger, would you?" Adelaide peered out the window. "There's no chance of a storm with that kind of sky, is there?"

Jean shook his head. "You wouldn't think so, but we don't take chances." He smiled at her with a sweetness that showed Ariel he had come to love her aunt.

A kaleidoscope of emotions swept over Adelaide's face. "What if you get caught out overnight?" Her face flamed. "Wouldn't there be gossip?"

Tom gave Adelaide a reassuring look. "Folks here know how sudden a squall can come up or fog roll in like gray velvet—so thick that boat lights aren't much help. Besides, Ariel's reputation is such that anyone who casts a slur on her has a lot more to deal with than Jean and me."

An hour later the young couple boarded the *Sea Witch*, hearts thrilling with the simple joy of being alive and together for a day. Hands raised high in farewell, they headed away from shore. Jean steered with one hand, held Ariel in the crook of his other arm. A mist came to Tom's eyes. So had he sailed with the woman he loved, who at times still seemed very near.

Two hours later, a yellow telegram came for Ariel Dixon, who would not receive it for many long, turbulent hours.

Seven

Blissfully unaware that impending trouble perched on the prow of the *Sea Witch*, Ariel and Jean made the run south from Ketchikan to Dixon Cove in record time. "You'll want to stay in Ketchikan for Christmas, won't you?" Jean asked a bit diffidently. "I know what it means for you to be with Tom."

Ariel blinked at his thoughtfulness. "It would be wonderful." A new thought struck her. "My goodness, aren't we a couple of silly snow geese! We haven't talked about where we're going to live. Will it be with Dad?"

Jean shook his dark head. His laugh rang over the water. "My dear girl, the fine young man you plan to marry is the possessor of a mansion, well, not a mansion, but a comfortable home not far from your father's."

"Really? Where? When did you get it? Why didn't

you tell me? How——?"

His face blazed with joy. "When I came back, I learned your father purchased my family's home shortly after we moved. I bought it from him."

Ariel gasped. "I didn't know that." She wrinkled her forehead, trying to remember. "For a long time after you left I wouldn't go near the place. I knew I'd cry. When I finally went, the emptiness hurt me." She laid a hand over her heart. "It was even worse when a new family moved in. If I thought about it at all, I suppose I accepted they bought it. Instead, they must have rented it from Dad." She rested her chin on a shapely hand. "I wonder why he bought it. Or why he didn't sell it during all these long years?"

Jean's awe-filled voice sounded choked. "Your father told me deep in his heart he always felt I'd come back." He hesitated and expertly swung the cabin cruiser toward the dock at Dixon Cove. "Tom also told me he hoped I'd come back unmarried and before you had chosen your life companion."

Ariel's eyes stung. "All these years and he kept silent!"

"He wouldn't trespass behind the wall you set up, even when he saw you look east a hundred times. If only Mother had told me sooner!" Anguish filled the cry.

Her heart echoed the wish, but Ariel tenderly said, "I wish she had, yet perhaps we wouldn't appreciate our love so much if we hadn't come so close to losing it." She leaned against his shoulder and laughed shakily.

"Now, Mr. Jean Thoreau, you have me for the rest of our lives. That is, if you'll unwrap a sandwich before I starve to death!"

Regret floated away on a cloud of healing laughter. Fed and happy, they inspected the "honeymoon house," as Jean called it. They built a fire in the big fireplace to chase away the winter chill and Jean kissed her when she blushed. "I love you, my darling. Ariel—lioness of God, that's what your name means. Will you defend me like a lioness defends its young?"

"You remembered what my name means?" she exclaimed. "Oh, Jean!" After a moment she whispered, "I will defend you to the death. How thankful I am your name is Jean for Jean means God is gracious and He truly is. If I hadn't known that before, He has proved it to me anew by allowing me to become your wife."

"And He will always be Head of our household," Jean promised. "Our sons and daughters will learn of Him in the cradle my father carved for his firstborn."

A tremor went through the girl, like a small cloud appearing in her sky of happiness. "If God chooses not to bless us with children, will you still love me?"

Jean's eyes flashed fire, the way she remembered from years before when she questioned him on a sensitive point. "Have I not been faithful these many years?"

"More so than I." Tears clogged her throat and her pale-gold head drooped.

"Forgive me, dear." He caught her close. "If you had not

believed yourself forgotten by the boy who left you, neither Emmet Carey nor any other man would have caught your fancy. I believe your heart has always been mine."

"It has, even when I did not know it." Jean's tender kiss forever sealed the question of whether he begrudged the girl he loved her temporary defection.

Lost in the past, the two who had been trained to be alert for changes in the weather made a serious mistake. They ignored the weather. Northern skies jealously demand complete and undivided attention, especially in winter. Storms take delight in swooping down on the unwary. In the time Jean and Ariel opened their hearts to one another in the "honeymoon house," the gray-velvet fog Tom had described to Adelaide crept over the horizon and banked there.

The snap of a burned-through log in the fireplace roused Ariel from her reverie. For a long while, she and Jean had sat side by side, staring into the fire and dreaming dreams. She shifted position, then sprang to her feet.

"What is it?" Cat-like, Jean leaped up.

"Look." Ariel pointed to the window, where tiny wraiths of fog curled.

"How could I have been so careless?" Jean strode to the door and cast a weather-wise gaze over the water. "Come. I think we can beat it."

She obediently trotted after him. "Don't blame yourself. Just because I've been in California doesn't excuse me for not watching." She smiled and nimbly jumped aboard the *Sea Witch*.

Jean hesitated. "Ariel, I have a bad feeling about this. No one can predict how fast the fog's moving or how quickly it will reach us. We're better off here than halfway back to Ketchikan. We can't depend on finding shelter the way we once could. A new element has surfaced, one that laughs at the law of the north. Carl and Swen told me last winter they got caught in a sudden squall. They fought their way to shore and to a shack always stocked for emergencies." His lips pressed together grimly. "It wasn't." The succinct words fell like rocks. "Someone had robbed the cache. Fish pirates, or maybe a fugitive. Carl and Swen had enough food aboard to see them through, but they would have been in trouble if they'd lost their boat or the storm had gone on for several days."

Hot Alaskan blood rose to Ariel's cheeks. "A thief up here is as bad as a murderer," she exploded. "Anyone who steals a cache will have to answer to both the law and God." She stared over the water, dulled now by gunmetal skies. "You're right. We'll stay. Let's pack up what we need from the *Sea Witch* while we can still see her. As Dad said, these things can happen."

By the time they finished carrying food and the extra blankets to the house, the fog had rolled to shore like a juggernaut. Smoke-like wraiths became a solid bank, obliterating sea, sky, and even the well-secured *Sea Witch*. Jean staggered under the weight of an enormous log and heaved it into the fireplace. Flames roared up the chimney. He also started fires in the small wood stoves in both bedrooms. Ariel warmed bedding in front of the living room fireplace and made up their beds, humming while she worked. "This is deluxe camping out," she called to Jean, who had obligingly offered to start supper.

Leaving a kettle of water to boil on the enormous kitchen wood stove, he came to the door of the bedroom and lounged against the jamb. "Ariel, you know you'll be as safe with me as though I were your father."

"Of course." Astonished, she glanced up from smoothing a pillowcase.

"Good." He smiled and went back to the kitchen, leaving her to thank God for the integrity of Jean Thoreau's big, wonderful heart.

They spent a happy evening discussing their Christmas Eve wedding; how they'd return to Dixon Cove Christmas afternoon; how terribly Ariel missed not being in Alaska for the previous summer's fish run and canning season. They talked of excursions, always in the north. Ariel could hardly wait to get back on snowshoes and skis, perhaps one day train and enter a dog sled race—although not the Iditarod. They made plans to visit or revisit every inch of the state they loved.

When Jean kissed her goodnight, he said, "Next time we'll be together."

In perfect love and trust, Ariel gazed into his dark

eyes. "I know." The look he gave her remained in her dreams, long after she fell asleep.

Cheated of possible prey, the capricious fog fled before a brisk wind that sprang up shortly after a pallid, winter sun appeared. Only a few festoons remained, hanging like the gray moss that beards giant trees in the forests of the south. Jean and Ariel made short work of breakfast and packing. Their return trip to Ketchikan proved uneventful, until they swung in and docked near a dozen lounging men, Carl and Swen among them.

"Morning," Jean called.

A hateful laugh sounded from one of the men who stood back of the others. Ariel recognized Thad Olson, her father's cannery superintendent who had gone over to Big Tom's fiercest competitor. According to Carl and Swen, he'd been nursing a grudge ever since because Jean Thoreau stepped in and put up a record pack. Now Thad elbowed his way between the others and sneered, "Come far?"

"Dixon Cove," Jean briefly explained. "Fog caught us yesterday afternoon."

"Shut up, Olson, you're drunk," someone warned. Tension heightened.

"Not so drunk I can't see and I ain't seen no fog. Have you fellers?" The venomous look he shot Jean was as much an insult as what he said.

Jean sprang to the dock, but not fast enough. Swen got to Olson first. A mighty thud was followed by a loud splash when Olson's heavy body hit the water. He bobbed to the surface, bellowing like an enraged polar bear and cursing at the top of his lungs.

"Shut your dirty trap, or I'll finish what my pard started," Carl bellowed back. Swen stood menacingly near, nursing his skinned knuckles.

"If he can't, the rest of us will," someone else threatened. "No one talks that way about Ariel Dixon. Jean Thoreau, either. They say there was fog, it's true. Haul yourself outa there and apologize, Olson, or plan to be on the next steamer. We ain't forgot you walkin' out on Tom Dixon on the eve of last year's run."

A low menacing murmur went through the crowd. The men surged forward.

"Wait!" Ariel breathlessly ordered. "He's drunk and not worth listening to." She cast Olson a withering glance that brought dull red to his face. Half-sobered by his unexpected bath, Thad's eyes showed fear. He struggled to shore, muttered, "Sorry" and shambled away.

"Thanks, boys." Jean put his arm around Ariel. His smile gleamed white in his lean, tanned face. "I guess some folks just judge everyone by themselves. By the way, you're all invited to a wedding come Christmas Eve. Ariel and—"

"That isn't necessary," an irritated voice cut in. "Such a small service surely doesn't require that kind of reward."

Jean's fingers bit into Ariel's shoulders and he took

an involuntary step backward. "Who are you?" he hoarsely demanded over the top of her head. "What right do you have to say who shall or shall not come to the wedding?"

"Every right," the smug voice went on. "I am Emmet Carey, Miss Dixon's fiancé. Now if you will excuse us, we have a previous engagement."

Carl and Swen pushed close, followed by a mumbling crowd. "Want we should dunk him, too, Ariel?" Swen muttered.

"Yeah, give it to him, the stuck-up swell," a loyal Dixon employee called.

Ariel tore herself free from Jean's grip and whirled. She wasn't having a nightmare after all. Emmet Carey stood a few feet away, perfectly turned-out and the blackest frown she had ever seen cutting deep lines between his brows. "What are you doing here?" she demanded, in a voice cold and jagged as broken icicles.

Emmet stroked his smooth chin. "I think my telegram explained sufficiently. I do not intend to engage in a lengthy explanation in front of these men or this buccaneer who has the audacity to lay hands on your person." He glared at Jean.

"Wot's he talking about?" Carl wanted to know.

"Beats me." Swen scratched his head with a long, callused finger. "But we're standing by in case she needs us."

Ariel ignored him. Never in her life had she been angrier. She glanced at Jean. To her amazement, not a trace of fury flickered in his expressive eyes. What a contrast between the self-important Californian in all his sartorial glory and Jean, carelessly clad, with a crimson kerchief at his neck.

A laugh rumbled deep in Jean's throat. It bubbled out like lava from a volcano. Every man there recognized the laugh of a conqueror, a man who refused to allow lesser mortals to drag him to their level. Ariel's silver chime of mirth aligned her with those with whom she had grown up. "This buccaneer's name is Jean Thoreau, the man I'm going to marry," she announced.

Eight

When Emmet only stared, Ariel repeated, "I am going to marry Jean." The fishermen cheered, until all but the intruder joined in the thunder of mirth and congratulations. When he could make himself heard, Emmet said, "I will speak with you at the home of your father. Perhaps your aunt can talk reason into you." He turned on the heel of one polished shoe and marched away. Carl, the irrepressible, fell in a few paces behind him in a ludicrous caricature of Emmet's walk that set the watching men roaring again.

Jean cocked an eyebrow. "Shall we beard the lion in his den?"

"Yes, and it isn't going to be easy!" She bit her lip to keep from having hysterics. An unpleasant interview lay before them. Yet why should it be? She had broken with Emmet before she knew Jean Thoreau was still alive. She owed the man nothing. *Father, give me the wisdom to handle this,* she prayed. As they climbed the steep streets and wound along Tyee Hill to the Dixon home Jean gave her a reassuring grin.

Armed with prayer and love, Ariel smiled and entered her home. The living room looked like the stage setting in a melodrama. Big Tom relaxed in a chair. Adelaide lay in her nest of blankets. Molly's brown face peered in from the kitchen and Emmet paced the floorboards with military precision, now and then stumbling over the giant bearskin rug before the fireplace.

"Here you are at last," he said scathingly when they came in. "Before you explain your actions, I suggest you read this. Aloud, if you like, since it hasn't been opened."

"We aren't in the habit of opening messages not addressed to us," Tom said.

Ariel felt anger spurt but opened the yellow telegram and read, *You win. Stop. Arrive by plane tomorrow. Stop. Find missioner to marry us. Stop. Won't affect Mother's plans. Stop. Real wedding Valentine's Day, as planned. Have gone to great expense and inconvenience because of your stubbornness.*

Missioner! Was he so ignorant of Alaska he thought the only ministers available were the traveling priests and missionaries of gold rush days? Ariel threw the paper to the floor. "I can't understand why you came at such expense and inconvenience. I made it clear in

California I didn't intend to marry you. No, don't leave," she sharply said when the others moved restlessly. "Emmet has drawn you all into this and you have a right to hear the end of it."

Her former fiancé stopped pacing and gave her a thin smile. "The end will be when we get out of this accursed country and back to civilization. Can you imagine how I felt, finding you cause for a brawl by a bunch of louts?" He shuddered and rolled his eyes. "I considered bringing Mother with me. Thank God, I did not. She wouldn't tolerate such a scene."

Ariel's outflung hand stopped a hot-eyed Jean midstride, but she could not stop his indignant words. "Those so-called louts would defend Ariel's honor to the death."

"If Ariel had been here waiting for me, where she should have been, there'd have been no need for such a degrading performance," Emmet obstinately said. "Neither would she be the subject of gossip." His nostrils flared.

Like a bolt of lightning, Ariel knew what to do. Thankfulness poured through her. "The important thing is not what others think, Emmet. Do you believe Jean and I are guilty of wrongdoing, even in the slightest degree?"

Dull color suffused his patrician face. "Are you mad? Of course not! No woman in her right mind would risk losing the Carey fortune by smirching her reputation with an escapade." He drew himself to his fullest imposing height. "Anyone can see Thoreau's in love with you. I trust that will be reason enough for him to keep mum." He shrugged. "Anyway, it's a long way from Ketchikan to San Diego. I doubt the gossip will reach Mother."

Big Tom Dixon rose from his chair in one mighty bound. "That will be about enough of that, you insolent pup. My daughter and son—" He bent a glance toward Jean, held back only by Ariel's slender strength. "Their actions are beyond reproach. Yours aren't. Now clear out before I forget I'm a God-fearing, peace-loving man and throw you through the front door!"

"I'll help," Adelaide grimly volunteered.

Emmet whipped toward her, clearly aghast at high treason from the one he'd counted as chief ally. His mouth worked, but no words came.

Not so with Ariel. Jean's laughing question from the day before rang in her ears, loud as if he had just spoken. *Ariel—lioness of God, that's what your name means. Will you defend me like a lioness defends its young?* Her vow: *I will defend you to the death.* The first chance to keep her vow had come.

Ariel leaned against Jean's strong chest, arms outspread to keep him from attacking. She felt his heart beat, the great heart that shed insults to himself but gave no quarter for one toward her. "Dad, Jean, I'll handle this." Exaltation filled her. "Emmet, Jean Thoreau is farther removed from the tawdry world in which men and women dally with the sacred things of life than Ketchikan is from California. Jean would die before uttering one word or committing one act that would cast reproach on my name."

"Bravo for him." The red in Emmet's smooth-shaven face receded to pallor but he refused to bow to the inevitable. The next instant, he abandoned his sarcasm and donned the boyish, winning smile that had once set Ariel's heart fluttering. "This place has mesmerized you, Ariel. Think. What has this fisherman to offer you, compared with my wealth and—love?" The word slipped out as if reluctant to drop from his lips. "I do love you, you know."

Anger fled. Pity filled her tender heart. It stilled the accusations that hovered on her tongue, truths she had fully intended to hurl against his arrogance. Jean's love for her was pure and selfless, enduring, akin to God's love for the world. Emmet based his love on her outward appearance, how well she would fit into his world, the children she would bear to follow in his footsteps. Rare insight told her Emmet would never understand.

"Forgive me for not knowing my own feelings earlier," Ariel impulsively said. "If I had, all this unpleasantness would have been avoided." She held out a shapely hand in comradely fashion, saw him struggle between anger and the sportsmanship required by good breeding.

"You actually care for this man?" Emmet demanded.

"With all my heart." Ariel turned to Jean, who magnificently rose to the occasion and extended his hand. "I loved him as a child, but thought him dead all these long years." Pain twisted her face.

Emmet set his lips and raised his head. Never had Ariel admired him more than when he gripped her hand, then Jean's. "Congratulations, Thoreau. I won't admit the better man has won but you're the man she wants. May God bless you." He dropped his hand and looked at his watch, the very watch they had gone to pick up the day the snowflake came to San Diego—and Ariel. "I believe my pilot can still reach Vancouver if we start now." He turned a haggard face toward Tom, then Adelaide. "Forgive me for my breach of good manners in your home." He wheeled and went out, shoulders military-straight.

When his footfalls across the wide veranda and down the steps ceased, Adelaide cleared her throat. "That's that. Now let's talk about the wedding."

Every passing hour erased a little more of Emmet's visit. Thad Olson decided to spend the rest of the winter elsewhere. Faithful Carl and Swen refrained from commenting, although Ariel and Jean laughed at their unusual tact. December scurried toward the twenty-fourth with blusters of rain and wind, occasional snow, and brilliant winter days that set Ariel's heart singing. She had refused Adelaide's offer of a complete trousseau, laughing and saying, "I have everything I need, even a wedding dress. Remember that gorgeous ivory silk from San Diego?"

"Are you sure you don't want white, beaded with pearls?" Adelaide asked.

"Jean likes me in ivory." A blush mantled her cheek.

"Then ivory it shall be." Mist crept into Adelaide's eyes. Ariel knew her aunt was remembering the day she became wife to her beloved Frederick.

"Most of Ketchikan wants to come," Tom complained at one point. "What are we going to do with them?"

"Hold the wedding in the biggest hall in town and invite 'em all," Adelaide advised. "Ariel and Jean are part of this town. Folks deserve to be at their wedding." She sniffed. "You're not sending out engraved invitations with admittance cards, are you?"

Tom threw his hands in the air at her suggestion and Ariel giggled, but sobered when she saw a wary look in Jean's eyes. "I know you don't regret giving up Emmet, but are there any twinges over the lack of fuss and feathers?" he whispered when they were alone.

"Not a twinge." She happily leaned against his shoulder. "I'm right where I belong. Besides, I have the fuss and feathers. Auntie fusses over the details, and Molly's giving us a patchwork quilt with wild geese flying. She made it and put it away for me when she heard I was engaged months ago." Ariel's laughter trilled. "Can you imagine the heir to the house of Carey sleeping under a homemade patchwork quilt? You don't mind, do you, that it was originally meant for a different groom?"

"Who says it was?" Jean looked mysterious. "Maybe Molly, like your father, knew I'd come back some day." His black eyes twinkled. "She always did have a spot in her heart for me warmer than her big cook stove!"

❧

Early Christmas Eve, Ariel and Jean stood before a white-haired minister who had known them both since childhood. A sifting of snow gently fell outside the packed hall. Candles by the score cast their soft light on faces of many hues. Outdated dress suits and once-elegant gowns rubbed shoulders with plaid mackinaws and soft chamois shirts. Yet San Diego in all its splendor could not compete as far as Jean and Ariel were concerned. They took their vows in steady voices, pledging love and devotion to one another and God. When he slipped a plain gold band on Ariel's ring finger, no memory of the great diamond she once wore rose to spoil the moment.

To Ariel's surprise, Jean added another ring when they turned from the minister to face Ketchikan and the future as Mr. and Mrs. Jean Thoreau. A curiously carved stone of Alaska jade, translucent and holding all the mystery of the land from which it came, rested in a simple golden setting. All through the toasts, manfully drunk by many who secretly longed for something stronger but stoutly insisted the fruit punch was nectar itself, Ariel sneaked glances at her wonderful ring. It caught and reflected the shimmering candlelight, making her feel she wore a rainbow on her finger.

Adelaide, so resplendent in gray taffeta at least three of Tom Dixon's bachelor associates cast wistful glances her way, at last announced in her ladylike voice, "Thank you all for coming. I'm sure you want to get home and spend the rest of Christmas Eve with your families. Tom, my coat, please." She led a general exodus toward the front door, giving Ariel the opportunity to slip out the back into the gently falling snow.

Ariel's heart beat fast when Jean caught her in his arms at the door and ran with her to the brand new red Ford parked behind the building, motor started. "Wedding present from Tom and Adelaide," he whispered, carefully tucking warm robes around her. "Wife, don't think we're going to be accepting such gifts in the future. We'll make our own way."

He hastily kissed her, then hurried around the car and hopped behind the wheel. "Good. No one's seen us." He laughed gleefully. "They won't recognize us if they do. Not in this car."

A short drive up the narrow, winding streets Ariel knew and loved brought them to the Thoreau home. A candle in a dimly lit window flickered, as if dancing with joy over their arrival. Jean expertly parked the car, then came around to open Ariel's door. His hand brushed her face. "Tears, Ariel?"

"It's just that for so long I couldn't come here," she choked. "I know." He caught her close, blankets and all, and carried her across the wide porch. He stepped inside and shoved the door closed with his foot. "Welcome home, wife." Jean set her on her feet and bent his dark head. His lips felt cool against her own, but warmed her as much as the blaze in the fireplace.

At last he released her and unwound the enveloping

wraps. Ariel stood before him, ivory-clad, golden hair shining in the firelight, gray-green eyes filled with love. The soft swish of snow falling like a curtain sounded sweeter in her ears than the finest symphony.

Jean knelt and held out his hands. Ariel joined him, her ivory skirts a billow on the wolf skin pelt in front of the fire. Jean took her hands in his. "We dedicate our life together to Thee, oh God, who has brought us home."

Ariel could only brokenly whisper, "Amen." She raised her bowed head and looked into the dark gaze that held her happiness. Tomorrow, they would go to church and celebrate the birth of the Savior of all who accepted Him. Afterward, God and the weather permitting, they would board the *Sea Witch* and sail to Dixon Cove.

But tonight, a thousand snowflakes fell, shutting them away from the world in their own brief and hallowed winterlude.

Colleen L. Reece is one of the most prolific authors writing today. With over seventy books published, Colleen has established herself as one of the most popular writers of inspirational romance. Twice voted "Favorite Author" in the annual **Heartsong Presents** readers' poll, Colleen has an army of fans that continues to grow. Colleen lives in Auburn, Washington, where she writes full-time.

Heartfelt wishes for the most
blessed Christmas "holy-day"
season ever.

In His love,
Colleen

Dakota
Destiny

Lauraine Snelling

One

"Mary's home! Mary's home!" Daniel, the youngest of the Moen brood, left off swinging on the gate to the picket fence and leaped up the porch steps to the door. "Mother, did you hear me?"

"Only me and half the town. Must you yell so?" Ingeborg Moen made her way down the steep stairs and bustled over to the door. "Did you see her or was it the little bird that told you?"

"I saw. . ." A gloved hand clamped gently over his mouth.

"Hello, Mother." Mary stood in the doorway. At seventeen, she had shed the little girl and donned the young woman. Golden hair fell in curls down her back, held back from her oval face with a whalebone clasp, high on the back of her head. Eyes the blue of a Dakota

261

summer sky still shone with the direct look that made students in her Sunday school classes squirm, much as her younger siblings had for years.

There was something about Mary that not only commanded attention but also made one look again. Was it the straightness of her carriage fostered by years of Mrs. Norgaard insisting the girls of Soldahl walk and stand tall no matter what their height? Or the firmness of her chin that bespoke of a will of her own? Or was it the twinkle that hid under long, dark lashes and flirted with the dimple in her right cheek whenever she was trying not to laugh—which was often?

Ingeborg gathered her eldest chick in her arms and hugged her as if they'd been apart for years instead of months. "Oh, my dear, I have missed you so. The house, nay even the town, is not the same without my Mary." She set the young woman a bit away and studied the girl's eyes. "How have you been, really? Has the school been hard for you? And the train trip home— all went well?"

"Mother, how can I answer so many questions at once? This has been a most marvelous year, and when I finish this time next spring, I will be able to teach school anywhere in North Dakota. Isn't that the most, the most. . ." Mary threw herself back into her mother's arms. "Oh, much as I love school, I have missed you all sorely."

Daniel thumped her valise on the waxed wooden floor. "Did you bring anything for all of us?"

"Of course I did, and how come you're not in school?" She hugged her ten-year-old brother. "You're not sick, are you? You don't look it."

He pulled away, already at the age of being embarrassed by being hugged in public. "Naw, not much anyway."

Mary looked a question at her mother. This, the baby in the family, had suffered many ailments in his short life. He seemed to catch anything that visited the school or the neighboring children, and with him it always lasted longer and took more of a toll.

"He'll be going back tomorrow." A shadow passed over Ingeborg's placid features. She lived by the creed that God loved his children and would always protect them. She'd taught that belief to her children all their lives, both she and the Reverend John, her husband. But sometimes in the dead of night when this one of her brood was near death's door, her faith had been tried—and wavered. But such doubts never lingered longer than the rise of the new day, for she believed implicitly in the mansions Jesus had gone to prepare.

Mary sniffed once and then again. "You baked apple pies."

"The last of the barrel. I'd been saving them for you, hoping they would last."

"I helped peel."

Mary stroked Daniel's pale cheek. "And I bet you are the best apple peeler in Soldahl. Now, let me put my things away and we will sample some of Mother's crust cookies, or did you eat them all?"

He shook his head so hard, the white blond hair swung across his forehead. "I din't."

Mary headed for the stairs. "And you, my dear Mor, will fill me in on all the happenings of town and country since your last letter."

"Will came by yesterday." Daniel struggled up the steps with the heavy valise.

"He did, eh?" Mary looked up to catch a nod from her mother. A thrill of pleasure rippled up Mary's back. *Will, soon I will see Will again. And we will have an entire summer to find out how deep our friendship really goes.*

She turned back to her little brother, "Here, let's do that together. That bag is so burdened with books, no wonder we can't lift it." Mary settled her hand next to Daniel's on the leather grip, and together they lugged it up the steep stairs—Mary laughing and teasing her little brother all the way. They set the case down, and with a sigh of happiness, Mary looked around the room she'd known all her life.

The first nine-patch quilt she'd made with her mother covered the bed, and the rag rug on the floor had warmed her feet since she was ten. Stiffly starched white Priscilla curtains crossed over the south-facing windows, and an oak commode held the same rose-trimmed pitcher and bowl given her by her bestamor, her mother's mother. The ceiling still slanted the same, its rose wallpaper now fading in places.

Daniel stood silently, intuitive as ever of his eldest sister's feelings. When she finished looking around, he grinned up at her. "Didja see anything new?"

Mary looked again. The kerosene lamp still sat on the corner of her dresser. As soon as she unpacked, the brush and hand mirror would go back in place. She looked down at her brother. "What's up, Danny boy?"

He looked at the ceiling directly above her head. She followed his gaze and her mouth fell open. "Electric lights. Far put in the electricity."

"The church board voted."

Since they lived in the parsonage, all improvements were at the whim and financial possibilities of the Soldahl Lutheran Church. They'd all grown up under that edict.

Mary reached up and pushed the button on the bare bulb hanging from a cord. Light flooded the room. "Now I can read in bed at night." She spun in place, arms outstretched as if to embrace the entire world, or at least her home and family. She swooped Daniel up and hugged him tight. *He is so thin,* she thought. *Has he been worse than mother told me?* He hugged her back and whispered in her ear. "I've missed you so."

"And me you, Bug. Let's go down and have some of that apple pie, if Mor will cut it before dinner." His childhood nickname slipped out; she hadn't called him that in years, but today, today was a time for remembering. Who knew what a magical day like today would bring?

Mary and Daniel, hand in hand, were halfway down the stairs when the front door opened again and the Reverend John Moen entered, removing his well-used black Fedora as he came. Mary put her finger to her lips, and she and Daniel froze in place.

"So, Mother, what's the news? Ummmm, something surely smells good."

As he walked toward the kitchen, Mary and Daniel tiptoed down the stairs.

"Apple pie? For me?"

"Get your fingers out of the crust." The laughter in Ingeborg's voice could be heard by the two creeping nearer.

Mary silently mouthed, *one, two, three,* and she and Daniel burst around the corner. "Surprise!"

"Land sakes alive, look who's here!" John grabbed his chest in mock shock. "Mary, come home at last." He spread his arms and Mary stepped into them, forcing herself to regain some sort of decorum. "Lord love you, girl, but I was beginning to think you were never coming home." He hugged her close and rested his cheek on smooth golden hair. "When did you go and get so grown up?"

Mary blinked against the tears burning the backs of her eyes. Her father had aged in the months she'd been gone. Deep lines bracketed his mouth, and the few strands of gray at his temples had multiplied. She stepped back, the better to see his dear face. "I'm never too grown up to come home to my family. Even though I've been so busy I hardly have time to turn around, I've missed you all so much."

"Come now, we can visit as we eat. Daniel, John, go wash your hands. Mary, put this in the center of the table please." Ingeborg handed her daughter a plate of warm rolls, fresh from the oven. Setting a platter with a roast surrounded by potatoes next to her place, Ingeborg checked to make sure everything was to her liking.

"Mother, you've gone to such trouble. I'll be around here for months." Mary clasped her hands over the back of the chair that had always been hers. "Oh, it feels so good to be home." She counted the places set and looked over at her mother. "Who else is coming?"

"You'll know soon enough." A knock at the door brightened Mor's eyes. "Go answer that while I bring on the coffee."

Mary gave her a puzzled look and went to do as bid.

"Hello, Mary." Will Dunfey's carrot hair had turned to a deep auburn that made his blue eyes even bluer. The smile on his face looked fit to crack the square jaw that he could set with a stubbornness like a bear trap. His shoulders now filled out a blue chambray shirt, open at the neck and with sleeves buttoned at strong wrists.

"Will!" Mary warred with the desire to throw herself into his arms. Instead she stepped back and beckoned him in. He took her hand as he passed, and a shiver went up her arm and straight to her heart. When he took her other hand and turned her to face him, the two shivers met and the delicious collision could be felt clear to her toes.

"So you're finally home." Had his voice deepened in the last months or was her memory faulty?

"Yes." *Say something intelligent, you ninny. This is only Will, you remember him, your best friend?*

"Invite him to the table, daughter." The gentle prompting came from her mother.

"Oh, I'm sorry." She unlocked her gaze from the deep blue pools of his eyes and, finally coming to herself, gestured him toward the table. "I believe Mother invited you for dinner."

Will winked at her, nearly undoing her again, and dropping her hands, crossed the room to shake hands with her father. After greeting the Reverend and Mrs. Moen, he took the place next to Mary's as if he'd been there many times.

The thought of that set Mary to wondering. When she started to pull out her chair, Will leaped to his feet to assist her. Mary stared at him. *What in the world?* She seated herself with a murmured "thank you" and a questioning look over her shoulder. Where had Will, the playmate hero, gone, and when had this exciting man taken his place?

Dinner passed in a blur of laughter, good food, and the kind of visiting that said this was not an unusual occurrence. Daniel treated Will much like his bigger brothers, and Ingeborg scolded the young man like one of her own.

Mary caught up on the news of Soldahl as seen through the loving eyes of her father, the slightly acerbic gaze of her mother, and the humorous observations of Will, who saw things from the point of view of the blacksmith and livery, where he worked for Dag Weinlander.

"The doctor was the latest one," Will was saying. "I'm going to have to go to mechanic's school if this drive to buy automobiles continues. You know, at first Dag thought they were a fad, but now that Mrs. Norgaard owns one and expects him to drive her everywhere, he thinks they're the best."

"Mrs. Norgaard bought an automobile?" Mary dropped her fork. "At her age?"

"Now dear, seventy isn't so old when one is in good health." Ingeborg began stacking the dishes.

"She says she has too much to do to get old," John said with a chuckle. "When I think back to how close she was to dying after her husband died. If it hadn't been for Clara, she would have given up for sure."

"That seems so long ago. I remember the classes we had at her house to learn to speak better English. Mrs. Norgaard was determined all the girls would grow up to be proper young ladies, whether we wanted to or not."

"She took me in hand. If it hadn't been for her and Dag, I would have gotten on the next train and kept on heading west." Will smiled in remembrance. "I thought sure once or twice she was going to whack me with that cane of hers."

"Did she really—whack anyone that is?" Daniel's eyes grew round.

"Not that I know of, but for one so tiny, she sure can put the fear of God into you."

"Ja, and everyone in town has been blessed by her good heart at one time or another." John held up his coffee cup. "Any more, my dear?"

Ingeborg got to her feet. "I'll bring the dessert. You stay right there, Mary."

"Thanks to her that I am at school." Mary got up anyway and took the remainder of the plates into the kitchen.

"And that the church has a new furnace."

"And the school too." Daniel added.

"Is Mr. Johnston happy here?" Mary had a dream buried deep in her heart of teaching in the Soldahl school, but that could only happen if the current teacher moved elsewhere.

"Very much so. His wife is president of the Ladies' Aid, such a worker." Ingeborg returned with the apple pie. "I'd hate for them to leave. Their going would leave a real hole in the congregation."

Mary nodded. So much for her dream. Surely there would be a school near Soldahl available next year.

They all enjoyed the pie and coffee, with Will taking the second piece Ingeborg pushed at him. He waved away the third offering.

"Mother, you are the best pie maker in the entire world." Mary licked her fork for the last bit of pie juice. She looked sideways at Will, but he seemed lost in thought of his own. Was something wrong?

When she looked at her father at the foot of the table, a look that matched Will's hovered about his eyes. What was going on?

"I better get back to the church. I have a young couple coming by for marriage counseling." John pushed his chair back. "You want to walk with me, son?"

"Sure." Daniel leaped to his feet.

"I better be getting back to work too," Will said with a sigh. "Thank you for such a wonderful meal, Mrs. Moen. I will remember these get-togethers for all time."

"Thank you, Will. Mary, why don't you walk Will to the gate? I'll do the cleaning up here." Ingeborg smiled, but the light didn't quite reach her eyes.

A goose just walked over my grave, Mary thought as she sensed something further amiss.

She locked her fingers behind her back as Will ushered her out the door. An intelligent word wouldn't come to her mind for the life of her.

"So, did you enjoy the last half of school?" Will leaned against the turned post on the porch.

"I loved most every minute of it. I had to study hard, but I knew that." Mary adopted the other post and turned to face him, her back against the warm surface.

Will held his hat in his hands, one finger outlining the brim. When he looked up at her, the sadness that had lurked in the background leaped forward. "Mary, there is so much I wanted to say, have wanted to say for years, and now. . ." He looked up at the sky as if asking for guidance.

"Will, I know something is wrong. What is it?"

He sat down on the step and gestured for her to do the same. "First of all, I have to know. Do you love me as I love you—with the kind of love between a man and a woman, not the kind between friends and kids?"

Mary clasped her hands around her skirted knees. All the dreaming of this time, and here it was: no preparation, just boom. "Will, I have always loved you." Her voice came softly but surely.

"I mean as more than friends."

"Will Dunfey, understand me." She turned so she faced him. "I love you. I always have, and I always will."

"I had hoped to ask you to marry me." He laid a calloused hand over hers.

"Had hoped?" She could feel a knot tightening in her breast.

"I thought by the time you graduated I would perhaps own part of the business or one of my own so I could support you."

"Will, you are scaring me." Mary laid her hand over his.

Will looked up at her, his eyes crying for understanding. "I signed up last week."

"Signed up?"

"Enlisted in the U.S. Army to fight against the Germans. They say this is the war to end all wars and they need strong young men."

Mary felt a small part of her die at his words.

Two

"**O**h, Will, you can't leave!" The cry escaped before Mary could trap it.

He studied the hat in his hands. "You know I don't want to."

"Then don't." Mary clasped her hands together, her fingers winding themselves together as if they had a mind of their own. "I. . .I just got home."

"I know." He looked up at her, his eyes filled with love and longing. "But they need men like me to stop the Huns. I couldn't say no. You wouldn't really want me to."

Yes I would. I want you here. I've been looking forward to this summer for months. It made the hard times bearable. But she wouldn't say those words, couldn't say them. No one had every accused Mary Moen of being selfish.

"Of course not." Now she studied her hands. If she looked at him, he would see the lie in her eyes.

A bee buzzed by and landed on the lilac that had yet to open its blossoms.

Will cleared his throat. "I. . .I want you to know that I love you. I've wanted to tell you that for years, and I promised I would wait until we—" His voice broke. He sighed. "Aw, Mary, this isn't the way I dreamed it at all." He crossed the narrow gap separating them and took her hands in his. "I want to marry you, but that will have to wait until I come back. No, that's not what I wanted to say at all." He dropped her hands and leaned against the post above her. "What I mean is—"

"I don't care what you mean, Will darling. I will be here waiting for you, so you keep that in your mind. I will write to you every day and mail the letters once a week, if I can wait that long." She grasped the front of his shirt with both hands. "And you will come back to me, Mr. Will Dunfey. You will come back." She lifted her face to his for the kiss she had dreamed of in the many lonely nights away at school.

His lips felt warm and soft and unbearingly sweet. She could feel the tears pooling at the back of her throat. *Dear God, please bring him home again. Watch over him for me.*

"We will all be praying for you," she murmured against his mouth. "I love you. Don't you ever forget that."

"I won't." He kissed her again. When he stepped

back, he clasped her shoulders in his strong hands. "I'll see you tonight?"

She nodded. "Come for supper."

She watched him leap off the porch and trot down the walk to the gate. When the gate swung shut, the squeal of it grated on Mary's ears. It sounded like an animal in pain. Maybe it was her.

"Did he say when he was leaving?" Ingeborg asked when Mary finally returned to the kitchen.

Mary shook her head. "And I forgot to ask." She slapped the palms of her hands on the counter. "It's. . . it's just not fair."

"Much of life isn't."

"But why should our young men go fight a war in Europe?" She raised a hand. "I know, Mother. I read the newspapers too. Some want us to be at the front and some want us to pretend it's not there. I just never thought we would be affected so soon. Are others of our boys already signed up too?"

Ingeborg shook her head. "Not that I know of."

"Then why Will?"

"Now that he has, others will follow. He's always been a leader of the young men—you know that."

"But I had such dreams for this summer—and next year. . ." Her voice dwindled. "And for the years after that."

"No need to give up the dreams." Ingeborg watched her beloved daughter wrestling with forces against which she had no power.

"But. . .but what if. . ."

The ticking clock sounded loud in the silence. Ashes crumbled in the freshly blacked cast-iron range.

Mary lifted tear-filled eyes and looked directly at her mother. "What if he doesn't come back?"

"Then with God's strength and blessing you go on with your life, always remembering Will with fondness and pride." Ingeborg crossed to her daughter. "You would not be the only woman in the country with such a burden to bear. Or the world, for that matter. Perhaps if our boys get in and get the job done, there won't be so many women longing for husbands, lovers, and sons."

"How will I do this?" Mary whispered.

"By the grace of God and by keeping busy making life better for others. That is how women always get through the hard parts of life."

Mary looked up at her mother, wondering as always at the quiet wisdom Ingeborg lived. Her mother didn't say things like that lightly. She who so often sat beside the dying in the wee hours of the morning had been there herself when one child was stillborn and another died in infancy. Mary put her arms around her mother's waist and pillowed her cheek on the familiar shoulder. "Oh, Mor, I've missed you more than words could say."

Ingeborg patted her daughter's back. "God always provides, child, remember that."

After supper that night, Mary and Will strolled

down the street in the sweet evening air. They'd talked of many things by the time they returned to her front fence, but one question she had not been able to utter. Finally she blurted it out.

"When will you be leaving?"

"Next week, on Monday."

"But this is already Thursday."

"I know."

Mary swallowed all the words that demanded speech. "Oh." Did a heart shatter and fall into pieces, or did it just seem so?

Three

Would her heart never quit bleeding? Mary stood waving long after the train left. Will had hung half out the side to see her as long as he could. The memory of the sun glinting off his hair and him waving his cap would have to last her a good long time. She had managed to send him off with a smile. She'd promised herself the night before that she would do that. No tears, only smiles.

"We are all praying for him," a familiar voice said from behind her.

"Mrs. Norgaard, how good of you to come." Mary wiped her eyes before turning around. She sniffed and forced a smile to her face.

"He's been one of my boys for more years than I care to count," Mrs. Norgaard said with a thump of her

278

cane. "And I'll be right here waiting when he returns too." A tear slid down the parchment cheek from under the black veil of her hat. With her back as ramrod straight as ever, Mrs. Norgaard refused to give in to the ravages of time, albeit her step had slowed and spectacles now perched on her straight nose.

"Now, then, we can stand here sniveling or we can get to doing something worthwhile. I know you were praying for him as I was, and we will continue to do that on a daily, or hourly if need be, basis. God only knows what's in store for our boy, but we will keep reminding our Father to be on the lookout." She stepped forward and, hooking her cane over her own arm, slid her other into Mary's. "Mrs. Olson has coffee and some kind of special treat for all of us, so let us not keep her waiting."

And with that the Moens, Dag and Clara, the doctor and his wife, and several others found themselves back at "the mansion," enjoying a repast much as if they'd just come for a party. With everyone asking her about school and life in Fargo, Mary felt her heart lighten. If she'd done what she planned, she'd have been home flat out across her bed, crying 'til she dried up.

Dr. Harmon came up to her, tucking a last bite of frosted cake into his mouth. Crumbs caught on his mustache, and he brushed them away with a nonchalant finger. "So, missy, what are you planning for the summer?"

"I was planning on picnics with Will, helping my mother with the canning and garden, and going riding with Will."

Doc nodded his balding head. "That so." He continued to nod. "I 'spect that's changed somewhat." The twinkle in his eye let her know he understood how she felt. "You given thought to anything else?"

Mary looked at him, her head cocked slightly sideways. "All right, let's have it. I've seen that look on your face too many times through the years to think you are just being polite."

"He's never been 'just polite' in his entire life." Gudrun Norgaard said from her chair off to the side. "What is it Harmon? Is there something going on I don't know about?"

"How could that be? You got your nose into more business than a hive's got bees."

"Be that as it may, what are you up to?" Mrs. Norgaard crossed her age-spotted hands over the carved head of her cane. Dag had made the cane for her the year her husband died when she hadn't much cared if she'd lived either.

"I think the two of you are cooking something up again." Clara Weinlander, wife of Dag and mother of their three children, stopped beside her benefactress's chair. "I know that look."

Doc attempted an injured air but stopped when he saw the knowing smile lifting the corners of Gudrun's narrow lips. "All right," he said to the older woman. "You know the Oiens?"

"Of course, that new family that moved into the Erickson property. He works for the railroad, I believe.

And she has some kind of health problem—ah, that's it." Gudrun nodded as she spoke. "A good idea, Harmon."

Mary looked from one to the other as if a spectator at that new sport she'd seen at school. Even the women played tennis—well, not her, but those who had a superfluous amount of time and money.

Clara came around to Mary and slipped an arm through hers. "Why do I get the feeling they are messing with someone else's life again?"

"It never did you any harm, did it?" Doc rocked back on his heels, glancing over to where Dag, owner of the local livery and blacksmith, now stood talking with the Reverend Moen. Sunlight from the bay window set both their faces in shadow, but the deep laugh could only come from Dag.

"No, that it didn't." Clara agreed. It had taken her a long time to get Dag to laugh so freely. "So, what do you have planned for Mary here?"

"I thought since she didn't have a position for the summer, she might be willing to help the Oiens care for their children. There are two of them: a boy four and the girl two. And perhaps she could do some fetching for the missus. Mrs. Oien resists the idea of needing help, but I know this would be a big load off her mind."

"What is wrong with her?" Mary asked.

"I just wish I knew. She keeps getting weaker, though she has some good days. You think you could help them out?"

"I'll gladly do what I can."

"I figured as much. After all, you are your mother's daughter." Doc Harmon gave her a nod of approval. "I'll talk with them tomorrow."

That night Mary wrote her first letter to Will, telling him about the party at the mansion and how it looked like she would be very busy that summer after all. As her letter lengthened, she thought of him on the train traveling east. Hoping he was thinking of her as she was him, she went to stand at her window.

"Look up to the Big Dipper every night," he'd said, "and think of me standing right on that handle, waving to you."

Mary closed her eyes against the tears that blurred the stars above. *Oh, God, keep him safe, please and thank You.* She looked out again, and the heavens seemed brighter, especially the star right at the end of the dipper handle.

Each morning she greeted the day with, *Thank You for the day, Lord, and thank You that You are watching over Will.* After that, she was usually too busy to think.

❧

The Erickson house sported a new coat of white paint, and the yard had not only been trimmed, but the flower beds along the walk were all dug, ready for planting the annuals now that the likelihood of a last frost was past.

I could do that for them, Mary thought as she lingered so as to arrive at the time Doc Harmon had set. After all, two little children won't take all my time. And Mrs. Norgaard said a woman came to clean and do some of the cooking. I know Clarissa will come help me if I need it. Clarissa was her younger sister, after Grace. With six kids in their family, there was always someone to help out, even with all the work they did around home.

The two cars arrived at nearly the same time. The man getting out of the first wore a black wool coat as if it were still winter. A homburg hat covered hair the color of oak bark and shaded dark eyes that seemed to have lost all their life. His smile barely touched his mouth, let alone his eyes. Tall and lean, he stooped some, as if the load he bore was getting far too heavy.

Dr. Harmon crossed the grass to take Mary's arm and guide her to meet her host. "Kenneth Oien, I want you to meet Mary Moen, the young woman who has agreed to help you for the summer." As the introductions were completed, Mary studied the man from under her eyelashes. Always one to bring home the stray and injured—both animals and people—Mary recognized pain when she saw it.

"Thank you for coming on such short notice. As the doctor might have told you, my wife, Elizabeth, has not wanted to have help with the children. I finally prevailed upon her to let me hire a woman to clean and do some of the cooking. I'm hoping you can make her days a bit easier. She frets so."

"I hope so, too."

"I. . .I haven't told her you were coming."

Mary shot a questioning look at the doctor, who just happened to be studying the leaves in the tree above. *I thought this was all set up. What if she hates me?*

"Perhaps you could just meet her and visit awhile, then come back tomorrow after I see how she responds?"

"Of course." Mary answered, still trying to catch the good doctor's attention.

"I'd best be going then—got a woman about to deliver out west aways." Doc tipped his hat. "Nice seeing you, Kenneth, Mary." He scooted off to his automobile before Mary could get in a word edgewise.

Mr. Oien ushered Mary into the front room of the two-story square home. "Elizabeth, I brought you company."

"Back here," the call came from a room that faced north and in most houses like this one, was a bedroom. A child's giggle broke the stillness, followed by another.

When they entered the room, the little ones were playing on a bench at the foot of the bed where Elizabeth lay.

"I'm sorry, Kenneth, I was so weak, I had to come back to bed before I fell over."

"Did you eat something?"

She shook her head.

"Have the children eaten?"

"We ate, Papa." The little boy lifted his head from playing with the Sears Catalogue.

The little girl scooted around the bed and peeped over the far side.

"Elizabeth, Jenny and Joey, I brought you some company. This is Mary Moen, just returned from college where she is studying to be a teacher."

Elizabeth smoothed her hair back with a white hand. "I. . .I wasn't expecting company. Please forgive me for . . .for. . ." She made a general gesture at her dishevelment and the toys spread about the room.

"I'm sorry, but I have to get back to my job. There is no one else there, you see, and I. . ." Mr. Oien dropped a kiss on his wife's forehead, waved to the children, and vanished out the door.

Mary heard the front door close behind him. So much for that source of help. She looked around for a chair to draw up to the bed. None. The little girl, Jenny, peered at her from across the bed, nose buried in the covers so all Mary could see was round brown eyes and uncombed, curly hair.

"Jenny don't like strangers," Joey announced from his place on the bench.

"I'm sorry, Miss Moen, I. . ." Elizabeth sighed. "I know Kenneth is trying to help, but he so often doesn't know how." She shook her head. "But then who would?"

"Sometimes talking to another woman helps." Mary came closer to the bed. "Doctor said you have a woman who comes in to clean."

"She is nice enough, a good worker, but she speaks Norwegian, and I don't. My grandmother came from Sweden, and Kenneth's grandparents from Norway. He only knows the table grace and a few phrases. I don't know what we are going to do."

Mary nodded. "Well, I know what I am going to do. I didn't come here just to visit. I came to help, and you and I will do much better if we are honest up front. Dr. Harmon and Mrs. Norgaard have a habit of fixing things in people's lives, and they decided I could help you and that way I would be too busy this summer to miss my Will who left on the train three days ago to fight the Germans."

She felt a thrill at saying the words my Will out loud. In the secret places of her heart, he'd been my Will since she was ten and he stuck up for her the first time. She looked around the room again. "How about if I move a chair in here for you to sit in while I fix your hair? Then you can hold Jenny while I brush hers."

"I combed my own hair." Still Joey didn't look up. Though he just kept turning the pages of the catalogue, he was obviously keeping track of the conversation.

"Are you sure you want to do this?" Elizabeth asked, the ray of hope peeping from her eyes belying the words.

"Ja, I am sure."

By noon when Kenneth came home for dinner, his wife had a smile on her face, Jenny wore a ribbon in her hair, and Joey had helped set the table. Mary took the chicken and dumplings from the stove and set the pot in the middle of the table.

"My land, why I. . .I. . ." He clasped his wife's hand and sat down beside her at the table.

"Thank you, Kenneth. You brought us a miracle worker."

"Mary said. . ." Joey slid into his place.

"Miss Moen," his father corrected him.

"Oh." A frown creased his forehead. "She said her name was Mary."

Mary set a platter of sliced bread next to the stew pot. "Okay, we can all say grace and then eat. How's that?" She took the chair closest to the food, just as her mother had always done, so she could serve.

"Mary, you are indeed an answer to prayer," Elizabeth said, extending her hand when Mary was ready to leave for home.

"You want me to come back then?"

"With all my heart."

Mary thought about the Oien family as she walked home in the late afternoon. Mr. Larson, the banker, tipped his hat as he passed her on the way home. Mrs. Johnson called hello from the door of the general store, and Miss Mabel waved from behind her display of hats in the ladies' shoppe. How good it felt to be home where she knew everyone and everyone knew her.

That night around the supper table, Knute, the oldest of the Moen boys, announced, "I want to enlist like Will did, before there ain't no more Germans to fight."

Mary's heart sprung a new crack. Not her brother too.

Four

"**Y**ou have a letter!" Daniel met her halfway home a few evenings later.

"From Will?" Mary broke into a run to meet him. A raised eyebrow from the hotel manager made her drop back to a decorous walk.

Daniel skidded to a stop, his cheeks pink from the exertion. "It is, it is! Read it aloud."

"How about if I read it first to myself and then to you?"

"Awww, Mary. I want to know how he is. Does he like being a shoulder?"

"Soldier, Danny boy, soldier." Mary grinned down at him. She slit the envelope with care and pulled out a flimsy sheet of paper. Well, Will certainly wasn't one to waste words on paper any more than he did in person.

Working with Dag Weinlander had taught him many things through the years, including how to conserve energy and speech.

My dearest Mary. The word dearest sent a thrill clear to the toes of her black pointed shoes. *I cannot tell you how much I miss the sight of your sweet face. When you were away at school, I always knew that if I grew desperate enough, I could take a train to Fargo and see you, if only briefly. Now I am clear across the continent from you, and so I commend you to the care of our loving God, for He can be with you when I cannot.*

Mary dug in her bag for a handkerchief.

"Is Will sick? Something is wrong." Daniel backpedaled in front of her so he could watch her face.

"No, silly, it's just that I miss him."

"Oh." He turned and walked beside her, slipping his hand in hers in spite of being out in public.

Mary continued reading. *I never dreamed people could be so ferocious with each other. The sergeants here shout all the time and expect us to do the same. When I think we are being trained to kill our fellow men, my soul cries out to God to stop this war before anyone else dies. But the Huns must be stopped or the world will never be a safe place in which to love and raise our children.*

Mary tucked the letter in her pocket. She would have to read it later when she could cry along with the heartfelt agony of the man she loved. Will had never been afraid to stand up for the weaker children, and he was carrying that same strength into the battle for freedom.

That night she could not see the Big Dipper; clouds covered the sky.

Within a week Mary had both Joey and Jenny waiting by the front windows for her arrival. Mrs. Oien brightened when her young friend walked into the room, and she seemed to be getting stronger. While she sometimes slipped into staring out the window, she more often read to the children and would pinch her cheeks to bring some color to them before Mr. Oien returned home for dinner.

"How would it be if I took the children home to play with my brothers and sisters this afternoon?" Mary asked after dinner one day. "We have a big swing in our backyard, and the cat in the stable has new kittens."

"Kittens." Joey looked from his father to his mother, his heart in his eyes.

"Now, no pets. Your mother has plenty to do already." Mr. Oien effectively doused the light in the child's eyes.

"You can play with them at my house; they are too little to leave their mother yet." Mary stepped into the breach. As far as she was concerned, an animal might make things more lively in this often silent home. Her mother had never minded when the children brought home another stray—of any kind. In fact, she frequently brought them home herself.

"Perhaps you would like to come too," she said to Elizabeth. "I know you would love visiting with my mother."

"Another time, dear, when I am feeling stronger."

Elizabeth smiled at her children. "But you two go on and have a good time."

Walking down the street with a child's hand in each of hers, Mary pointed out the store, the post office, and the hotel. But when she passed the livery, all she could think was that Will wasn't the one pounding on the anvil out back, most likely fitting shoes to one of the farmer's horses.

Jenny refused to leave the kittens. She plunked her sturdy little body down by the nest the cat had made in the hay under the horse's manger and giggled when the kittens nursed. She reached out a fat little finger and stroked down the wriggling kittens' backs.

Ingeborg had come out to the stable with Mary to watch. "I can't believe one so little would have the patience to sit like that. She is just enthralled with the kittens."

Joey had looked them over and then gone to see what the boys were doing. Knute was hoeing weeds in the garden and Daniel followed behind on hands and knees, pulling out the weeds too close to the plants for the hoe to work. He showed Joey which were weeds, and the little boy had followed the older one from then on. When they found a worm, Joey cupped it in his hands and brought it to Mary.

"Did you ever see such a big worm?" he asked.

"I think tomorrow we will dig in your flower beds and perhaps find some there." Mary stroked the hair back from the boy's sweaty forehead. Pulling weeds in the June sun could be a hot task.

"Not this big. This is the biggest worm ever. Can I take it home to show Mama?"

Mary nodded. But when Joey stuck the wriggling worm in his pocket, she shook her head. "He'll die there. Come on, let's find a can for him, and you can put dirt in it." By the time Ingeborg called the children in for lemonade, Joey had several more worms in his can.

"Mor, could we take Joey fishing?" Daniel asked, wiping cookie crumbs from his mouth. All had gathered on the porch for the afternoon treat.

Ingeborg looked up. "I don't see why not. Mary, where is Jenny?"

Mary put her finger to her lips and pointed to the barn. When she and her mother tiptoed into the horse stall, they saw Jenny on the hay, sound asleep. The mother cat and kittens were doing the same.

"I checked on her a few minutes ago and decided to leave her there. Isn't she a darling?"

"You children used to love to sleep in the hay too. How is their mother, really?"

Mary shook her head. "She scares me sometimes, Mor. It's as though she isn't even there, and other times she is so sad. I don't know what to do to help her." Mary pondered the same question that night when she added to the week's letter to Will. "I wonder about Elizabeth Oien," she wrote. "She loves her husband and children but seems to be slipping away from them. What makes one person have such a strong will to live, like Mrs. Norgaard, and another unable to overcome a bodily weakness? Doc says she has never been the same since Jenny was born. I guess it was a hard time and she nearly died. But the children had such fun at our house."

She went on to describe the afternoon. She closed the letter as always, "May God hold you in His love and care, Your Mary."

Joey caught two fish and a bad case of hero worship. Jenny pleaded every day, "Kittens, pease see kittens." Daniel spent as much time at the Oiens as he did at home. And Mr. Oien paid Mary double what they'd agreed.

"I cannot begin to tell you what a difference you have made in our lives," he said one evening when he handed her the pay envelope. "Elizabeth and I are eternally grateful."

છે

The Fourth of July dawned with a glorious sunrise, and the rest of the day did its best to keep up. The parade started in the schoolyard and followed Main Street to the park where a bandstand had been set up. There would be speeches and singing, races for the children, carnival booths set up to earn money for various town groups like the Lutheran church ladies who sold fancy sandwiches and good strong coffee. Mary had worked in that booth since she was old enough to count the change.

The Grange sold hot dogs, the school board ice cream that was being hand-cranked out behind the booth by members of the board, and the Presbyterian church made the best pies anywhere. Knute won the pie eating contest for the second year in a row, and one child got stung by a bee. The fireworks that night capped a day that made Mary dream of Will even more. Last year they'd sat together, hands nearly touching while the fireworks burst in the sky to the accompaniment of the band. Did they have fireworks in the training camp he was in?

The next day an entire train car of young men left, waving to their families and sweethearts. They were on their way to an army training camp.

Mary stood next to her father, who had given the benediction at the ceremony. "Soon we won't have any young men left," she said softly. "Who is going to run the farms and provide food for the troops if all the workers leave?"

"Those of us left at home. It is the least we can do." John Moen blew his nose. "God have mercy on those boys." He used his handkerchief to wipe the sweat from his forehead. "Unseasonable hot, isn't it?"

"Yes, Father, it is hot, but you can't fool me. That wasn't all sweat you wiped from your face."

"You are much too observant, my dear. You will make a fine teacher; the children will accuse you of having eyes in the back of your head." John took his daughter's arm on one side and his wife's on the other. "Let's go home and make ice cream. I only got a taste yesterday."

The heat continued, made worse by air so full of moisture it felt like they were breathing under water. Heat lightening danced and stabbed, but it failed to deliver the needed rain. How hot it was became the talk of the town. When the farmers came in to shop on Saturdays, their horses looked as bone weary as the people.

Mary tried to entertain the Oien children, but Jenny fussed and pleaded to go see the kittens. Mrs. Oien lay on the chaise lounge on the back porch, where it was coolest, but daily Mary watched the woman weaken.

If only it would rain. Dust from the streets coated everything, including the marigolds and petunias she had planted along the front walk. Early each day she carried water to the struggling plants, praying for rain like everyone else.

The corn fields to the south of town withered in the heat. Storm clouds formed on the western horizon but always passed without sending their life-giving moisture to the ground below.

One day Mary came home from the Oiens to find Daniel lying in bed, a wet cloth on his forehead. He looked up at her from fever-glazed eyes. "I don't feel so good, Mary."

The letter lying on the hall table had no better news. Will was boarding the ship to Europe in two days. She checked the postmark. He was already on the high seas.

Five

"He's a mighty sick boy, Ingeborg, I won't deny that." Doc Harmon looked up after listening to Daniel's labored breathing with his stethoscope. "People seem to fall into a couple of characteristics. Everything seems to settle in the chest for some, in the stomach for others. I don't understand it, but with Daniel here, it's always the chest. Onion plaster might help; keep his fever down and thump on his chest and back like this to loosen the mucus up." He cupped his hand and tapped it palm down on the boy's back.

Daniel started to cough after only a couple of whacks, giving the doctor a look of total disbelief.

"I know, son, but you will breathe better this way. Make sure he drinks a lot of water, and keep him as cool as possible. That plaster will heat him up some." He looked Daniel in the eye. "Now you do as your mother says and make sure you eat. Lots of broth—both chicken and beef—are good for building him back up."

He looked back up at Ingeborg. "You take care of yourself too. This summer complaint is affecting lots of people. What we need is a good rain to clear the air."

The rains held off.

Daniel was finally up and around again but more than willing to take afternoon naps. His favorite place was next to Mary. Mrs. Oien seemed better too, at least in the early morning and after the sun went down. Mr. Oien bought a newfangled gadget called an electric fan. Everyone wanted to sit in front of it, even when it only moved hot air around. Mary set a pan of water in front of the fan, and that helped them cool more.

July passed with people carrying water to their most precious plants and the farmers facing a year of no crops. At the parsonage, that meant there was no money in the church budget to pay the pastor, and Mary's wages became the lifeline for the Moens.

The weather changed when walnut-sized hail stones pounded the earth and all upon it. What the drought hadn't shriveled, the hail leveled. Ingeborg and Mary stood at the kitchen window and watched the garden they'd so faithfully watered be turned to flat mud and pulp.

"Guess we take God at His Word and trust that He

will provide." Ingeborg wiped a tear from her eye and squared her shoulders. "The root crops will still be good, and we already had some beans put up. I lived without tomatoes for years, so I know we can do so again. And the corn, well, next year we'll have corn again. At least the early apples were plentiful and perhaps we can buy a barrel from Wisconsin or somewhere later in the fall."

Mary knew her mother was indulging in wishful thinking. There would be no money for apples this year. "Mor, I could stay home from school and keep working for the Oiens."

Ingeborg shook her head. "No, my dear, your school is paid for, and you must finish. If it comes to that, I could go take care of her and those little ones."

Her face lost the strained look of moments before. "See, I said the Lord provides. What a good idea. All of ours are in school all day. Why I could do all their cleaning and cooking and perhaps—no, I couldn't cause someone else to lose their job. We will make do."

Mary knew this talking to herself was her mother's way of working things out, whether anyone else listened or not. She often found herself doing the same thing. Each night when she wrote her letters to Will, she sometimes spoke the words as she wrote them, as if that made him hear them sooner. Or rather see them.

It rained for two days, much of the water running off because the earth was too hard to receive it. At night she stood in front of her window and let the cool breeze blow over her skin. Cool, wet air—what a blessing. But she had to remember where the handle to the Big Dipper lay because she couldn't see it through the clouds.

Why hadn't she heard from Will? Where was he?

She still hadn't heard from him when she packed her trunk for the return to school. She wrapped the three precious letters carefully in a linen handkerchief and tied them with a faded hair ribbon. While she'd about memorized the words, she'd reread the pages until the folds were cracking from repeated bending.

Each week she mailed another letter to him, in care of the U.S. Army. Was he getting her letters? They hadn't come back.

The night before she was to leave, she walked to the mansion and up to the front door. Fireflies pirouetted to the cadence of the crickets. Mosquitos whined at her ear, but she brushed them away. She barely raised her hand to knock when Dag swung open the door.

"Come in, come in. Gudrun has been waiting for you." He turned to answer over his shoulder. "Yes, it is Mary." When he ushered her in, he whispered. "I told you she'd been waiting."

"Sorry, I should have come sooner."

"She's in the library."

Mary nodded. She loved coming to this house with its rich velvets and artfully carved sofas and whatnot tables. The embossed wallpaper gleamed in the newly installed electric lights that took the place of the gas jets.

Mrs. Norgaard sat behind the walnut desk that had belonged to her husband when he owned the bank. While she still owned the Soldahl Bank, she employed a manager who ran it and only reported to her quarterly, unless of course, there was an emergency.

"Come in, my dear and sit down." She took off her spectacles and rubbed the bridge of her nose. "I'm glad you could humor an old woman like me this last night you have with your family."

"They will see me off in the morning." Mary took in a deep breath and voiced something that had been on her heart and mind for the last weeks. "If paying my school expenses is a hardship for you this year, I could stay—"

"Absolutely not. You will finish your year out, and then you can teach. The children of North Dakota need teachers like you. If you think a few months of drought and then a hailstorm will wipe out commerce around here, you just don't understand the world yet.

"Companies make a great deal of money during wartime—I sometimes think that is why men start them—and our bank has invested wisely. I can afford your schooling, and you will not hear of my bank foreclosing on the farmers because they can't make their payments on time this year. Or anyone else for that matter. Do I hear your mother is going to take over at the Oiens?"

Mary nodded.

"That is good. But I have a feeling you've been worrying about the church paying your father's salary." She tipped her head to look over the tops of her gold wire spectacles.

"Some. My mother says they will make do, but I know it is hard to feed seven mouths, and five of the children are growing so fast we can't keep them in shoes."

"You are not to worry. If I'd known John hadn't gotten paid last month, it never would have happened, and you can bet your life it won't happen again." Mrs. Norgaard sat up straighter. "Those men can bungle things up so bad sometimes, it takes me weeks to just figure it out."

Mary knew she referred to the deacons who ran the business of the congregation. "How'd you find out?" Curious, Mary leaned forward in her chair.

"I have my ways, child."

"Doc Harmon?" Mary shook her head. "No, he's not on the board. Mr. Sommerstrum?" At the twinkle in Gudrun's eye, Mary laughed. "Mrs. Sommerstrum."

"I'll never tell, but it's a good thing some men talk things over with their wives, even if it's only to share the gossip."

Mary nodded. "I see. I've often wondered how you keep such good tabs on the goings on in Soldahl when you don't go out too often. Mrs. Sommerstrum tells Mrs. Olson, and Mrs. Olson tells you." Mrs. Olson had been the housekeeper at the mansion ever since Mary could remember.

Gudrun nodded. She reached in a drawer, removed an envelope, and handed it across the shiny surface of the desk. "Here. And I don't want you scrimping and going without to send part of that money home, you understand me?"

Mary nodded, guilt sending a flush up her neck. *How did she know what I'd been thinking of?*

"Ah, caught you, did I?" At the girl's slight nod, Gudrun continued. "Now that we have that out of the way, I have a very personal question to ask. Have you heard from Will?"

"No, not since early July, and that letter had been written while he was on the ship."

"Neither have we. That's not like our Will." She stared at the desk before her. "Did he say anything about where they were sending him?"

Again, Mary shook her head.

Gudrun nodded and rose to her feet. "Well, as the old saying goes, no news is good news. Come, let's have a last cup of coffee and some of Mrs. Olson's angel food cake. I think she has a packet ready to send with you too."

By the time Mary said good-bye to the family in the mansion, she could hardly hold back the tears. It wasn't like she was going clear around the world or anything, but right now Fargo seemed years away.

The next morning was even worse. Daniel clung to

her until they were both in tears. John finally took the child in his arms while Ingeborg hugged her daughter one last time. Mary smiled through her tears and ruffled Daniel's hair while at the same time hugging her father. She went down the line, hugging each of her brothers and sisters. "Now, promise me, all of you, that when I ask your teacher at Christmas time how you are doing, he will have a good report for me."

They all nodded and smiled at her.

"Hey, I'm not leaving forever, you know."

"It just seems like it."

The train blew its whistle, and the conductor announced, "All aboard."

Mary stepped on the stool and up the stairs. She waved one last time and hurried inside so she could wave again out the window. Slowly the train pulled out of the station, and when she could see them no more, she sank back in her seat to wipe her eyes. Why was leaving so hard when she had so much to look forward to?

As the miles passed, she thought back to the last night she had seen Will. The small package she'd given him contained one of her treasures, the New Testament given her by her parents on her twelfth birthday. "Will you keep this with you to remind you always how much I love you and how much more God loves you?"

"I will keep it in my shirt pocket," he'd replied, never taking his gaze from hers while he put the Testament next to his heart. "But I need no reminder."

The kiss they'd shared had been only sweeter with the small book tucked between them.

At Grand Forks, two of Mary's friends from the year before boarded, and they spent the remainder of the trip catching up on their summers. When Mary told them Will had gone to war, Janice said her brother had left too. Dorie shook her head. "I can't believe all our boys are going over there. What if they don't come home? Who will we marry?"

Mary rolled her eyes. "Leave it to you to keep the most important things right out front." The three laughed, but Mary felt a pang of fear. What if Will didn't come home?

One evening, toward the middle of October, she returned to her room to find a message saying there was a gentleman waiting in the parlor. He wanted to talk with her. Mary flew back down the stairs, her heart pounding. Perhaps it was Will!

But when she slid open the heavy door, her father and Dag Weinlander sat in the armchairs facing the fireplace. From the looks on their faces, she knew.

"He's dead, isn't he?" How could she say the words? Dead, what did that mean?

John shook his head. Dag cleared his throat. "We hope not." He extended the letter bearing an official seal at the top.

Mary read it quickly, then went back to read each word one at a time. *We regret to inform you that Private First Class Willard Dunfey is missing in action and presumed dead.* The date was three months earlier.

Six

"Then he isn't dead." Mary went to stand in front of the fire. She wanted to throw the horrible letter in and let the flames devour it.

"We can pray that he isn't." John said. He stepped closer and wrapped an arm around her shoulders.

"Father, wouldn't I know if Will no longer lived on this earth? I mean, he can't have been dead for three months and me not sense it, could he?"

"I don't know, child." John shook his head. "I just don't know. The Almighty hasn't seen fit to let me know many things."

Mary looked up at her father. The lines had deepened in his face and his hair showed white all over. "What's been happening?"

"I had two funerals last week of boys shipped home

305

to be buried. The oldest Gustafson boy and Teddy Bjorn. What can I say to those grieving parents—that this was God's will?"

He laid his cheek on the top of her head, now nestled against his shoulder. "I cannot say that war is God's will, that He is on the side of the right. He loves the Germans too, not just the Americans and the English and French. We are all his children, so how can we go about killing each other?" His voice had softened on the last words. "How?"

Mary felt the shudder that passed through him. Her gentle father, who loved all the children of the parish and their parents and relatives. Who never preached the fire and brimstone of other churches because he said God is love and His grace is made perfect in our human weakness. This man now had to bury the ones he loved because of man's inhumanity to man.

But was war really human? She'd sat through many discussions and heard heart-stirring speeches about fighting for freedom, but did freedom have to come at the cost of so many lives? She had no answers, only questions.

Had Will really gone to his heavenly home, or was he on earth, suffering some unspeakable agony? If he were alive, wouldn't he have contacted her?

"You may have to accept the fact that he is gone." John drew his arms away and stepped back so he could see her face more clearly.

"But not now!"

"No, not now."

Mary straightened her shoulders, reminiscent of Mrs. Norgaard. She forced a smile to her quivering lips. "How is Daniel? And mother with the Oiens? Did Mr. Oien give in yet and let Jenny have a kitty? She loves them so. How have you been? You're looking tired." Before he could answer, she turned to Dag, who had been sitting quietly. "How is Mrs. Norgaard and Clara?" Perhaps if she asked enough questions, the greater one would disappear.

"We are all fine," her father finally managed to insert. "In fact, with the cooler weather, Daniel has been doing well. Hasn't missed a day of school but he would have today if he could have hidden out in my pocket to come along. He is counting the days until you come home for Christmas. Said to tell you he prays for Will every night."

That nearly undid her. She blinked several times and stared into the fire until she had herself under control. "Have you had supper?" When they shook their heads, she looked up at the carved clock on the mantel. "I'm sure Mrs. Killingsworth will let me fix you something in the kitchen. Where are you staying?"

"We aren't. We will catch the eleven o'clock back north. I just felt it important to give you this news in person, not through a letter or over the telephone."

Mary placed a hand on his arm. "Father, you are so kind. How lucky I am that I was born to you and Mor." She spun away before he could answer. "Let me check on supper for you."

An hour later she waved them on their way. "Thank you for coming along with him, Dag. You are a good friend."

He tipped his black felt hat to her. "Mrs. Norgaard just wanted me to check up on her investment; this seemed as good a time as any." The twinkle in his eye let her know he was teasing.

"Well, then, since this was a business trip, thank you for bringing my father along." She hugged her father one last time. "Pass that on to everyone, okay?"

She kept the smile in place as long as they looked back, but when she closed the door, the tears could no longer be held back. She stumbled against the lower step of the staircase and sat down. Leaning her head against the newel post, she couldn't have stopped the tears had she tried.

One by one the other young women in the boarding house came down the stairs and clustered around her. One offered a handkerchief; another went for a glass of water. Still another slipped into the music room and, sitting down at the piano, began playing the hymns they'd learned as children.

As the music washed over them, soon one began humming and then another.

When the storm of tears finally abated, Mary listened to the humming in harmony. Had a chorus of angels come just to give her strength? She closed her eyes and leaned against the post. They drifted from melody to melody as the pianist did, until she finally let the last notes drift away.

"Amen." As the notes died away, Janice took Mary's arm and tugged her to her feet. Together, arms around each other's waists, they climbed the stairs to the bedroom they shared.

"Thank you, all." Mary whispered. Talking loudly would have broken the spell.

When despair grabbed at her in the days to come, she remembered that peaceful music and the love of her friends. In spite of the official letter, each evening Mary added tales of the day to her own letters to Will. She continued to send them, refusing to allow herself to speculate about what was happening to them.

"I guess I'm afraid that if I quit, Will will be dead, and if I keep on, there's a chance he is alive," she explained to Janice one night. They'd been studying late because exams were coming up.

"How can you keep on going and not let it drag you down?" Janice tightened the belt of her flannel robe. "The not knowing. . ." She shook her head so her dark hair swung over one shoulder. She combed the tresses with her fingers and leaned back against the pillows piled at the head of her bed. "Makes me glad I don't have a sweetheart yet."

"I wouldn't trade my friendship and love for Will for all the men on campus."

"There are several who would ask if you gave them the chance."

"Janice!" Mary turned in her chair and locked her hands over the back. "I haven't treated any one of them as more than a friend."

"I know that. You act like you are already married, for heaven's sake. I'm just telling you what I see. And hear."

"Oh, pooh, you're making that up." Mary turned back to her books. "Be quiet, I have to get this memorized."

But Mary recognized that her skirts hung looser about her waist and the shadows that lurked beneath her eyes grew darker, as if she hadn't enough sleep. Each night she committed Will to her heavenly Father's keeping and waved goodnight to him on the last star of the handle.

Two days before she left for home, she received a letter from her mother. *My dear Mary,* she read. *I have some sad news for you. Mrs. Oien, my dear friend Elizabeth, died from pneumonia two days ago. Dr. Harmon said she had no strength to fight it, and I could see that. I was with her when she breathed her last, as was Mr. Oien.*

He is so broken up, I want to take him in my arms like I do Daniel, to comfort him. The funeral is tomorrow. The children are with us for the time being, as Kenneth can't seem to know what to do with them. He stayed home from work for the first day but said he was going crazy in that house without her.

The rest of us are eagerly waiting for your return. God keep you, my dear. Your loving mother.

Mary laid the paper in her lap and looked out the

window into the blackness. A street light up by the corner cast a round circle of light on the freshly fallen snow. Clouds, pregnant with moisture, covered the twinkling stars. The night felt heavy, like the news in her lap.

"Oh, Elizabeth," Mary whispered, "how you must have fought to stay with your children. And your poor husband. Good-bye, my friend. Go with God." She sat down and wrote a letter of condolence to Mr. Oien, knowing she would get back to town nearly as soon as the letter but feeling she needed to write it anyway.

"What happened now?" Janice asked when she came in some time later.

Mary handed her the letter.

"Oh, that poor man." Janice looked up from her reading. "He'll need someone to care for his children." She tilted her head slightly sideways and looked at Mary. "You won't think you have to stay home next term and care for them?"

"No, I promised Mrs. Norgaard I would finish this year. I just grew to care for her so much last summer, and the children, Joey and Jenny, will be lost."

"Not if your mother has anything to do with it."

"Or Doc Harmon and Mrs. Norgaard. They'll probably have him married off in a month or two." Mary's smile slipped. "Men do that you know—marry again right away. I don't know how they can."

"For some I think marrying is like changing underwear. You do what's necessary."

"Janice Ringold!" Mary, feeling her jaw hit her chest, looked at her friend. The shock of the words made them both laugh. "You are outrageous, you know that?"

"I know. My mother always said my mouth would get me in trouble. 'Men don't like outspoken young ladies.' If I heard her say that once, I heard her a thousand times."

"Didn't help much, did it?" They chuckled again.

But before Mary fell asleep that night, she added an extra prayer for the Oien family along with her others, and as always, she gave Him Will.

≥≥

The house smelled like cinnamon and freshly baked bread when Mary tiptoed in through the front door. Candles in the windows were ready to be lit on Christmas Eve, a pine tree from Minnesota filled the usual spot in the corner of the parlor, and garlands of cedar trimmed the doorway. Mary felt a pang; she'd missed the house decorating again. If only she'd had her last exam early in the week like many of the others, she could have left sooner. She could hear her mother in the kitchen, removing something from the oven.

Mary shut the door softly, hoping there would be no squeak, and when that was accomplished, she crossed the room to the kitchen. "Surprise!"

"Oh, my heavens!" Ingeborg grabbed at the sheet of cookies that was headed for the floor. When she had the cookies safely on the table, she put her hand to her heart. "What are you trying to do, you naughty child, give your mother a heart attack?" But the smile that took in her whole face, and her outstretched arms made light of her scolding words. "Land sakes, Mary, I didn't think you were ever coming."

A child's whimper came from the bedroom.

"Now see what you did—woke up Jenny. Joey won't be far behind."

"They are here?" Mary hugged her mother and began unwinding the bright red scarf about her neck. She hung it and then her coat on the rack by the door and reached outside for her valise. "You think they will remember me?"

"With Daniel telling them every day that Mary is coming, what do you think?" Ingeborg cocked her head and listened. "I think she'll settle down again. Give us time for a cup of coffee and some catching up."

"I have another box at the station, it was too heavy to carry."

"Mary, you didn't spend your money on Christmas presents, did you?"

"Some, and some I made, like always. There are some books there for my classroom—when I get a classroom, that is." She sat down at the table and watched her mother take down the good china cups. They only came down for special company and the Ladies Aid. Ingeborg set the one with tiny rosebuds around the rim in front of her daughter. It had been her favorite since when she was little and they had tea once in a great while.

313

Oh, I'm home, Mary thought. *I never know how much I miss it and my family until I come back.* But this time there would be no Will to come sweep her off her feet. She sighed. A bit of the sunlight went out of the day. *You knew better,* she scolded herself. *You knew he wasn't here, so behave yourself. Don't take your feelings out on Mor who is so happy to see you.*

After Ingeborg poured the coffee, she took her daughter's chin in gentle fingers and tilted her face toward the light. "Have you been sick?"

Mary shook her head.

"Working too hard and not sleeping enough?" She tilted the girl's head down and kissed the forehead. "Grieving for Will?" Her words were soft as the ashes falling in the stove.

"Oh, Mor." Mary flung her arms around her mother's waist and buried her face in the flour-dusted apron. "I can't believe he's dead. Wouldn't I know, some part of me down in my heart? Wouldn't I know for sure?"

Ingeborg stroked the soft curls and brushed the wisps of hair back that framed Mary's face. "I've heard tell of that, of mothers with their children, sometimes of those who've been married for many years, but . . ." She bent down and laid her cheek on Mary's head. "My dear, I just don't know."

They stayed that way, comforting each other for a time. Finally Mary drew away.

Ingeborg brushed some flour off her daughter's cheek. "Now the coffee is gone cold. Let me heat it up." She poured the brown liquid back in the pot and set it on the front burner again. "One thing I do know. When the time comes, you say good-bye, knowing that you loved him and he loved you and love goes on forever. But Will wouldn't want you to grieve over long; he'd want you to get on with your life."

"I'll be teaching next year. Isn't that getting on with my life?"

"Ja, it is. God, I know, has special plans for you, and when we cry, He says He is right here with us. As He is all the time."

Mary watched the peace on her mother's face and heard the faith in her voice. Ingeborg's faith never wavered. Could she ever be strong like that?

૨૦

"Mary's home!" The cry rang through the house when school let out and the children ran in through the door. Jenny and Joey came out of their rooms, rubbing their eyes, and after a moment joined the others in the circle around Mary. Everyone talked at once until the ceiling echoed with happy laughter.

Supper that night continued in the same vein. When Mr. Oien came to pick up his children, Ingeborg invited him to stay for a bite to eat. They pulled out the table and set in another leaf so there would be room.

Once or twice his smiles at the antics of the younger Moen children nearly reached his eyes. "Thank you so much," he said as he readied to leave after the meal was finished.

"You're welcome to stay longer." John leaned back in

his chair and crossed his legs at the ankles.

"I. . .I'd best be going—put these two to bed, you know." He nodded toward Joey and Jenny, who were being bundled up by the Moens. "Again, thank you." He put his hat on and picked up Jenny. "Come, Joey." He took the boy's hand, and the three went down the walk to where he had parked his automobile at the front gate.

"He should have started that contraption first." Ingeborg shut the door and peeked through the lace curtain. "Knute, why don't you go out and help him crank that thing?"

The oldest Moen son did as asked. When he returned, he rubbed his hands together. "If it weren't for cranking those things, I'd want one the worst way."

"Wanting never hurt anyone." John winked at Mary. "I was hoping since you were home, you would read to us tonight."

"Of course. What are you reading?" She took the book her father handed her. "Oh, Charles Dickens and old Scrooge. How I love it." As soon as the dishes were washed and put away, the family gathered in the parlor and Mary began to read. After the chapter was finished, she picked up the Bible that lay on the end table and opened it to the Psalms. "I keep going back to this one. 'Oh Lord, thou has searched me, and known me.' "

"Psalm 139." Daniel beamed at being the first to recognize it. They'd played this game of guessing the Scripture all the years of their lives, until now they were all well-versed in Bible knowledge.

Mary continued reading and, when she finished, closed the book. "Far, will you pray tonight?"

John nodded. "Father in heaven, Thou dost indeed know us right well. We ask You to forgive us our sins and fill us with Your Holy Spirit so that we may do the works Thou hast given us." When he came to the end, he finished with a blessing and they all said, "Amen."

"Now I know I am home for sure." Mary said with a sigh and a smile.

She felt that same way in church a few nights later when they gathered to celebrate the birth of the Christ child. Singing the old hymns and hearing the words embedded in her memory from eighteen Christmases made her want to wrap her arms around every person in the room. *Please, God, if You will, send me a sign that Will is either here on earth or up there with You. I want to do Your will, and I thank You that You sent Your Son to walk this earth. All I ask, dear Father, is a small sign.*

Christmas passed in a blur of happiness, only saddened when Mary thought of Will and what he was missing. Two days later, Dag came to see them.

"I have something that came in the mail today." He stopped, swallowed hard, and continued.

Mary felt an icy hand grip her heart.

Dag held out something metal on his hand. "They say these are Will's dog tags, taken from a body buried in Germany."

Mary couldn't breathe.

Seven

"Mary, are you all right?"

She heard the voice as if from a great distance. "I. . .I'm fine. Why?" Had she been sitting in the chair when. . .? Memory crashed back and she whimpered. "No, no, please no." *Dear God, please. . . that's not the sign I wanted. I know I asked for a sign but. . .*

Dag stood before her, his hand clenched at his side, a small piece of chain dangling between thumb and forefinger.

Now, why would I notice something like that? Chains don't matter at this point. But that one did. The chain that Will had worn so proudly now brought agony to his beloved.

"Mary." Her father's face swam before her eyes. He cuddled her cold hands in his warm ones and waited for her to respond.

"Yes." She left off studying the shimmering hairs on the backs of his hands and looked at him. The tears fighting to overflow his blue eyes undid her. She threw herself into his arms and wept.

Minutes later—but what seemed like hours—she accepted the handkerchief from her mother and mopped at her eyes. "I wanted him to come home. I asked God, and you said God always answers our prayers. I prayed that He would bring Will home."

"I know. I did too."

"And me." Dag lowered himself into a chair and leaned forward. "All of us prayed for that."

"Then why?" She shouted her question, shaking her fist in the face of God. "Why did He let Will die? Others are coming home—why not Will?"

John bent his head. "I don't know. I do not understand the mind of God or some of His purposes. All I know is that His heart breaks too and He holds us close. Close like me holding your hand and even closer. And the other thing I know with all certainty is that you will see Will again."

"I know about heaven, but I want him here." Tears dripped down her face.

"I know that too."

Mary felt her mother's hands on her shoulders, warm and secure.

"God could have saved Will." Again she felt like lashing out.

"Ja, He could have." The hands on her shoulders

rubbed gently.

"Then why didn't He?" Mary hiccuped on the last word.

"I 'spect every wife, mother, friend, feels the same. None of us want someone we love to be killed." John rubbed the back of her hands with his thumbs.

"Am I being selfish?"

"No more'n anyone else. But death comes. It is part of life, and we look forward to heaven all the time."

Mary sat silently. Then she shook her head. "It's not fair. Will is such a good man."

"Yes, he was. You can be proud he was your friend and loved you with all his heart."

It bothered her that her father said "was." She couldn't think of Will as "was." He is! Her rebellious mind insisted. Will is.

When she awoke in the middle of the night, after alternately praying and crying, she found her mother sitting by the bed, sound asleep. Mary fought back tears again. This was so like her mother, keeping watch over those she loved and those who needed her. Her presence comforted the girl, and she drifted back to sleep.

Each day felt like she waded through Spring gumbo three feet deep. Every part of her felt heavy, even to her eyelids and the tops of her ears. She pushed her hair back and finally braided it and coiled the braid in a bun at the base of her head to keep the weight of it from pulling her over. All she really wanted to do was sleep, for only in sleep did the knowledge disappear. But on waking, it always returned. They said Will was dead.

"You can stay home, you know." Ingeborg helped fold the undergarments to put in Mary's traveling valise.

"Would it be any better?" Mary turned from sorting through her books and deciding which had to go back with her.

"It would for me, because then I could make sure you eat and get enough rest and—"

"And cluck over me like one of your chicks?"

"You are one of my chicks." Ingeborg smoothed a ribbon into place on a nightgown. "No matter how grown up you get—even when you have a family of your own—you will always be my eldest chick."

"But I have to grow up, and learning to keep going is part of that, isn't it?"

"Ja, and I know our heavenly Father will watch over you and keep you safe."

I hope He does a better job with me than He did with Will. Mary was horrified at her thoughts. They just snuck up on her and dashed off before she could rope them in and discipline them to behave.

Later, her bags all packed, Mary bundled up to walk over to the mansion to say good-bye to Mrs. Norgaard. The north wind bit her cheeks and tried to burrow into her bones.

"Come in, my dear, come in." Clara swung the door wide open. "Are you about frozen clear through out walking in this cold?"

Mary stamped the snow from her boots and smiled

at the diminutive dynamo in front of her. Clara Weinlander often reminded Mary of her mother. If there was something that needed doing, those two women would take it on.

"Herself is waiting for you." Mrs. Olson secretly used that nickname for her employer, and at times, so did half the town. "We'll bring the coffee right in."

After their greetings, Mrs. Norgaard beckoned Mary to sit beside her on the sofa in front of the south windows. "I want to say something to you before the others come in."

Mary sat and turned to face her benefactress. "Yes."

"Losing one you love is one of the hardest things in life, but there's something I learned through all that. The Bible says, 'This too shall pass,' and it will. Right now you doubt me, but in a few weeks, months, the pain will be less and there will be some days when you surprise yourself because you didn't think of missing him at all."

Gudrun covered Mary's hands with her own. "Trust me, child, I know it is true. And one day you will think of Will, and the memory will be sweet. For you see, he will be closer now than he could have been when he was alive."

Mary felt the tears burning and closed her eyes. "But . . .but I still feel he might be alive, somewhere, somehow."

"I know, the mind plays tricks like that on us. Oh, how often I thought my husband would be home in half an hour. But he was gone, and finally I came to accept that. And that's when I began to live again." She looked up to see Clara and Mrs. Olson with the serving trays. "And much of that is thanks to these two. They bullied me into wanting to live again."

"That we did." Mrs. Olson set the tray down. "And would again."

"Just think of all the exciting things you would have missed." Clara sat in the chair and leaned forward to pour the coffee from the silver pot. "Mary, help yourself to those cookies. Mrs. Olson baked them just for you, and there's a box for you to take with you."

In spite of herself, Mary left the mansion feeling a little less weighed down by life.

&

With papers to write and new classes, Mary found herself busier than ever. Her friends gathered round her and made sure she ate and went with them to the lectures on campus and to hear the suffragettes trying to get the suffrage bill passed through Congress. When it was defeated, they all held a wake.

When General Pershing made his triumphant entrance into Paris, they all listened to the speeches on the radio in the parlor. Surely peace would be coming soon.

But the war continued, and school drew to a close. The entire Moen tribe came down on the train for Mary's graduation from normal school. She would now be able to teach grades one through high school in the state of North Dakota. Mary almost, but not quite, kept from looking for Will in the well-wishers.

"To think, a daughter of mine has graduated from teaching school." Ingeborg clasped her hands at her waist.

"I won't be the last." Mary removed the square black mortar board that crowned her head. "I will help pay for the next one who wants to go. Has Knute talked about what he wants to do?" Her brother next in line was due to graduate from high school at the end of May. She looked down at the brother tugging on her arm. "Yes, Daniel?"

"Far said if you were to change, we could go have ice cream."

"Oh, he did, did he? Well, let me congratulate my friends over there, and we will all walk to the soda fountain."

"I think we need a place like this in Soldahl," Ingeborg said after they took their places in two adjoining booths.

"That's right, Mother, you need something else to do." Mary shook her head.

"I didn't say I should do it." She looked around at the scroll-backed metal chairs and the small round tables. "But think what—"

"Don't even think such a thing." John leaned across the table to bring his face closer to his wife's. "You have far too much to do right now."

"Well."

"Mother!" Mary couldn't tell if her mother was serious or just teasing. After the young man took their order, Ingeborg leaned back against the high-backed wooden bench and turned to her daughter. "So, how are you, really?" She studied Mary's face, searching for the truth.

"I am much better. Mrs. Norgaard was right. Only by looking back can I tell how far I've come. I'm not angry at God anymore—or anyone else. I can read His Word and let it bless me again. But I still write my letters every night to Will and collect them in a box. I guess that has become my diary." She didn't tell them of not looking for the Big Dipper any more. She still had a hard time looking up at the night sky at all. Invariably when she did, her eyes filled with tears and she couldn't make out the stars anyway.

"I could tell a difference in your letters. Your father and I want you to know how proud we are of you."

The sodas arrived, and the conversation turned to how good they tasted and what everyone was planning for the summer.

"Mr. Oien has been writing and asking if I would care for the children again this summer."

"I know," Ingeborg responded. "I think he sees that with all of my own children home, his two little ones might be too much."

"He doesn't know you very well then, does he?" Mary sipped on her straw. Her mother's straw hat had just been knocked askew by an arm belonging to one of the boys who had been reaching over the back of the bench. Mary gave the hand a pinch and smiled at the "yeow" that her action provoked. Her mother righted the hat with a laugh and a threat to fix the perpetrator good. The booth full of children laughed at her words, knowing their mother would get even somehow, sometime when they least expected it.

Mary felt a glow settle about her heart. How she had missed them, mostly without even knowing it.

"So what will you do?" Ingeborg finally asked.

"I will care for his house and children and keep on searching for my school. I have my application in four different places, so time will tell."

"And that is what you want?"

Mary nodded. "This is what I want. Since God made sure I got through school, He must have a place in mind for me."

But the summer passed swiftly, and still Mary hadn't heard. By the end of August, she had a hard time keeping doubts at bay. Would she get a school? If not, what would she do?

Eight

The letter arrived on a Wednesday.

Mary stared at the postmark, then slit open the envelope with a shaking finger. Grafton lay in the next township, but the school they mentioned was not in town. If they hired her, she would be teaching first through fourth at a country school with two class-rooms. Could she come for an interview on Friday?

Could she come for an interview? Did cows give milk? Did the moon follow the sun? An interview! She finally had an interview. And she wouldn't be clear on the other side of the state. She could see the dear faces of her family on weekends—that is, if she could afford the train. She hurried home to tell her family.

Questions bubbled to the surface. Where would she live? Oh, not with a family that made her share a room and bed with one of their children. Sometimes that was

327

the arrangement. In some places families still took turns boarding the teacher. She'd heard some terrible stories about situations like that. Her feet slowed. If only she could teach right here in Soldahl.

"Mary, that is wonderful." Ingeborg clasped her hands in delight. "And so close by."

Mary read the letter out loud, the actual sound of the words making it more of a reality. "So, will you care for the children on Friday for me?" she asked her mother.

"Of course. You must call the people in Grafton and tell them what time your train will arrive. This is late for hiring a new teacher. I wonder what happened there? I hope it was not an illness of the teacher they already had."

Or she didn't want to go back and found a position elsewhere. Mary shook her head. Thoughts like that were better barricaded behind steel doors.

On Friday, Mary boarded the early train and returned home in time for supper, the proud owner of a teaching position. She would report for duty in two weeks in order to have her classroom ready for her pupils.

"So, why did they need a teacher at this late date?" Ingeborg asked after the children were all in bed.

"Miss Brown's mother became ill in Minnesota and she had to go be with her. A man teaches the older grades—has for a long time. I will be staying with a widow about a mile from the schoolhouse and helping her in exchange for board. I met with her, and she seems very nice. She's a bit hard of hearing and speaks

German as much as English, but we should do fine."

"Any one who has you to help them is very blessed indeed. Helping doesn't mean milking cows and such, does it?" Ingeborg wiped her hands on her apron. "You never have had to do farm labor."

"If you ask me, her sons just want someone living with their mother. She said she didn't want to go live with them." Mary's eyes danced. "I think she doesn't want anyone bossing her around." She caught her mother by the hands and whirled around the kitchen with her. "Oh, Mr. Gunderson, the head of the school board, told me three times that they didn't want any fooling around. 'Our teachers must be a model of decorum.' " She deepened her voice to mimic the gentleman. "Mother, this is the twentieth century for pity's sake. He must still be back in the dark ages."

"So what did you tell him?"

Mary's smile slipped. "I told him my fiancé was killed in the war and all I was interested in was teaching children the three Rs."

The next afternoon when Mr. Oien came home from work, Mary gave him her good news.

"I'm so very happy for you," he said, but his face showed shock and what was it—bewilderment?

"You knew I planned on teaching school if I could find a position?"

"I did. But since you hadn't said anything, I'd hoped you would stay." He sank down in a chair by the door. "My mother will watch the children again." Mary stepped to the window to check on the two who were playing outside in the sandbox. They were so sweet, and she would indeed miss them.

"That is not the problem." He paused, then continued in a rush. "I had not planned to mention this yet, what with your grieving for Will and all, but you love my children and you are so good with them and you are such a lovely person, and would you consider marrying me?"

"What did you say?"

"I asked you to marry me." He smoothed his sandy hair back with his hands. A smile came to his face. "I did it. I asked you to marry me."

"But you don't love me."

"How do you know? I love having you here with Joey and Jenny when I come home. I love seeing you play with them. I love hearing you laugh and I—"

"But I don't love you." Mary said the words softly, gently.

"You could, you know. I make a good living, you wouldn't have to teach school, you'd be near to your family whom I know you love dearly, you would have a nice house, and. . ."

Mary's slow shaking of the head forced him to run down.

"Please," he quickly amended, "don't say no right now. Give it some thought. Let me visit you, take you for drives. We could have a picnic—a. . .a. . ."

Mary stared at him. The thought of marrying

someone other than Will brought a knot to her throat and tears to her eyes. "I have to go. Thank you for. . . for. . ." She turned and bolted out the door.

&

"What happened to you?" Ingeborg's eyes widened when she saw her daughter's face.

"He. . .he asked me to m. . .marry him." Mary put a hand to her throat.

"A bit of a surprise, that?" Ingeborg shook her head. "Well I never." She stirred the kettle simmering on the stove. "Hmm, that idea has possibilities."

"Possibilities! Mother, I don't love Kenneth."

"Yet. Sometimes the best marriages are when two people grow into love."

"Mother! You want me to marry someone I don't love?"

"I didn't say that. But I can see it is a natural choice from his point of view. You are lovely, you are familiar, you know his home, and you love his children. Many men would say that's more than enough basis for marriage. Women have married for a lot less, you know."

Mary felt like she was talking with a total stranger who somehow wore her mother's face. She turned on her heel and climbed the stairs to her bedroom. Flinging herself across her bed, she buried her face in her hands. *Oh, Will, why did you have to go and die?*

ↄ

Time took wings during the days until Mary left, making her breathless most of the time. So much to be finished. In spite of her feelings of misgivings, she continued to care for Joey and Jenny, bringing them back to her mother's on the afternoons when she had errands to run. She wanted her classroom just perfect for her new pupils and spent hours preparing calendars and pictures, lesson assignments, and flash cards for numbers. Mr. Gunderson had said the school didn't have a large budget for supplies—the year had been hard for the farmers, in spite of the high prices for grain due to the war.

Mrs. Norgaard insisted that Dag would drive Mary to her new home so she wouldn't have to take all her things on the train. "God will be with you, child, as you share His love for those children. Don't you forget it."

"I'm not about to." Mary gave the old woman a hug. "You take care of yourself now while I'm away."

"Humph." Gudrun straightened her back, as if it needed it. "I've been taking care of myself since before your mother and father were born. I surely won't stop now." But the twinkle in her faded blue eyes turned the tear that shimmered on her lashes brilliant. She waved one slender hand. "You drive careful now, Dag, you hear?"

Clara, too, stood in the doorway, waving them off. "We'll keep supper for you, Dag. Enjoy the day."

"I wish she could have come." Mary settled back in her seat. The wind whipped the scarf she'd tied around her hat and blew the ends straight out behind her. The thrill of driving such speeds! *One day*, she promised herself, *I will have a car of my own to drive.* The picture of the black roadster driven by Kenneth Oien flashed through her mind. What would it be like, married to him? She liked him well enough. In fact, they could probably be friends. She shrugged the thoughts away. He'd said he'd write and gladly drive up to bring her home for a weekend. She deliberately pushed the thoughts out of her mind.

"So, how goes the blacksmithing?" She turned in the seat so Dag could hear her above the roar of the automobile and the rushing wind.

"Slow. I know I will have to convert more and more to repairing tractors and automobiles and trucks. With the engines improving all the time, we will see more changes than we ever dreamed of."

"I agree." She sought for another topic, but let it lie. Talking above the noise took too great an effort.

Dag carried all her boxes into the schoolroom, and then took the suitcases into the Widow Williamson's two-story square farmhouse and up the stairs to the large bedroom facing east. When he straightened, his head brushed the slanted ceiling so he ducked a bit.

"This is very nice."

"I think so." Mrs. Williamson had even brought up a desk and chair to set in front of the window. Carved posts stood above a white bedspread, and extra pillows nearly hid the oak headboard. Braided rag rugs by the bed and in front of the high dresser would keep Mary's feet off cold floors in the winter, and there was more than enough space for her simple wardrobe in the double-doored oak chifforobe. A picture of Jesus the Shepherd hung by the door.

"Well, I'd best be on my way." Dag extended his hand. "You call if you need anything. I saw a telephone on the wall downstairs."

"Thank you for all your help." Mary walked him down the stairs, turning at the landing and on down. When his car roared to life and he drove away, she stood on the porch waving long after the dust had settled. She was on her own now—just what she had always wanted. Or had she?

Mary fell in love with her pupils the instant they shuffled through the door. She had sixteen all together: four in the first grade, all so shy they couldn't look up at her; three in the second; five in the third; and four in fourth. The fourth graders already bossed the younger ones, but when she rapped for order, they all sat at attention.

"We will stand for the flag salute." She checked her seating chart. "Arnold, will you lead us?" She put her hand over her pounding heart. Were they as nervous as she? She nodded at the boy on the outside row.

"I pledge allegiance to the flag. . ." They stumbled through the words, some having forgotten them and others having not yet learned.

One of the first graders broke into tears when Mary asked them to repeat the Lord's Prayer. And when they sang the "Star Spangled Banner," she mostly sang solo. These children had a lot to learn.

She had planned on standing in front of them and quizzing them on their reading and numbers, but at the sight of the tears, she called all the children to the side of the room and, sitting down on a chair, told them to sit in front of her. She smiled at each one when she called their names again.

"I need to know who you are, so could you please tell me something you like to do?"

The older children looked at each other wide eyed.

"Arnold, we'll start with you. What do you like?" And so she went around the group, and by the time she reached the youngest ones, they smiled back at her. One little towhead girl stared at her teacher with her heart in her eyes.

"You are so pretty," she whispered. "I like you."

Mary felt her heart turn over. "And I like you." She laid the tip of her finger on the little girl's button nose. "Now, let's all learn the pledge of allegiance because we are going to start every day saluting our flag."

"My brother went to war for our flag." One of the boys said. "He never comed home."

Mary knew she was going to have heart problems for certain. "That has happened to many of our young men, so when we salute the flag, we are remembering them at the same time." Thoughts of a star in the Big Dipper handle twinkled through her mind. Remembering. Yes, the sweetness promised by Mrs. Norgaard had finally come.

"A very dear friend of mine went to Europe to fight

too and never came home." She laid a hand on the head of a little boy who had gravitated next to her knee. "Now, repeat after me, I pledge allegiance to the flag. . ." And so the morning continued. By the time recess came around, Mary felt like running outside to play anti-over with the children.

"The first day is always the hardest." Mr. Colburn, his graying hair worn long over the tops of his ears, stood in her doorway. His kind brown eyes and smile that made his mustache wiggle invited her to smile back.

"Is that a promise?" Mary stretched her shoulders. "Mr. Colburn, everyone spoke so highly of you, I feel honored to share your building."

"Yes, well, I try, and the honor is mine. I think we will do well together. My wife insisted I bring you home for supper one night soon. She is so curious about the new teacher, I made her promise not to come see you for herself. We've lived here for ten years, and we are still not considered part of the community. She's hoping you can be friends."

"Isn't that nice? I never turn down the offer of friendship."

"I'll go ring the bell." Mr. Colburn left, and immediately the bell in the tower bonged twice. The children flew to form a line starting with the larger ones and going to the smallest and marched into the building.

Mary took a deep breath and dived back in.

The days fell into a pattern. Up before dawn to make breakfast while Mrs. Williamson did the outside chores. Then walk to school, teach all day, and walk home. Evenings after she'd washed the supper dishes were spent preparing for the next day. On Saturday they cleaned house, and on Sunday, Mrs. Williamson's sons took turns driving them to church.

Mary didn't have time to be lonely. She continued to write her letters to Will each night, but now she planned to send them to her mother. Ingeborg would love to hear the stories of her daughter and her small charges.

When Mr. Colburn discovered she could play the piano, he rolled the heavy instrument into her room on the condition that she teach music. The students at Valley School loved to sing. So every afternoon, if all had done their assignments, everyone gathered in Mary's classroom for singing and then Mr. Colburn read to them. His mellow voice played the parts as he read first *The Jungle Book*, by Rudyard Kipling, and then *Oliver Twist*, by Charles Dickens. Mary was as entranced as the children.

Letters came weekly from Kenneth Oien, and Mary grew to look forward to them. While she had yet to go home to visit, his letters were like a window into the life of Soldahl. He wrote of the antics of Joey and Jenny and their new friend, Mews, a half-grown cat that had shown up on their doorstep one day. He described the changing of the colors with the frost, and the geese flying south. He said they all missed her and looked forward to her coming home.

There's a poet hiding in that man's soul, Mary thought as she read the latest letter. *But can I ever think of him as more than a friend?*

When the phone rang one evening and Mrs. Williamson called up the stairs to say it was for her, Mary felt her heart leap into her throat. Was something wrong at home? Was Daniel sick again?

"Hello?" She knew she sounded breathless, only because she was.

"Mary, this is Kenneth."

"Kenneth? Oh, Mr. Oien. . .uh, Kenneth." She felt like an idiot. Surely they could be on a first-name basis by now, in fact should have been a long time ago.

"I wondered if I could come and get you on Friday afternoon, if you would like to come home, that is. I would take you back on Sunday, after church. I. . .ah, that is."

Mary took pity on his stammering. "I would love that. Thank you for the invitation."

"Would you like me to come to the school?"

"No, I'll meet you here at Mrs. Williamson's." She gave him the directions and hung up the receiver. She'd heard a click on the party line. Now everyone around would know the new teacher had a beau. Whether he was or not did not matter.

≈

"I think of you a lot," Kenneth said when he stopped the automobile in front of the parsonage that Friday night. Dark had fallen before they reached Soldahl and traveling the rough roads by lamplight had made them drive even more slowly.

What could she say? "I enjoy reading your letters.

And thank you for the ride home. Will you be coming to dinner on Sunday?"

"Yes." He smiled at her in the dimness. "And we have been invited to supper on Saturday at the mansion. That is, if you would like to go."

"Why of course." Mary fumbled for her purse. "Thank you again for the ride."

He got out and came around to open her door, leaving the motor running. "Til tomorrow then." He helped her out and carried her valise to the door. "Jenny and Joey hope you will come see them while you are in town."

"Oh." Mary wondered what had happened to her tongue. Suffering from a lack of words was a new experience for her.

Looking back, she couldn't remember having a nicer time in a long while. While she was fully aware that all her friends and family were playing matchmakers, she couldn't fault them for it. Kenneth Oien was a very nice man.

But a few weeks later, when he asked her to consider marriage, she shook her head.

"Please don't pressure me," she whispered. "I just cannot answer that yet."

"Yet?" His eager voice came through the darkness. He'd just brought her back from another weekend at home. He touched her cheek with a gentle caress.

Mary held herself still. If that had been Will, the urge to throw herself in his arms would have made her shake. All she felt was a longing to feel more. What was the matter with her?

Nine

The world went crazy on Tuesday, November 11, 1918. Victory Day. The war to end all wars was over.

School bells rang, radio announcers shouted, the people cheered. Some sobbed at the thought their sons might still make it home in one piece. Others cried for those who would never return.

Mary was one of the latter. While her head said, *Thank You Father for finally bringing peace,* her heart cried for the young man she had seen leave for war.

While the children were out on the playground after eating their lunches, she walked out beyond the coal shed and leaned against the building wall. Letting the tears come, she sobbed until she felt wrung out. When she could finally feel the cold wind biting her cheeks and tugging at her hair, she wiped her eyes and lifted her face to the sun that played hide and seek in the clouds.

"Will," she whispered, "I loved you then and I love you now, but I guess it is about time I got on with my life. One more Christmas is all I will ask for, and then if God wants me to marry Kenneth Oien, I will follow His bidding." She waited, almost hoping for an answer, but all she heard was the wind, and it was too light to look for that star.

Kenneth and the children joined the Moens for Thanksgiving dinner after the church service. Pastor Moen had thanked God for bringing peace to a world torn asunder by war, and the congregation heartily agreed. Mary refused to let the tears come again. She sat in the front pew but didn't dare look directly up at her father, for she knew the love in his eyes would be her undoing. Why was it always so hard to keep from crying in church?

Several of the boys, now turned men, had returned from the service already, making it easy for some families to give thanks. One even brought back a French wife, and if that didn't start the gossips buzzing . . . .

Mary felt sorry for the shy young woman. If only she could speak French to help her out.

They had stuffed goose for dinner, two given them by one of the hunters in the congregation. Ingeborg had been cooking for a week, or so the amount of food on the table testified. Afterward they played charades, and when the two little ones woke up from their naps, they played hide the thimble. Jenny ignored the game and came to sit on Mary's lap, leaning her head back against Mary's chest.

Mary looked up to catch a glance between her parents. *Please, don't push me,* she wanted to cry. Cuddling Jenny was so easy. Would cuddling with her father be as simple?

"You know, Kenneth is a fine young man." John said after the company had left.

"Yes, Father, I know you like him." Mary bit off the colored thread she was using to embroider a rose on a handkerchief for Mrs. Williamson. Making Christmas presents had begun.

"He will make a fine husband," Ingeborg said without looking up from her knitting.

"All right. I know how you feel and I know how he feels. All I want to know now is how God feels."

"And what about you?" John kept his finger in his place in the book. "How do you feel?"

"Like I cannot make a decision yet."

John nodded. "You don't have to."

"I want to go through Christmas first. I will make a decision after the first of the year. Then it will have been a year since we got the final word. But I know one thing for sure, no matter what my decision, I will finish my year at Valley School."

John and Ingeborg both nodded. Daniel wandered back down the stairs, rubbing the sleep out of his eyes. "I heard you talking, and it made me hungry."

Mary laughed as she rose to cut him another piece of pumpkin pie. "You should be as big as Knute with all that you eat."

The weeks before Christmas passed in a blur of preparing a school program and party for the families around Pleasant Valley. They decorated a Christmas tree someone brought from Minnesota and hung chains made from colored paper around the room. But the music made Mary the most proud. The children sang like the angels had from on high, and during the performance even the most stoic fathers dabbed at their eyes more than once.

Mary left for home with her presents completed and bearing treasures given her by her students. Her favorite, if she were allowed to pick, was a card decorated with pressed wild flowers and lettered, "To my teechur."

A snow storm hung on the northern horizon, so she took the train, rather than allowing Dag or Kenneth to come for her. While it would take a lot of snow to stop the train, automobiles buried themselves in drifts with the ease of children finding a mud puddle.

Her father met her at the station with his horse and buggy. He took her valise and wrapped an arm around her shoulders. "Do you have anything more?"

"Father, at Christmas?" Her laugh pealed out. She pointed to two boxes tied up tightly with twine. "Those are mine. What happened to all the fancy automobiles?"

"Too much snow." John loaded the boxes into the

area behind the seat and helped her up. "I sure hope we don't have a blizzard for Christmas."

She told him about the school program on the way home, her arm tucked in his and a robe covering their knees. When her story finished, she said, "You know one good thing about horses?"

"No, what's that?"

"You can talk and hear the other person answer." She leaned closer to him. "Without shouting."

"I know. Sometimes I think if the congregation offered me one, I'd turn it down." He slapped the reins, clucking the gray gelding into a trot. "General, here, and I, we've been through a lot together. An automobile won't take me home if I fall asleep after a late call or listen to me practice my sermon. If he doesn't like one, he shakes his head and snorts. Then I know I need to go back to the desk and keep writing."

Big white flakes drifted before the wind, glistening and dancing in the street lights. Two days until Christmas. This year they could truly say peace on earth and good will to men.

They spent the next two days baking julekake, the Norwegian Christmas bread, sandbaklse, and krumkake and frying fatigman and rosettes. The house smelled of nutmeg and cardamon, pine and cedar. No one was allowed to open a door without knocking or peek into closets or on shelves.

Ingeborg spent the late hours of Christmas Eve afternoon beating rommegrote, a rich pudding, until the melted butter from the cream rose to the surface. When anyone tried to sneak tastes, she batted them away with her wooden spoon. "If you want some, you'll have to wait or make your own." She'd been saying the same thing every year that Mary could remember.

When they finally trooped off on the walk to church, Mary stayed in the midst of her family. Kenneth finally sat in a pew a few rows behind them, a look of puzzlement on his face.

With Daniel glued to one side and Beth, her youngest sister, on the other, Mary put her arms around them and let them hold the hymnal. She didn't need to see the words; she'd known the carols all her life. And for a change she could sit with her family since other people now played the piano and organ Mrs. Norgaard had donated two years earlier. The music swelled, and the congregation joined in. "Silent night, holy night, all is calm, all is bright."

Two people stood to read the Christmas story. " 'And it came to pass in those days. . .' "

Mary could say the words along with the readers. " 'And they laid the babe in the manger for there was no room for them in the inn.' "

A hush fell as Reverend John stepped into the pulpit. He stood there, head bowed.

Mary heard a stir in the back but kept her eyes on her father. When he raised his head, he gasped. He looked to Mary and then to the back of the room.

The buzz grew with people shifting and murmuring.

Mary turned and looked over her shoulder.

The man coming up the center aisle walked as if he knew the way. Well he should. He'd helped lay the carpet.

He stopped at the end of the pew. "Hello, Mary. Merry Christmas."

"Will." She rose to her feet. Her gaze melded with his. Her heart stopped beating and then started again, triple time. She shifted so there was room for him to sit beside her. Hands clamped as if they'd never let go, they raised their faces to the man standing openmouthed in the pulpit.

"Dearly beloved," John's voice broke. He blew his nose and tucked his handkerchief up the sleeve of his robe. "I'm sorry, folks, but never have those words been more true." He wiped his eyes with the back of his hand. "We have been given a gift, as you all know. Welcome home, Will Dunfey."

Mary heard no more of the sermon. *Will is alive. Thank You, God, thank You.* Over and over the words repeated in her mind. Tears ran unchecked down her cheeks, and while her chin quivered, she couldn't quit smiling. Not that she wanted to.

When the benediction sounded, she rose to her feet along with the others. At the final amen, when the organ poured out its triumphal notes, she turned to Will and melted into his arms. Proper or no, the kiss they shared spoke of all their heartache and all their joy. Will Dunfey had come home.

"It was my destiny," he said later after he'd shaken every hand and been clapped on the back a hundred times by all the congregation. He and Mary were sitting in the parlor at the parsonage with all the Moens, the Weinlanders, and Mrs. Norgaard. "I told Mary I would come home, and Dag taught me to always keep my word."

A chuckle rippled through the room.

"Where were you?" Daniel held the place of honor at Will and Mary's feet.

"In a prisoner-of-war camp. I lost my dog tags, and for a long time I didn't know who I was. I've been trying to get home ever since the signing of the peace. Kept me in a hospital for a while, then told me I was dead." He raised his left hand, leaving his right hand still holding firmly on to Mary's. "I said I might have been, but I was alive now and my name was still Willard Dunfey."

Mary laid her head on his shoulder. "Everyone insisted you were dead, but my heart didn't believe it. I thought I was going crazy, so I asked God for a sign and a couple of days later, your dog tags arrived."

"When that happened, we were sure they had buried you over there." Mrs. Norgaard took a lace handkerchief from the edge of her sleeve and wiped her eyes again. "Must be something in the air."

"Of course," Dag managed to say with a straight face.

"They would have except for this." Will took the Testament Mary had given him from his shirt pocket and held it up. A hole showed through the upper half.

"It slowed the bullet so it couldn't penetrate my ribs. I bled like a stuck pig, but flesh wounds heal. So you see, Mary, you saved my life."

"The Word of God is powerful in more ways than one." Gudrun wiped her eyes again. "Pesky cold."

Later when everyone else had gone home or gone to bed, Mary and Will put on their coats and stepped out on the porch. The storm had blown over, and the stars shone like crystals against the black sky. Will pointed to the end of the Dipper.

"You don't need to look for me up there anymore because I am right here, and here I will stay. My love for you has only grown deeper, your face kept me from ever giving up, and," he patted his chest, "I have a scar to remind me how close I came to losing you."

Mary laid her hand over his. "And I you."

When he kissed her this time, she could have sworn she heard someone laughing. Was it that man dancing on the last star in the handle of the Big Dipper? Or the angels rejoicing with them?

Lauraine Snelling is the best-selling author of "The Golden Filly" and "High Hurdles" series (Bethany House Publishers) for teen readers, as well as *An Untamed Land*, Book 1 in the new "Red River of the North" (Bethany House Publishers) series for adults. A talented writer, teacher, and conference speaker, Lauraine lives with her husband in Martinez, California.

Here's wishing you
a Blessed Christmas
and a wonder-
filled New Year.
        Lauraine Snelling
I John 1: 1-2

Coming Spring 1997

Summer Dreams

A collection of four inspirational
romance novellas including:

Summer Breezes
by Veda Boyd Jones

A la Mode
by Yvonne Lehman

King of Hearts
by Tracie Peterson

No Groom for the Wedding
by Kathleen Yapp

A Letter To Our Readers

Dear Reader:

In order that we might better contribute to your reading enjoyment, we would appreciate your taking a few minutes to respond to the following questions. When completed, please return to the following: Susan Johnson, Managing Editor, Barbour & Company, P.O. Box 719, Uhrichsville, OH 44683.

1. Did you enjoy reading *Christmas Treasures*?
   ❑ Very much, I would like to see more books like this.
   ❑ Moderately—I would have enjoyed it more if _____
   _____
   _____

2. What influenced your decision to purchase this book?
   (Check those that apply)
   ❑ Cover   ❑ Back cover copy   ❑ Title   ❑ Price
   ❑ Friends   ❑ Publicity   ❑ Other_____

3. Which story was your favorite? ❑ An Ozark Christmas Angel
   ❑ Christmas Dream   ❑ Winterlude   ❑ Dakota Destiny

4. Please check your age range:
   ❑ Under 18   ❑ 18-24   ❑ 25-34
   ❑ 35-45   ❑ 46-55   ❑ Over 55

5. How many hours per week do you read? _____

Name _____
Occupation _____
Address _____
City_____ State_____ Zip _____

Heartsong Presents
Love Stories Are Rated G!

That's for godly, gratifying, and of course, great! If you love a thrilling love story, but don't appreciate the sordidness of some popular paperback romances, **Heartsong Presents** is for you. In fact, **Heartsong Presents** is the *only inspirational romance book club*, the only one featuring love stories where Christian faith is the primary ingredient in a marriage relationship.

Sign up today to receive your first set of four, never before published Christian romances. Send no money now; you will receive a bill with the first shipment. You may cancel at any time without obligation, and if you aren't completely satisfied with any selection, you may return the books for an immediate refund!

Imagine. . .four new romances every four weeks—two historical, two contemporary—with men and women like you who long to meet the one God has chosen as the love of their lives. . .all for the low price of $9.97 postpaid.

To join, simply complete the coupon below and mail to the address provided. **Heartsong Presents** romances are rated G for another reason: They'll arrive *Godspeed!*
